BOOKS BY D. MICHAEL MARTINDALE

Brother Brigham
Celeste & the White Dragon
Gospels the Novel

Twisted Stories series
Twisted Mind
Twisted Soul

What readers have said about D. Michael's stories

"I found Martindale's writing exciting and compelling. He created a world of nations, customs, and peoples that blends magic with the gods of the lands. It's an exciting read, carefully constructed with sequences and twists to sustain a series. I'm looking forward to the second book of the series."

— *Doug Gibson, writer, blogger*

"It reminds me of Heinlein in his juvenile years. That's meant as high praise. It's captivating, moves fast, is worth reading a second time immediately after finishing."

— *Joe Buchman, adventure traveler*

"It's very clean. It gets right into the action, and it keeps up throughout. I think it's a great story."

— *Henry Knudsen, screenwriter*

"Exciting, clever, and action packed. A great story and a great ending. This is going to be such a hit!"

— *Sharon Dodge, database administrator*

"The story drew me in right from the beginning. I was so engrossed in the first chapters when I read them that I knew I wouldn't be able to put the book down again."

— *Karen Crapo, caretaker*

"I absolutely loved it! It was a great read and kept me interested throughout. I can't wait to start the second."

--*Valerie Kahler-Cordova, artist*

"Jack London once made my heart pound, but Michael Martindale is the first writer to rock me back in my chair in wide-eyed amazement."

— *Preston McConkie, journalist*

"Like Stephen King, Martindale captures the earthy rhythms of daily life as the characters get caught up in bizarre, harrowing events."

— *Christopher Kimball Bigelow, author and editor*

"The story still lingers in my mind. It was a real page-turner!"

—*Eileen Stringer, reader*

"Outrageous, provocative, insightful, courageous and thoughtful. Michael Martindale reminded me of the sensitivities of Orson Scott Card in his novel *Saints*."

— *Eugene Kovalenko, blogger*

"Martindale's frank sensuality...is not salacious; it's simply a matter of fact. A lesser book would have found a way to ignore it completely. It is frustrating when people, in life and in fiction, say what they think should be said instead of what they feel. In that light, Martindale's relative profundity is refreshing."

— *Sam Vicchrilli, In Utah This Week Magazine*

"Reading this fast-paced and quickly changing story is like embarking on a river rafting trip that starts out in placid shallows, never suspecting that around the next corner whitewater rapids wait, anxious to engulf you. The ride never slows down until the last few pages."

—*Jonathan Neville, writer*

"One of the things that a novelist, especially one who writes fantasy fiction, is required to do, is get the reader to suspend disbelief, and then sustain that suspension... This is where Martindale succeeds hands down."

— *David Birley, reader*

"His captivating storytelling keeps the plot moving without being predictable or trite. His descriptions ring true."

— *Wife of reader*

"Skillfully written, creating a realistic, complex, difficult world where everything is not as it initially seems. It's a page-turner, a real heavy weight."

—*Mahonri Stewart, playwright*

"D. Michael has an incredible talent for writing. I was utterly wowed by his characters' inner thoughts."

— *Brian Sheets, digital media specialist*

"I had a hard time putting it down, and as a result I read it surprisingly quickly. I had to know how the whole mess was going to end. It's deep, well thought out, and opens up some interesting and thought-provoking ideas."

—*Lee Penrod, systems programmer*

"Martindale...paints a scenario at once believable and shudderingly delusional."

— *Kim Madsen, readers group coordinator*

GOSPELS THE NOVEL

THE FOUR GOSPELS
SYNTHESIZED INTO ONE NARRATIVE
PRESENTED IN NOVEL FORMAT

EDITED BY D. MICHAEL MARTINDALE

Worldsmith Stories
Salt Lake City, Utah

King James Version of Bible text is in the public domain

Modifications to KJV text and additional content
© 2024 by Martindale Family Trust

All rights reserved

ISBN: 978-1-970065-08-4

Published by
Worldsmith Stories
1042 Fort Union Blvd. Suite 109
Midvale UT 84047

info@worldsmithstories.com
https://worldsmithstories.com

Artwork courtesy of **Pixabay**
pixabay.com

TABLE OF CONTENTS

In the Beginning, D. Michael Created *Gospels the Novel*	1
Prolog	5
The First Twelve Years	6
The Way Prepared	15
The First Year of the Ministry	21
The Second Year of the Ministry	33
The Third Year of the Ministry	69
The Final Journey to Jerusalem	112
The Last Week	122
The Resurrection	164
Epilog	173
Bonus Novelette: The Apostles	175
About the Editor	237

IN THE BEGINNING, D. MICHAEL CREATED
GOSPELS THE NOVEL

At some point in my teenaged years, I discovered a thing called "Harmony of the Gospels." It was at the end of my personal copy of the Bible. It consisted of four columns on each page, one column per gospel. It listed the verses of each gospel in chronological order, side by side, matching up verses on the pages so verses coincided with the timeline.

The really interesting part was when more than one gospel told the same story. You could see the verses lined up in their columns and compare the details of the story that the respective gospels told, the similarities and the differences.

Of course you'd have to keep looking up each verse to do the comparison. Tedious! It would have been nice to actually print the verses themselves on each column, not just the verse references, and compare them at a glance.

Then I thought, you know what would be cool? To actually combine the verses into one narrative that you could read straight through from beginning to end. Get a real feel for the story of the life of Jesus organically from beginning to end. Combine all the details from all the gospels into one narrative.

Then I thought, you know what would be even cooler? Preserve the King James language of my King James Version, but write it up as if it were a modern novel. Chapters (the novel kind, not the Bible kind) complete with chapter titles. Sections within the chapters to break up the long narrative. Paragraphs grouping together concepts rather than verses arbitrarily breaking up the sentences.

And funnest of all, modern punctuation. It's no secret the King James translators wrote in what's now an archaic version of English. I wanted to preserve that language because it's the traditional language English speakers have experienced the Bible in for so long, and it seems clear the translators went out of their way to make the language beautifully poetic.

It also happened to be the translation I had conveniently in hand.

More modern translations use a more familiar English translation for modern readers, and tend to be more accurate than the translators back in the year 1611. But that's significant for Bible study. That was not my goal. My goal was to have an emotional, even a spiritual, experience reading the life of Jesus like a novel. I do not recommend my edit of the gospels as a resource for academic or spiritual study.

I completed my "novelization" of the four gospels several decades ago, then let it sit on the shelf for decades. Recently it occurred to me, hey, I could publish it! As I read through it again, I was struck with how impactful reading the four gospels in this format is. I felt like I was reading a novel or watching a movie that played in my mind, feeling all the feels one would expect from such experiences. It brought the story of Jesus to life for me more than reading the four gospels separately in a study session or something.

It also occurred to me that the story doesn't end with the end of the gospels. There's one more book in the New Testament that continues the story. So I added a bonus chapter called "The Apostles" that novelizes Acts of the Apostles.

I hope reading *Gospels the Novel* will provide you with as moving an experience as it gave me.

Changes made in the process of combining the four gospels

I combined the gospels by combining the verses, sentences, phrases, even down to words as I saw fit, to provide as natural a narrative flow as I could without changing the words of the Bible. I'm a novelist, so I combined everything with an ear to mimic the feel of a novel. These are the sorts of changes I made:

* Formatting in novelistic chapters and paragraphs rather than Bible chapters and verses.

* Jumbling sentence, phrase, and word orders around to mimic a more modern storytelling style, but not changing or adding words.

* Removing superfluous words at the beginning of sentences like *and, now,* or *then*. The amount of such spurious words the KJV translators used could fill the Mediterranean Sea.

* Playing fast and loose with punctuation. The KJV translators used a lot of exotic punctuating, flooding the text with colons, semicolons, and excessive commas, enough to cover the surface of the Mediterranean Sea. I used my own experience as a novelist to punctuate as I saw fit to improve the flow of reading for modern audiences.

* In particular, I added quotation marks to indicate what was dialog. I feel like that addition was one of the more significant influences in making the narrative feel modern.

Gospels the Novel

* Other more technical changes with examples:

ae to *e*	Judaea	Judea
Capitalize letter after ?	this? for	this? For
ou to *o* (sorry, Brits)	favoured	favored
-ck to *-c*	publick	public
Two words to one compound	any thing	anything
Greek names to Old Testament	Esaias	Isaiah
	Messias	Messiah
Modernize spelling	inclosed	enclosed
	stedfastly	steadfastly
	cloke	cloak
	subtilty	subtlety
Add hyphenation	daughter in law	daughter-in-law
	Syrophenician	Syro-phoenecian
Split compound word	fellowdisciple	fellow disciple
No capital letter after comma	I say unto you, Hereafter	
	I say unto you, hereafter	
an to *a* before h-	an horn	a horn

("an hungred" was not changed because "a hungred" sounds weirder)

Most importantly, every page has a column on the right that lists references to the verses that every part of the narration is derived from. That way those readers who want to study precisely how I combined the four gospels can look them up themselves and see what I did to blend them together—if you're masochistic enough to inflict that upon yourself!

Every word in the narrative comes from somewhere out of the four gospels, except for a tiny, tiny handful of words I needed to add just to make the English sentences flow better. Every one of those added words are placed within [square brackets] to indicate they were added.

PROLOG

In the beginning was the Word, and the Word was with God, and the Word was God. The same was in the beginning with God. All things were made by him, and without him was not anything made that was made. In him was life, and the life was the light of men. And the light shineth in darkness, and the darkness comprehended it not. There was a man sent from God whose name was John. The same came for a witness to bear witness of the Light, that all men through him might believe. He was not that light, but was sent to bear witness of that light. That was the true Light which lighteth every man that cometh into the world. He was in the world, and the world was made by him, and the world knew him not. He came unto his own, and his own received him not. But as many as received him, to them gave he power to become the sons of God—even to them that believe on his name—which were born, not of blood, nor of the will of the flesh, nor of the will of man, but of God.	John 1:1-13
John bare witness of him and cried, saying, "This was he of whom I spake, 'He that cometh after me is preferred before me, for he was before me.'" Of his fulness have all we received, and grace for grace. For the law was given by Moses, but grace and truth came by Jesus Christ. No man hath seen God at any time. The only begotten Son, which is in the bosom of the Father, he hath declared him.	John 1:15-18
The Word was made flesh and dwelt among us. We beheld his glory, the glory as of the only begotten of the Father, full of grace and truth.	John 1:14

THE FIRST TWELVE YEARS

1

There was in the days of Herod, the king of Judea, a certain priest named Zacharias of the course of Abia. His wife was of the daughters of Aaron, and her name was Elisabeth. They were both righteous before God, walking in all the commandments and ordinances of the Lord blameless. They had no child because that Elisabeth was barren, and they both were now well stricken in years.

It came to pass that, while he executed the priest's office before God in the order of his course according to the custom of the priest's office, his lot was to burn incense when he went into the temple of the Lord. The whole multitude of people were praying without at the time of incense.

There appeared unto him an angel of the Lord standing on the right side of the altar of incense. When Zacharias saw him he was troubled, and fear fell upon him.

But the angel said unto him, "Fear not, Zacharias, for thy prayer is heard. Thy wife Elisabeth shall bear thee a son, and thou shalt call his name John. Thou shalt have joy and gladness, and many shall rejoice at his birth.

"For he shall be great in the sight of the Lord and shall drink neither wine nor strong drink. He shall be filled with the Holy Ghost, even from his mother's womb.

"Many of the children of Israel shall he turn to the Lord their God. He shall go before him in the spirit and power of Elijah, to turn the hearts of the fathers to the children and the disobedient to the wisdom of the just, to make ready a people prepared for the Lord."

Zacharias said unto the angel, "Whereby shall I know this? For I am an old man, and my wife stricken in years."

The angel answering said unto him, "I am Gabriel that stand in the presence of God, and am sent to speak unto thee and to shew thee these glad tidings. Behold, thou shalt be dumb and not able to speak until the day

Luke 1:5-80

that these things shall be performed, because thou believest not my words which shall be fulfilled in their season."

The people waited for Zacharias and marvelled that he tarried so long in the temple. When he came out, he could not speak unto them. They perceived that he had seen a vision in the temple, for he beckoned unto them and remained speechless.

It came to pass that, as soon as the days of his ministration were accomplished, he departed to his own house. After those days his wife Elisabeth conceived and hid herself five months, saying, "Thus hath the Lord dealt with me in the days wherein he looked on me, to take away my reproach among men."

In the sixth month the angel Gabriel was sent from God unto a city of Galilee named Nazareth, to a virgin espoused to a man whose name was Joseph of the house of David. The virgin's name was Mary. The angel came in unto her and said, "Hail, thou that art highly favored. The Lord is with thee. Blessed art thou among women."

When she saw him, she was troubled at his saying and cast in her mind what manner of salutation this should be.

The angel said unto her, "Fear not, Mary, for thou hast found favor with God. Behold, thou shalt conceive in thy womb and bring forth a son and shalt call his name JESUS.

"He shall be great and shall be called the Son of the Highest. The Lord God shall give unto him the throne of his father David. He shall reign over the house of Jacob forever, and of his kingdom there shall be no end."

Then said Mary unto the angel, "How shall this be, seeing I know not a man?"

The angel answered her and said, "The Holy Ghost shall come upon thee, and the power of the Highest shall overshadow thee. Therefore also that holy thing which shall be born of thee shall be called the Son of God. Behold thy cousin Elisabeth. She hath also conceived a son in her old age, and this is the sixth month with her who was called barren. For with God nothing shall be impossible.

Mary said, "Behold the handmaid of the Lord. Be it unto me according to thy word."

The angel departed from her.

Mary arose in those days and went into the hill country

with haste, into a city of Judea, and entered into the house of Zacharias and saluted Elisabeth.

It came to pass that, when Elisabeth heard the salutation of Mary, the babe leaped in her womb. Elisabeth was filled with the Holy Ghost. She spake out with a loud voice and said, "Blessed art thou among women, and blessed is the fruit of thy womb. Whence is this to me that the mother of my Lord should come to me? For lo, as soon as the voice of thy salutation sounded in mine ears, the babe leaped in my womb for joy. Blessed is she that believed, for there shall be a performance of those things which were told her from the Lord."

Mary said, "My soul doth magnify the Lord, and my spirit hath rejoiced in God my Savior. For he hath regarded the low estate of his handmaiden. For, behold, from henceforth all generations shall call me blessed. For he that is mighty hath done to me great things, and holy is his name. His mercy is on them that fear him from generation to generation.

"He hath shewed strength with his arm. He hath scattered the proud in the imagination of their hearts. He hath put down the mighty from their seats and exalted them of low degree. He hath filled the hungry with good things, and the rich he hath sent empty away. He hath holpen his servant Israel in remembrance of his mercy, as he spake to our fathers, to Abraham, and to his seed forever."

Mary abode with her about three months and returned to her own house.

Now Elisabeth's full time came that she should be delivered, and she brought forth a son. Her neighbors and her cousins heard how the Lord had shewed great mercy upon her, and they rejoiced with her.

It came to pass that on the eighth day, they came to circumcise the child, and they called him Zacharias after the name of his father.

His mother answered and said, "Not so, but he shall be called John."

They said unto her, "There is none of thy kindred that is called by this name." They made signs to his father, how he would have him called.

He asked for a writing table and wrote, saying, "His name is John." And they marvelled all.

His mouth was opened immediately, and his tongue loosed. He spake and praised God. Fear came on all that dwelt round about them.

All these sayings were noised abroad throughout all the hill country of Judea. All they that heard them laid them up in their hearts, saying, "What manner of child shall this be!" And the hand of the Lord was with him.

His father Zacharias was filled with the Holy Ghost and prophesied, saying, "Blessed be the Lord God of Israel. For he hath visited and redeemed his people and hath raised up a horn of salvation for us in the house of his servant David. As he spake by the mouth of his holy prophets which have been since the world began, that we should be saved from our enemies and from the hand of all that hate us, to perform the mercy promised to our fathers, and to remember his holy covenant, the oath which he sware to our father Abraham, that he would grant unto us, that we being delivered out of the hand of our enemies might serve him without fear, in holiness and righteousness before him all the days of our life.

"And thou, child, shalt be called the prophet of the Highest, for thou shalt go before the face of the Lord to prepare his ways, to give knowledge of salvation unto his people by the remission of their sins through the tender mercy of our God. Whereby the dayspring from on high hath visited us to give light to them that sit in darkness and in the shadow of death, to guide our feet into the way of peace."

The child grew and waxed strong in spirit, and was in the deserts till the day of his shewing unto Israel.

2

The birth of Jesus Christ was on this wise:

Matthew 1:18-25

When as his mother Mary was espoused to Joseph, before they came together, she was found with child of the Holy Ghost. Then Joseph her husband, being a just man and not willing to make her a public example, was minded to put her away privily.

But while he thought on these things, behold, the angel of the Lord appeared unto him in a dream, saying,

"Joseph, thou son of David, fear not to take unto thee Mary thy wife. For that which is conceived in her is of the Holy Ghost. She shall bring forth a son, and thou shalt call his name JESUS,* for he shall save his people from their sins."

Yahweh is salvation

Now all this was done that it might be fulfilled which was spoken of the Lord by the prophet, saying, "Behold, a virgin shall be with child and shall bring forth a son, and they shall call his name Emmanuel,"* which being interpreted is, "God with us."

Isaiah 7:14

Then Joseph being raised from sleep did as the angel of the Lord had bidden him and took unto him his wife, and knew her not till she had brought forth her firstborn son. He called his name JESUS.

It came to pass in those days that there went out a decree from Caesar Augustus that all the world should be taxed. This taxing was first made when Cyrenius was governor of Syria. All went to be taxed, everyone into his own city.

Luke 2:1-18

Joseph also went up from Galilee, out of the city of Nazareth into Judea, unto the city of David which is called Bethlehem, because he was of the house and lineage of David, to be taxed with Mary his espoused wife, being great with child.

So it was that, while they were there, the days were accomplished that she should be delivered. She brought forth her firstborn son and wrapped him in swaddling clothes and laid him in a manger, because there was no room for them in the inn.

There were in the same country shepherds abiding in the field, keeping watch over their flock by night. Lo, the angel of the Lord came upon them, and the glory of the Lord shone round about them. They were sore afraid.

The angel said unto them, "Fear not, for behold, I bring you good tidings of great joy which shall be to all people. For unto you is born this day in the city of David a Savior which is Christ the Lord.

"This shall be a sign unto you. Ye shall find the babe wrapped in swaddling clothes, lying in a manger."

Suddenly there was with the angel a multitude of the heavenly host praising God and saying, "Glory to god in the highest, and on earth peace, good will toward men."

It came to pass, as the angels were gone away from

them into heaven, the shepherds said one to another, "Let us now go even unto Bethlehem and see this thing which is come to pass, which the Lord hath made known unto us."

They came in haste and found Mary and Joseph, and the babe lying in a manger.

When they had seen it, they made known abroad the saying which was told them concerning this child. All they that heard it wondered at those things which were told them by the shepherds.

And the shepherds returned, glorifying and praising God for all the things that they had heard and seen, as it was told unto them. | Luke 2:20

But Mary kept all these things and pondered them in her heart. | Luke 2:19

When eight days were accomplished for the circumcising of the child, his name was called JESUS, which was so named of the angel before he was conceived in the womb. | Luke 2:21-38

When the days of her purification according to the law of Moses were accomplished, they brought him to Jerusalem to present him to the Lord, as it is written in the law of the Lord, "Every male that openeth the womb shall be called holy to the Lord,"* and to offer a sacrifice according to that which is said in the law of the Lord, "A pair of turtledoves, or two young pigeons."* | *Exodus 13:2

*Leviticus 12:6-8

Behold, there was a man in Jerusalem whose name was Simeon. The same man was just and devout, waiting for the consolation of Israel, and the Holy Ghost was upon him. It was revealed unto him by the Holy Ghost that he should not see death before he had seen the Lord's Christ.

He came by the Spirit into the temple. When the parents brought in the child Jesus to do for him after the custom of the law, then took he him up in his arms and blessed God, and said, "Lord, now lettest thou thy servant depart in peace according to thy word. For mine eyes have seen thy salvation, which thou hast prepared before the face of all people, a light to lighten the Gentiles, and the glory of thy people Israel."

Joseph and his mother marvelled at those things which were spoken of him. Simeon blessed them and said unto Mary his mother, "Behold, this child is set for the fall and rising again of many in Israel, and for a sign which shall be spoken against, that the thoughts of many hearts may be revealed. Yea, a sword shall pierce thy own soul also."

There was one Anna, a prophetess, the daughter of Phanuel of the tribe of Aser. She was of great age and had lived with a husband seven years from her virginity. She was a widow of about fourscore and four years, which departed not from the temple, but served God with fastings and prayers night and day. She, coming in that instant, gave thanks likewise unto the Lord and spake of him to all them that looked for redemption in Jerusalem.

3

When Jesus was born in Bethlehem of Judea in the days of Herod the king, behold, there came wise men from the east to Jerusalem, saying, "Where is he that is born King of the Jews? For we have seen his star in the east and are come to worship him."   *Matthew 2:1-23*

When Herod the king had heard these things, he was troubled, and all Jerusalem with him. When he had gathered all the chief priests and scribes of the people together, he demanded of them where Christ should be born.

They said unto him, "In Bethlehem of Judea, for thus it is written by the prophet, 'Thou Bethlehem in the land of Judea art not the least among the princes of Judea. For out of thee shall come a Governor that shall rule my people Israel.'"*   **Micah 5:2*

Then Herod, when he had privily called the wise men, inquired of them diligently what time the star appeared. He sent them to Bethlehem and said, "Go and search diligently for the young child. When ye have found him, bring me word again, that I may come and worship him also."

When they heard the king, they departed. And lo, the star which they saw in the east went before them, till it came and stood over where the young child was. When they saw the star, they rejoiced with exceeding great joy.

When they were come into the house, they saw the young child with Mary his mother, and fell down and worshipped him. When they had opened their treasures, they presented unto him gifts, gold, frankincense, and myrrh.

Being warned of God in a dream that they should not return to Herod, they departed into their own country another way. When they departed, behold, the angel of the Lord appeareth to Joseph in a dream, saying, "Arise and take the young child and his mother and flee into Egypt. Be thou there until I bring thee word. For Herod will seek the young child to destroy him."

When he arose, he took the young child and his mother by night and departed into Egypt, and was there until the death of Herod, that it might be fulfilled which was spoken of the Lord by the prophet, saying, "Out of Egypt have I called my son."* *Hosea 11:1*

Then Herod, when he saw that he was mocked of the wise men, was exceeding wroth and sent forth and slew all the children that were in Bethlehem and in all the coasts thereof, from two years old and under according to the time which he had diligently inquired of the wise men.

Then was fulfilled that which was spoken by Jeremiah the prophet, saying, "In Rama was there a voice heard, lamentation and weeping and great mourning. Rachel weeping for her children and would not be comforted, because they are not."* *Jeremiah 31:15*

But when Herod was dead, behold, an angel of the Lord appeared in a dream to Joseph in Egypt, saying, "Arise and take the young child and his mother and go into the land of Israel, for they are dead which sought the young child's life."

He arose and took the young child and his mother and came into the land of Israel. But when he heard that Archelaus did reign in Judea in the room of his father Herod, he was afraid to go thither. Notwithstanding, being warned of God in a dream, he turned aside into the parts of Galilee. He came and dwelt in a city called Nazareth, that it might be fulfilled which was spoken by the prophets, "He shall be called a Nazarene."* *No reference* Luke 2:40-52

The child grew and waxed strong in spirit, filled with wisdom, and the grace of God was upon him.

Now his parents went to Jerusalem every year at the feast of the passover. When he was twelve years old, they went up to Jerusalem after the custom of the feast.

When they had fulfilled the days, as they returned, the child Jesus tarried behind in Jerusalem. Joseph and his mother knew not of it, supposing him to have been in the company.

They went a day's journey, and they sought him among their kinsfolk and acquaintance. When they found him not, they turned back again to Jerusalem, seeking him.

It came to pass that after three days they found him in the temple, sitting in the midst of the doctors, both hearing them and asking them questions. All that heard him were astonished at his understanding and answers.

When they saw him, they were amazed. His mother said unto him, "Son, why hast thou thus dealt with us? Behold, thy father and I have sought thee sorrowing."

He said unto them, "How is it that ye sought me? Wist ye not that I must be about my Father's business?"

They understood not the saying which he spake unto them.

He went down with them and came to Nazareth and was subject unto them. But his mother kept all these sayings in her heart.

Jesus increased in wisdom and stature, and in favor with God and man.

THE WAY PREPARED

1

In the fifteenth year of the reign of Tiberias Caesar, Pontius Pilate being governor of Judea, and Herod being tetrarch of Galilee, and his brother Philip tetrarch of Iturea and of the region of Trachonitis, and Lysanias the tetrarch of Abilene, Annas and Caiaphas being the high priests, the word of God came unto John the son of Zacharias in the wilderness. He came into all the country about Jordan, preaching the baptism of repentance for the remission of sins and saying, "Repent ye, for the kingdom of heaven is at hand."	Luke 3:1-3 Matthew 3:2-3
For this is he that was spoken of by the prophet Isaiah, saying, "The voice of one crying in the wilderness, 'Prepare ye the way of the Lord. Make his paths straight. Every valley shall be filled, and every mountain and hill shall be brought low. The crooked shall be made straight, and the rough ways shall be made smooth. And all flesh shall see the salvation of God.'"*	Luke 3:5-6 *Isaiah 40:3-4
The same John was clothed with camel's hair and a leathern girdle about his loins, and he did eat locusts and wild honey.	Matthew 3:4/ Mark 1:6
Then went out to him Jerusalem and all Judea and all the region round about Jordan, and were all baptized of him in the river of Jordan, confessing their sins.	Matthew 3:5/ Mark 1:5
But when he saw many of the Pharisees and Sadducees come to his baptism, he said unto them, "O generation of vipers, who hath warned you to flee from the wrath to come? Bring forth therefore fruits worthy of repentance, and think not to say within yourselves, 'We have Abraham to our father.' For I say unto you that God is able of these stones to raise up children unto Abraham.	Matthew 3:7 Matthew 3:9/ Luke 3:8
"Now also the axe is laid unto the root of the trees. Every tree therefore which bringeth not forth good fruit is hewn down and cast into the fire."	Luke 3:9-15
The people asked him, saying, "What shall we do then?"	

He answered and said unto them, "He that hath two coats, let him impart to him that hath none, and he that hath meat, let him do likewise."

Then came also the publicans to be baptized, and said unto him, "Master, what shall we do?"

He said unto them, "Exact no more than that which is appointed you."

The soldiers likewise demanded of him, saying, "And what shall we do?"

He said unto them, "Do violence to no man, neither accuse any falsely, and be content with your wages."

As the people were in expectation, and all men mused in their hearts of John, whether he were the Christ or not, John answered, saying unto them all, "I indeed baptize you with water unto repentance. But he that cometh after me is mightier than I, the latchet of whose shoes I am not worthy to stoop down and unloose. I indeed have baptized you with water, but he shall baptize you with the Holy Ghost and with fire, whose fan is in his hand, and he will thoroughly purge his floor and will gather the wheat into his garner. But the chaff he will burn with fire unquenchable." | Matthew 3:11/
Mark 1:7/
Luke 3:16
Matthew 3:11/
Mark 1:8
Luke 3:17-18

Many other things in his exortation preached he unto the people.

It came to pass in those days that Jesus came from Nazareth of Galilee unto John to be baptized of him in Jordan. But John forbad him, saying, "I have need to be baptized of thee, and comest thou to me?" | Matthew 3:13/
Mark 1:9
Matthew 3:14-15

Jesus answering said unto him, "Suffer it to be so now, for thus it becometh us to fulfil all righteousness."

Then he suffered him. And Jesus, when he was baptized, went up straightway out of the water. And praying, lo the heavens were opened unto him. He saw the Holy Ghost descending in a bodily shape like a dove and lighting upon him. | Matthew 3:16-17/
Luke 3:21-22

Luke 3:23
Mark 1:13/
Luke 4:1

A voice came from heaven, saying, "This is my beloved Son, in whom I am well pleased."

Jesus himself began to be about thirty years of age. He, being full of the Holy Ghost, returned from Jordan and was led by the Spirit into the wilderness, and was with the wild beasts.

When he had fasted forty days and forty nights, he afterward hungered. When the devil came to him, he said, | Matthew 4:2-4/
Luke 4:2-4

"If thou be the Son of God, command that these stones be made bread."

But Jesus answered and said, "It is written, 'Man shall not live by bread alone, but by every word that proceedeth out of the mouth of God.'"* *Deuteronomy 8:3*

Then the devil brought him to Jerusalem and set him on a pinnacle of the temple, and said unto him, "If thou be the Son of God, cast thyself down from hence. For it is written, 'He shall give his angels charge over thee, to keep thee, and in their hands they shall bear thee up, lest at any time thou dash thy foot against a stone.'"* Matthew 4:5/ Luke 4:9 Luke 4:10-11

Psalm 91:11-12

Jesus answering said unto him, "It is written again, 'Thou shalt not tempt the Lord thy God.'"* *Deuteronomy 6:16*

Again the devil, taking him up into an exceeding high mountain, shewed unto him all the kingdoms of the world and the glory of them in a moment of time. The devil said unto him, "All this power will I give thee and the glory of them, for that is delivered unto me and to whomsoever I will give it. If thou therefore wilt fall down and worship me, all these things shall be thine." Matthew 4:8-9/ Luke 4:5-7

Jesus answered and said unto him, "Get thee behind me, Satan, for it is written, 'Thou shalt worship the Lord thy God, and him only shalt thou serve.'"* Luke 4:8

Deuteronomy 6:13

Then the devil departed from him for a season. And, behold, angels came and ministered unto him. Matthew 4:11/ Luke 4:13

2

This is the record of John, when the Jews sent priests and Levites from Jerusalem to ask him, "Who art thou?" John 1:19

They which were sent were of the Pharisees. John 1:24

He confessed and denied not, but confessed, "I am not the Christ." John 1:20-23

They asked him, "What then? Art thou Elijah?"

He said, "I am not."

"Art thou that Prophet?"*

He answered, "No." *Deuteronomy 18:15,18*

Then said they unto him, "Who art thou, that we may give an answer to them that sent us? What sayest thou of thyself?"

He said, "I am the voice of one crying in the wilderness, 'Make straight the way of the Lord,' as said the prophet Isaiah."* *Isaiah 40:3*

They asked him and said unto him, "Why baptizest thou then, if thou be not that Christ, nor Elijah, neither that Prophet?"

John answered them, saying, "I baptize with water, but there standeth one among you, whom ye know not. He it is who coming after me is preferred before me, whose shoe's latchet I am not worthy to unloose."

These things were done in Bethabara beyond Jordan, where John was baptizing.

The next day John saw Jesus coming unto him and said, "Behold the Lamb of God, which taketh away the sin of the world. This is he of whom I said, 'After me cometh a man which is preferred before me, for he was before me.' I knew him not, but that he should be made manifest to Israel, therefore am I come baptizing with water."

John bare record, saying, "I saw the Spirit descending from heaven like a dove, and it abode upon him. I knew him not, but he that sent me to baptize with water, the same said unto me, 'Upon whom thou shalt see the Spirit descending and remaining on him, the same is he which baptizeth with the Holy Ghost.' I saw and bare record that this is the Son of God."

Again the next day after John stood and two of his disciples, and looking upon Jesus as he walked, he said, "Behold the Lamb of God!" The two disciples heard him speak, and they followed Jesus.

Then Jesus turned and saw them following, and said unto them, "What seek ye?"

They said unto him, "Rabbi,"—which is to say, being interpreted, *Master*—"where dwellest thou?"

He said unto them, "Come and see."

They came and saw where he dwelt and abode with him that day, for it was about the tenth hour.

One of the two which heard John speak and followed him was Andrew, Simon Peter's brother. He first found his own brother Simon, and said unto him, "We have found the Messiah," which is, being interpreted, *The Christ*. He brought him to Jesus.

When Jesus beheld him, he said, "Thou art Simon the son of Jonah. Thou shalt be called Cephas." Which is by interpretation, *a stone*.

John 1:25-51

The day following Jesus would go forth into Galilee and found Philip, and said unto him, "Follow me."

Now Philip was of Bethsaida, the city of Andrew and Peter. Philip found Nathanael and said unto him, "We have found him of whom Moses in the law and the prophets did write, Jesus of Nazareth, the son of Joseph."

Nathanael said unto him, "Can there any good thing come out of Nazareth?"

Philip said unto him, "Come and see."

Jesus saw Nathanael coming to him and said of him, "Behold an Israelite indeed, in whom is no guile!"

Nathanael said unto him, "Whence knowest thou me?"

Jesus answered and said unto him, "Before that Philip called thee, when thou wast under the fig tree, I saw thee."

Nathanael answered and said unto him, "Rabbi, thou art the Son of God. Thou art the King of Israel."

Jesus answered and said unto him, "Because I said unto thee, I saw thee under the fig tree, believest thou? Thou shalt see greater things than these." He said unto him, "Verily, verily, I say unto you, hereafter ye shall see heaven open, and the angels of God ascending and descending upon the Son of man."

3

The third day there was a marriage in Cana of Galilee; and the mother of Jesus was there. Both Jesus was called and his disciples to the marriage.

When they wanted wine, the mother of Jesus said unto him, "They have no wine."

Jesus said unto her, "Woman, what have I to do with thee? Mine hour is not yet come."

His mother said unto the servants, "Whatsoever he saith unto you, do it."

There were set there six waterpots of stone after the manner of the purifying of the Jews, containing two or three firkins apiece. Jesus said unto them, "Fill the waterpots with water."

They filled them up to the brim.

He said unto them, "Draw out now and bear unto the governor of the feast." And they bare it.

When the ruler of the feast had tasted the water that

John 2:1-12

was made wine and knew not whence it was—but the servants which drew the water knew—the governor of the feast called the bridegroom and said unto him, "Every man at the beginning doth set forth good wine, and when men have well drunk, then that which is worse. But thou hast kept the good wine until now."

This beginning of miracles did Jesus in Cana of Galilee and manifested forth his glory, and his disciples believed on him.

After this he went down to Capernaum, he and his mother, his brethren and his disciples. They continued there not many days.

THE FIRST YEAR OF THE MINISTRY

1

The Jews' passover was at hand. Jesus went up to Jerusalem and found in the temple those that sold oxen and sheep and doves, and the changers of money sitting. When he had made a scourge of small cords, he drove them all out of the temple, and the sheep and the oxen, and poured out the changers' money and overthrew the tables; and said unto them that sold doves, "Take these things hence. Make not my Father's house a house of merchandise."

His disciples remembered that it was written, "The zeal of thine house hath eaten me up."*

Then answered the Jews and said unto them, "What sign shewest thou unto us, seeing that thou doest these things?"

Jesus answered and said unto them, "Destroy this temple, and in three days I will raise it up."

Then said the Jews, "Forty and six years was this temple in building, and wilt thou rear it up in three days?"

But he spake of the temple of his body. When therefore he was risen from the dead, his disciples remembered that he had said this unto them, and they believed the scripture and the word which Jesus had said.

Now when he was in Jerusalem at the passover in the feast day, many believed in his name when they saw the miracles which he did. But Jesus did not commit himself unto them, because he knew all men and needed not that any should testify of man. For he knew what was in man.

There was a man of the Pharisees named Nicodemus, a ruler of the Jews. The same came to Jesus by night and said unto him, "Rabbi, we know that thou art a teacher come from God, for no man can do these miracles that thou doest except God be with him."

Jesus answered and said unto him, "Verily, verily, I say unto thee, except a man be born again, he cannot see the kingdom of God."

John 2:13-25

*Psalm 69:9

John 3:1-21

Nicodemus said unto him, "How can a man be born when he is old? Can he enter the second time into his mother's womb and be born?"

Jesus answered, "Verily, verily, I say unto thee, except a man be born of water and of the Spirit, he cannot enter into the kingdom of God. That which is born of the flesh is flesh; and that which is born of the Spirit is spirit.

"Marvel not that I said unto thee, ye must be born again. The wind bloweth where it listeth, and thou hearest the sound thereof, but canst not tell whence it cometh and whither it goeth. So is everyone that is born of the Spirit."

Nicodemus answered and said unto him, "How can these things be?"

Jesus answered and said unto him, "Art thou a master of Israel and knowest not these things? Verily, verily, I say unto thee, we speak that we do know and testify that we have seen, and ye receive not our witness. If I have told you earthly things and ye believe not, how shall ye believe if I tell you of heavenly things?

"No man hath ascended up to heaven, but he that came down from heaven, even the Son of man which is in heaven. As Moses lifted up the serpent in the wilderness, even so must the Son of man be lifted up, that whosoever believeth in him should not perish, but have eternal life.

"For God so loved the world that he gave his only begotten Son, that whosoever believeth in him should not perish, but have everlasting life. For God sent not his Son into the world to condemn the world, but that the world through him might be saved. He that believeth on him is not condemned, but he that believeth not is condemned already, because he hath not believed in the name of the only begotten Son of God.

"This is the condemnation, that light is come into the world, and men loved darkness rather than light, because their deeds were evil. For everyone that doeth evil hateth the light, neither cometh to the light, lest his deeds should be reproved. But he that doeth truth cometh to the light, that his deeds may be made manifest, that they are wrought in God."

2

After these things came Jesus and his disciples into the land of Judea. There he tarried with them and baptized. John also was baptizing in Aenon near to Salim because there was much water there, and they came and were baptized. For John was not yet cast into prison. | John 3:22-36

Then there arose a question between some of John's disciples and the Jews about purifying. They came unto John and said unto him, "Rabbi, he that was with thee beyond Jordan to whom thou barest witness, behold, the same baptizeth, and all men come to him."

John answered and said, "A man can receive nothing, except it be given him from heaven. Ye yourselves bear me witness, that I said, I am not the Christ, but that I am sent before him.

"He that hath the bride is the bridegroom, but the friend of the bridegroom, which standeth and heareth him, rejoiceth greatly because of the bridegroom's voice. This my joy therefore is fulfilled. He must increase, but I must decrease.

"He that cometh from above is above all. He that is of the earth is earthly and speaketh of the earth. He that cometh from heaven is above all. What he hath seen and heard, that he testifieth, and no man receive his testimony. He that hath received his testimony hath set to his seal that God is true. For he whom God hath sent speaketh the words of God, for God giveth not the Spirit by measure unto him.

"The Father loveth the Son and hath given all things into his hand. He that believeth on the Son hath everlasting life. He that believeth not the Son shall not see life, but the wrath of God abideth on him."

Many other things in his exhortation preached he unto the people. But Herod the tetrarch, being reproved by him for Herodias his brother Philip's wife and for all the evils which Herod had done, added yet this above all, that he shut up John in prison. | Luke 3:18-20

When therefore the Lord knew how the Pharisees had heard that Jesus made and baptized more disciples than John—though Jesus himself baptized not, but his disciples—[and] when Jesus had heard that John was cast into prison, he left Judea and departed again into Galilee. | John 4:1-2

Matthew 4:12/ John 4:3

And he must needs go through Samaria. Then came he to a city of Samaria which is called Sychar, near to the parcel of ground that Jacob gave to his son Joseph. Jacob's well was there. Jesus therefore, being wearied with his journey, sat thus on the well. It was about the sixth hour.

There came a woman of Samaria to draw water. Jesus said unto her, "Give me to drink." For his disciples were gone away unto the city to buy meat.

Then said the woman of Samaria unto him, "How is it that thou, being a Jew, askest drink of me which am a woman of Samaria? For the Jews have no dealings with the Samaritans."

Jesus answered and said unto her, "If thou knewest the gift of God and who it is that saith to thee, 'Give me to drink,' thou wouldest have asked of him, and he would have given thee living water."

The woman said unto him, "Sir, thou hast nothing to draw with, and the well is deep. From whence then hast thou that living water? Art thou greater than our father Jacob, which gave us the well and drank thereof himself, and his children, and his cattle?"

Jesus answered and said unto her, "Whosoever drinketh of this water shall thirst again, but whosoever drinketh of the water that I shall give him shall never thirst. But the water that I shall give him shall be in him a well of water springing up into everlasting life."

The woman said unto him, "Sir, give me this water that I thirst not, neither come hither to draw."

Jesus said unto her, "Go, call thy husband and come hither."

The woman answered and said, "I have no husband."

Jesus said unto her, "Thou hast well said, 'I have no husband,' for thou hast had five husbands, and he whom thou now hast is not thy husband. In that saidst thou truly."

The woman said unto him, "Sir, I perceive that thou art a prophet. Our fathers worshipped in this mountain, and ye say that in Jerusalem is the place where men ought to worship."

Jesus said unto her, "Woman, believe me, the hour cometh when ye shall neither in this mountain nor yet at Jerusalem worship the Father. Ye worship ye know not what. We know what we worship, for salvation is of the Jews.

John 4:4-42

"But the hour cometh and now is when the true worshippers shall worship the Father in spirit and in truth. For the Father seeketh such to worship him. God is a Spirit, and they that worship him must worship him in spirit and in truth."

The woman said unto him, "I know that Messiah cometh, which is called Christ. When he is come, he will tell us all things."

Jesus said unto her, "I that speak unto thee am he."

Upon this came his disciples and marvelled that he talked with the woman. Yet no man said, "What seekest thou?" or, "Why talkest thou with her?"

The woman then left her waterpot and went her way into the city, and said to the men, "Come, see a man which told me all things that ever I did. Is not this the Christ?"

Then they went out of the city and came unto him.

In the meanwhile his disciples prayed him, saying, "Master, eat."

But he said unto them, "I have meat to eat that ye know not of."

Therefore said the disciples one to another, "Hath any man brought him ought to eat?"

Jesus said unto them, "My meat is to do the will of him that sent me and to finish his work. Say not ye there are yet four months, and then cometh harvest? Behold, I say unto you, lift up your eyes and look on the fields, for they are white already to harvest. He that reapeth receiveth wages and gathereth fruit unto life eternal, that both he that soweth and he that reapeth may rejoice together.

"Herein is that saying true, 'One soweth and another reapeth.' I sent you to reap that whereon ye bestowed no labor. Other men labored, and ye are entered into their labors."

Many of the Samaritans of that city believed on him for the saying of the woman which testified, "He told me all that ever I did." So when the Samaritans were come unto him, they besought him that he would tarry with them. He abode there two days.

Many more believed because of his own word and said unto the woman, "Now we believe, not because of thy saying. For we have heard him ourselves and know that this is indeed the Christ, the Savior of the world."

3

After two days he departed thence and returned in the power of the Spirit into Galilee. Then when he was come into Galilee, the Galileans received him, having seen all the things that he did at Jerusalem at the feast. For they also went unto the feast.	Luke 4:14/ John 4:43 John 4:45
There went out a fame of him through all the region round about. He taught in their synagogues, saying, "The time is fulfilled, and the kingdom of God is at hand. Repent ye and believe the gospel."	Luke 4:14 Mark 1:15/ Luke 4:15
So Jesus came again into Cana of Galilee where he made the water wine.	John 4:46-54

There was a certain nobleman whose son was sick at Capernaum. When he heard that Jesus was come out of Judea into Galilee, he went unto him and besought him that he would come down and heal his son. For he was at the point of death.

Then said Jesus unto him, "Except ye see signs and wonders, ye will not believe." | Luke 4:16-30

The nobleman said unto him, "Sir, come down ere my child die."

Jesus said unto him, "Go thy way. Thy son liveth."

The man believed the word that Jesus had spoken unto him, and he went his way. As he was now going down, his servants met him and told him, saying, "Thy son liveth."

Then inquired he of them the hour when he began to amend. They said unto him, "Yesterday at the seventh hour the fever left him."

So the father knew that it was at the same hour in the which Jesus said unto him, "Thy son liveth," and himself believed, and his whole house.

This is again the second miracle that Jesus did, when he was come out of Judea into Galilee.

He came to Nazareth where he had been brought up. As his custom was, he went into the synagogue on the sabbath day and stood up for to read. There was delivered unto him the book of the prophet Isaiah.

When he had opened the book, he found the place where it was written, "The Spirit of the Lord is upon me, because he hath anointed me to preach the gospel to the poor. He hath sent me to heal the brokenhearted, to preach deliverance to the captives, and recovering of sight to the blind, to set at liberty them that are bruised, to preach the acceptable year of the Lord."* *Isaiah 61:1-2*

He closed the book, and he gave it again to the minister and sat down. The eyes of all them that were in the synagogue were fastened on him.

He began to say unto them, "This day is this scripture fulfilled in your ears."

All bare him witness and wondered at the gracious words which proceeded out of his mouth. They said, "Is not this Joseph's son?"

He said unto them, "Ye will surely say unto me this proverb, 'Physician, heal thyself. Whatsoever we have heard done in Capernaum, do also here in thy country.'"

He said, "Verily I say unto you, no prophet is accepted in his own country.

"But I tell you of a truth, many widows were in Israel in the days of Elijah, when the heaven was shut up three years and six months, when great famine was throughout all the land. But unto none of them was Elijah sent, save unto Sarepta, a city of Sidon, unto a woman that was a widow.* *1 Kings 17:9*

"And many lepers were in Israel in the time of Elisha the prophet, and none of them was cleansed, saving Naaman the Syrian."§ §*2 Kings 5:1,9-10,14*

All they in the synagogue, when they heard these things, were filled with wrath and rose up and thrust him out of the city, and led him unto the brow of the hill whereon their city was built, that they might cast him down headlong.

But he passing through the midst of them went his way. | Luke 4:30

Leaving Nazareth, he came and dwelt in Capernaum, a city of Galilee which is upon the sea coast in the borders of Zebulun and Naphtali, that it might be fulfilled which was spoken by Isaiah the prophet, saying, "The land of Zebulun and the land of Naphtali, by the way of the sea beyond Jordan, Galilee of the Gentiles. The people which sat in darkness saw great light, and to them which sat in the region and shadow of death light is sprung up."* | Matthew 4:13/ Luke 4:31 Matthew 4:14-16

Isaiah 9:1-2

4

Jesus, walking by the sea of Galilee, saw two brethren, Simon called Peter and Andrew his brother, casting a net into the sea, for they were fishers. When he had gone a little further thence, he saw other two brethren, James the son of Zebedee and John his brother, in a ship with Zebedee their father, mending their nets.

It came to pass that, as the people pressed upon him to hear the word of God, he saw [the] two ships standing by the lake, but the fishermen were gone out of them and were washing their nets. He entered into one of the ships, which was Simon's, and prayed him that he would thrust out a little from the land.

He sat down and taught the people out of the ship.

Now when he had left speaking, he said unto Simon, "Launch out into the deep and let down your nets for a draught."

Simon answering said unto him, "Master, we have toiled all the night and have taken nothing. Nevertheless at thy word I will let down the net."

When they had this done, they enclosed a great multitude of fishes, and their net brake. They beckoned unto their partners which were in the other ship that they should come and help them. They came and filled both the ships so that they began to sink.

When Simon Peter saw it, he fell down at Jesus' knees, saying, "Depart from me, for I am a sinful man, O Lord." For he was astonished, and all that were with him, at the draught of the fishes which they had taken. So was also James and John, the sons of Zebedee, which were partners with Simon.

Jesus said unto Simon and Andrew his brother, "Fear not. Follow me and I will make you fishers of men."

When they had brought their ships to land, they forsook all and followed him.

Straightway he called James the son of Zebedee and John his brother. They left their father Zebedee in the ship with the hired servants and followed him.

They went into Capernaum, and straightway on the sabbath day he entered into the synagogue and taught. They were astonished at his doctrine, for he taught them as one that had authority and not as the scribes.

Matthew 4:18	
Matthew 4:21/ Mark 1:19	
Luke 5:1	
Luke 5:2-9	
Matthew 4:19/ Mark 1:16/ Luke 5:10	
Luke 5:11	
Matthew 4:21-22/ Mark 1:20	

There was in their synagogue a man with the spirit of an unclean devil. He cried out with a loud voice, saying, "Let us alone! What have we to do with thee, thou Jesus of Nazareth? Art thou come to destroy us? I know thee who thou art, the Holy One of God."	Mark 1:23/ Luke 4:33 Mark 1:24
Jesus rebuked him, saying, "Hold thy peace and come out of him."	Mark 1:26-27/ Luke 4:35-36 Mark 1:21-28
When the devil had thrown him in the midst, torn him, and cried with a loud voice, he came out of him and hurt him not.	
They were all amazed, insomuch that they questioned among themselves, saying, "What thing is this? What new doctrine is this? For with authority and power he commandeth even the unclean spirits, and they do obey him."	
Immediately his fame spread abroad throughout all the region round about Galilee.	Mark 1:28-29
Forthwith when they were come out of the synagogue, they entered into the house of Simon and Andrew with James and John. Simon's wife's mother lay sick with a great fever, and they besought him for her.	Mark 1:30-32/ Luke 4:38-40
He came and stood over her, took her by the hand, lifted her up, and rebuked the fever. Immediately the fever left her, and she arose and ministered unto them.	
Now when the sun was setting, all they that had any sick with divers diseases brought them unto him, and them that were possessed with devils. All the city was gathered together at the door.	Mark 1:33 Matthew 8:16/ Luke 4:40
He laid his hands on every one of them that were sick and healed them, that it might be fulfilled which was spoken by Isaiah the prophet, saying, "Himself took our infirmities and bare our sicknesses."*	Matthew 8:17 *Isaiah 53:4
Devils also came out of many with his word, crying out and saying, "Thou art Christ the Son of God." He rebuking them suffered them not to speak, for they knew that he was Christ.	Matthew 8:16/ Luke 4:41
In the morning, rising up a great while before day, he went out and departed into a solitary place and there prayed. Simon and they that were with him followed after him. When they had found him, they said unto him, "All men seek for thee."	Mark 1:35-37
He said unto them, "Let us go into the next towns, that I may preach the kingdom of God to other cities also, for therefore am I sent."	Mark 1:38/ Luke 4:43

Jesus went about all Galilee, teaching in their synagogues, preaching the gospel of the kingdom, and healing all manner of sickness and all manner of disease among the people. His fame went throughout all Syria, and they brought unto him all sick people that were taken with divers diseases and torments, those which were possessed with devils, those which were lunatic, and those that had the palsy, and he healed them. There followed him great multitudes of people from Galilee, from Decapolis, from Jerusalem, from Judea, and from beyond Jordan. | Matthew 4:23-25

It came to pass, when he was in a certain city, there came a man full of leprosy who, seeing Jesus, fell on his face and besought him, saying, "Lord, if thou wilt, thou canst make me clean." | Mark 1:40-41/ Luke 5:12-13

Jesus, moved with compassion, put forth his hand and touched him, saying, "I will. Be thou clean."

As soon as he had spoken, immediately the leprosy departed from him, and he was cleansed. | Mark 1:42

Jesus straitly charged him, "See thou say nothing to any man, but go thy way, shew thyself to the priest, and offer for thy cleansing those things which Moses commanded for a testimony unto them." | Matthew 8:4/ Mark 1:43-44

But he went out and began to publish it much and to blaze abroad the matter, insomuch that Jesus could no more openly enter into the city, but was without in desert places. Great multitudes came together from every quarter to hear, and to be healed by him of their infirmities. | Mark 1:45/ Luke 5:15

He withdrew himself into the wilderness and prayed. | Luke 5:16

Again he entered into Capernaum after some days, and it was noised that he was in the house. It came to pass on a certain day, as he was teaching, that there were Pharisees and doctors of the law sitting by which were come out of every town of Galilee and Judea and Jerusalem. Straightway many were gathered together, insomuch that there was no room to receive them, no, not so much as about the door. He preached the word unto them, and the power of the Lord was present to heal them. | Mark 2:1
Mark 2:2/ Luke 5:17

Men brought to him a man sick of the palsy, lying on a bed which was borne of four. They sought means to bring him in and to lay him before him. When they could not find by what way they might bring him in because of the multitude, they went upon the housetop and uncov- | Matthew 9:2/ Mark 2:3/ Luke 5:18
Mark 2:4/ Luke 5:19

ered the roof where he was. When they had broken it up, they let him down through the tiling with his couch into the midst before Jesus.

Jesus seeing their faith said unto the sick of the palsy, "Son, be of good cheer. Thy sins are forgiven thee." | Matthew 9:2/ Luke 5:20

Certain of the scribes and the Pharisees sitting there began to reason in their hearts, saying, "Who is this which speaketh blasphemies? Who can forgive sins but God alone?" | Mark 2:6/ Luke 5:21

Immediately when Jesus perceived in his spirit that they so reasoned within themselves, he said unto them, "Why think ye evil in your hearts? For whether it is easier to say to the sick of the palsy, 'Thy sins be forgiven thee,' or to say, 'Arise and take up thy bed and walk'? But that ye may know that the Son of man hath power on earth to forgive sins..." He said to the sick of the palsy, "I say unto thee, arise, take up thy bed, and go thy way into thine house." | Matthew 9:4-5/ Mark 2:8-9 Mark 2:10-11

Immediately he arose, took up the bed, and went forth before them all to his own house, glorifying God. They were all amazed, and they glorified God which had given such power unto men, and were filled with fear, saying, "We have seen strange things today." | Mark 2:12/ Luke 5:25 Matthew 9:8/ Luke 5:26

After these things Jesus went forth again by the seaside, and all the multitude resorted unto him, and he taught them. | Matthew 9:9/ Mark 2:13-14/ Luke 5:27-28

As he passed by, he saw a man, a publican named Matthew the son of Alpheus sitting at the receipt of custom. He said unto him, "Follow me."

He left all, rose up, and followed him.

Matthew made him a great feast in his own house. As Jesus sat at meat in his house, many publicans and sinners came and sat down with him and his disciples, for there were many, and they followed him. | Matthew 9:9-10/ Mark 2:15/ Luke 5:29

But when the scribes and Pharisees saw him eat with publicans and sinners, they murmured, saying unto his disciples, "How is it that your Master eateth and drinketh with publicans and sinners?" | Matthew 9:11/ Mark 2:16/ Luke 5:30

But when Jesus heard it, he said unto them, "They that are whole have no need of a physician, but they that are sick. But go ye and learn what that meaneth, 'I will have mercy, and not sacrifice.'* For I came not to call the righteous, but sinners to repentance." | Matthew 9:12-13/ Mark 2:17

*Hosea 6:6

Then came to him the disciples of John and of the Pharisees, saying, "Why do we fast often and make prayers, but thy disciples eat and drink?"	Matthew 9:14/ Mark 2:18/ Luke 5:33
Jesus said unto them, "Can the children of the bridechamber mourn as long as the bridegroom is with them? As long as they have the bridegroom with them, they cannot fast. But the days will come when the bridegroom shall be taken away from them, and then shall they fast in those days."	Matthew 9:15/ Mark 2:19/ Luke 5:35
He spake also a parable unto them. "No man also seweth a piece of new cloth on an old garment, if otherwise then both the new piece that filled it up taketh away from the old, and the rent is made worse, and the piece that was taken out of the new agreeth not with the old.	Mark 2:21/ Luke 5:36
"Neither do men put new wine into old bottles, else the bottles break, and the wine is spilled, and the bottles will be marred. But new wine must be put into new bottles, and both are preserved.	Matthew 9:17/ Mark 2:22/ Luke 5:38
"No man also having drunk old wine straightway desireth new, for he saith, 'The old is better.'"	Luke 5:39

THE SECOND YEAR OF THE MINISTRY

1

There was a feast of the Jews, and Jesus went up to Jerusalem.

Now there is at Jerusalem by the sheep market a pool which is called in the Hebrew tongue Bethesda, having five porches. In these lay a great multitude of impotent folk, of blind, halt, withered, waiting for the moving of the water. For an angel went down at a certain season into the pool and troubled the water. Whosoever then first after the troubling of the water stepped in was made whole of whatsoever disease he had.

A certain man was there which had an infirmity thirty and eight years. When Jesus saw him lie and knew that he had been now a long time in that case, he said unto him, "Wilt thou be made whole?"

The impotent man answered him, "Sir, I have no man, when the water is troubled, to put me into the pool. But while I am coming, another steppeth down before me."

Jesus said unto him, "Rise, take up thy bed, and walk."

Immediately the man was made whole, and took up his bed and walked.

On the same day was the sabbath.

The Jews therefore said unto him that was cured, "It is the sabbath day. It is not lawful for thee to carry thy bed."

He answered them, "He that made me whole, the same said unto me, 'Take up thy bed and walk.'"

Then asked they him, "What man is that which said unto thee, 'Take up thy bed and walk?'"

He that was healed wist not who it was, for Jesus had conveyed himself away, a multitude being in that place.

Afterward Jesus found him in the temple and said unto him, "Behold, thou art made whole. Sin no more, lest a worse thing come unto thee."

The man departed and told the Jews that it was Jesus which had made him whole. Therefore did the Jews

John 5:1-47

persecute Jesus and sought to slay him, because he had done these things on the sabbath day.

But Jesus answered them, "My father worketh hitherto, and I work."

Therefore the Jews sought the more to kill him, because he not only had broken the sabbath, but said also that God was his Father, making himself equal with God.

Then answered Jesus and said unto them, "Verily, verily, I say unto you, the Son can do nothing of himself, but what he seeth the Father do. For what things soever he doeth, these also doeth the Son likewise. For the Father loveth the Son and sheweth him all things that himself doeth, and he will shew him greater works than these, that ye may marvel. For as the Father raiseth up the dead and quickeneth them, even so the Son quickeneth whom he will.

"For the Father judgeth no man, but hath committed all judgment unto the Son, that all men should honor the Son, even as they honor the Father. He that honoreth not the Son honoreth not the Father which has sent him.

"Verily, verily, I say unto you, he that heareth my word and believeth on him that sent me hath everlasting life and shall not come into condemnation; but is passed from death unto life.

"Verily, verily, I say unto you, the hour is coming and now is when the dead shall hear the voice of the Son of God, and they that hear shall live. For as the Father hath life in himself, so hath he given to the Son to have life in himself and hath given him authority to execute judgment also, because he is the Son of man. Marvel not at this, for the hour is coming in the which all that are in the graves shall hear his voice and shall come forth, they that have done good unto the resurrection of life, and they that have done evil unto the resurrection of damnation.

"I can of mine own self do nothing. As I hear, I judge, and my judgment is just, because I seek not mine own will, but the will of the Father which hath sent me.

"If I bear witness of myself, my witness is not true. There is another that beareth witness of me, and I know that the witness which he witnesseth of me is true.

"Ye sent unto John, and he bare witness unto the truth. But I receive not testimony from man, but these things I say that ye might be saved. He was a burning and a shining light, and ye were willing for a season to rejoice in his light.

"But I have greater witness than that of John, for the works which the Father hath given me to finish, the same works that I do bear witness of me, that the Father hath sent me. The Father himself which hath sent me hath borne witness of me. Ye have neither heard his voice at any time nor seen his shape. Ye have not his word abiding in you, for whom he hath sent, him ye believe not.

"Search the scriptures, for in them ye think ye have eternal life, and they are they which testify of me. And ye will not come to me that ye might have life.

"I receive not honor from men. But I know you, that ye have not the love of God in you. I am come in my Father's name, and ye receive me not. If another shall come in his own name, him ye will receive. How can ye believe, which receive honor one of another, and seek not the honor that cometh from God only?

"Do not think that I will accuse you to the Father. There is one that accuseth you, even Moses in whom ye trust. For had ye believed Moses, ye would have believed me, for he wrote of me. But if ye believe not his writings, how shall ye believe my words?"

2

It came to pass on the second sabbath after the first, that Jesus went through the corn fields, and his disciples were an hungred and began as they went to pluck the ears of corn and to eat, rubbing them in their hands. But when certain of the Pharisees saw it, they said unto him, "Why do ye that which is not lawful to do on the sabbath days?"	Matthew 12:1/ Mark 2:23/ Luke 6:1 Matthew 12:2/ Luke 6:2
Jesus answering them said, "Have ye never read what David did when he had need and was an hungered, and they that were with him? How he entered into the house of God in the days of Abiathar the high priest and did take and eat the shewbread, and gave also to them that were with him, which was not lawful for him to eat, neither for them which were with him, but only for the priests?*	Mark 2:25/ Luke 6:3 Matthew 12:4/ Mark 2:26/ Luke 6:4 *1 Samuel 21:2-6
"Or have ye not read in the law how that on the sabbath days, the priests in the temple profane the sabbath	Matthew 12:5-7

and are blameless?* But I say unto you that in this place is one greater than the temple.

"But if ye had known what this meaneth, 'I will have mercy and not sacrifice,'* ye would not have condemned the guiltless. The sabbath was made for man, and not man for the sabbath. For the Son of man is Lord even of the sabbath day."

When he was departed thence, it came to pass also on another sabbath that he entered into the synagogue and taught.

There was a man whose right hand was withered. The scribes and Pharisees watched him whether he would heal on the sabbath day, that they might find an accusation against him.

But he knew their thoughts and said to the man which had the withered hand, "Rise up and stand forth in the midst."

He arose and stood forth.

Then said Jesus unto them, "I will ask you one thing. Is it lawful to do good on the sabbath days, or to do evil? To save life, or to destroy it?"

But they held their peace.

He said unto them, "What man shall there be among you that shall have one sheep, and if it fall into a pit on the sabbath day, will he not lay hold on it and lift it out? How much then is a man better than a sheep? Wherefore it is lawful to do well on the sabbath days."

When he had looked round about on them with anger, being grieved for the hardness of their hearts, he said unto the man, "Stretch forth thy hand."

He stretched it forth, and it was restored whole, like as the other.

The Pharisees went forth filled with madness and straightway held a council with the Herodians against him, how they might destroy him.

But when Jesus knew it, he withdrew himself with his disciples from thence to the sea, and great multitudes from Galilee followed him, and from Judea, and from Jerusalem, and from Idumea, and from beyond Jordan, and they about Tyre and Sidon—a great multitude when they had heard what great things he did came unto him.

He healed them all that it might be fulfilled which was spoken by Isaiah the prophet, saying, "Behold my

---

*Numbers 28:9-10

*Hosea 6:6
Mark 2:27
Matthew 12:8

Matthew 12:9/
  Luke 6:6

Luke 6:7-8

Mark 3:4/
  Luke 6:9

Matthew 12:11-12

Matthew 12:13/
  Mark 3:5/
  Luke 6:10

Matthew 12:14/
  Mark 3:6/
  Luke 6:11

Matthew 12:15/
  Mark 3:7-8

Matthew 12:17-21

servant whom I have chosen, my beloved in whom my soul is well pleased. I will put my spirit upon him, and he shall shew judgment to the Gentiles. He shall not strive nor cry, neither shall any man hear his voice in the streets. A bruised reed shall he not break, and smoking flax shall he not quench, till he send forth judgment unto victory. And in his name shall the Gentiles trust."* *Isaiah 42:1-3

Unclean spirits when they saw him fell down before him and cried, saying, "Thou art the Son of God." He straitly charged them that they should not make him known. Mark 3:11-12

He spake to his disciples that a small ship should wait on him because of the multitude, lest they should throng him. For he had healed many, insomuch that they pressed upon him for to touch him, as many as had plagues. Mark 3:9-10

It came to pass in those days that he went out into a mountain to pray, and continued all night in prayer to God. Luke 6:12

When it was day, he called unto him his disciples, and they came unto him. Of them he chose and ordained twelve, whom he also named apostles, that they should be with him, and that he might send them forth to preach, and to have power to heal sicknesses, and to cast out devils. Mark 3:13-14/ Luke 6:13 Mark 3:15

Simon, whom he also surnamed Peter, and Andrew his brother, James the son of Zebedee, and John the brother of James. He surnamed them Boanerges, which is, *The sons of thunder.* Philip and Bartholomew, Matthew and Thomas, James the son of Alpheus, and Simon the Canaanite called Zelotes, and Judas the brother of James, and Judas Iscariot, which also was the traitor. Mark 3:16-18/ Luke 6:14-16

He came down with them and stood in the plain, and the company of his disciples, and a great multitude of people out of all Judea and Jerusalem, and from the sea coast of Tyre and Sidon, which came to hear him and to be healed of their diseases, and they that were vexed with unclean spirits. Luke 6:17-19

The whole multitude sought to touch him, for there went virtue out of him, and he healed them all.

3

Seeing the multitudes, he went up into a mountain, and when he was set, his disciples came unto him. He lifted up his eyes on his disciples and opened his mouth and taught them, saying:

"Blessed are the poor in spirit, for theirs is the kingdom of heaven.

"Blessed are they that mourn, for they shall be comforted.

"Blessed are the meek, for they shall inherit the earth.

"Blessed are they which do hunger and thirst after righteousness, for they shall be filled.

"Blessed are the merciful, for they shall obtain mercy.

"Blessed are the pure in heart, for they shall see God.

"Blessed are the peacemakers, for they shall be called the children of God.

"Blessed are they which are persecuted for righteousness' sake, for theirs is the kingdom of heaven.

"Blessed are ye that weep now, for ye shall laugh.

"Blessed are ye when men shall revile you, and persecute you, and separate you from their company, and shall say all manner of evil against you falsely for my sake. Rejoice ye in that day, be exceeding glad, and leap for joy, for great is your reward in heaven. For so persecuted they the prophets which were before you.

"But woe unto you that are rich! For ye have received your consolation.

"Woe unto you that are full! For ye shall hunger.

"Woe unto you that laugh now! For ye shall mourn and weep.

"Woe unto you when all men shall speak well of you! For so did their fathers to the false prophets.

"Ye are the salt of the earth. But if the salt have lost his savor, wherewith shall it be salted? It is thenceforth good for nothing but to be cast out and to be trodden under foot of men.

"Ye are the light of the world. A city that is set on a hill cannot be hid. Neither do men light a candle and put it under a bushel, but on a candlestick, and it giveth light unto all that are in the house. Let your light so shine before men that they may see your good works and glorify your Father which is in heaven.

Matthew 5:1
Matthew 5:2/
 Luke 6:20

Matthew 5:3-10

Luke 6:21
Matthew 5:11-12/
 Luke 6:22-23

Luke 6:24-26

Matthew 5:13-47

"Think not that I am come to destroy the law or the prophets. I am not come to destroy, but to fulfill. For verily I say unto you, till heaven and earth pass, one jot or one tittle shall in no wise pass from the law till all be fulfilled.

"Whosoever therefore shall break one of these least commandments and shall teach men so, he shall be called the least in the kingdom of heaven. But whosoever shall do and teach them, the same shall be called great in the kingdom of heaven. For I say unto you, that except your righteousness shall exceed the righteousness of the scribes and Pharisees, ye shall in no case enter into the kingdom of heaven.

"Ye have heard that it was said by them of old time, 'Thou shalt not kill,'* and 'Whosoever shall kill shall be in danger of the judgment.'§ But I say unto you that whosoever is angry with his brother without a cause shall be in danger of the judgment And whosoever shall say to his brother, 'Raca,'* shall be in danger of the council. But whosoever shall say, 'Thou fool,' shall be in danger of hell fire.

"Therefore if thou bring thy gift to the altar and there rememberest that thy brother hath ought against thee, leave there thy gift before the altar and go thy way. First be reconciled to thy brother, and then come and offer thy gift.

"Agree with thine adversary quickly whiles thou art in the way with him, lest at any time the adversary deliver thee to the judge, and the judge deliver thee to the officer, and thou be cast into prison. Verily I say unto thee, thou shalt by no means come out thence till thou hast paid the uttermost farthing.

"Ye have heard that it was said by them of old time, 'Thou shalt not commit adultery.'* But I say unto you, that whosoever looketh on a woman to lust after her hath committed adultery with her already in his heart.

"If thy right eye offend thee, pluck it out and cast it from thee. For it is profitable for thee that one of thy members should perish, and not that thy whole body should be cast into hell. And if thy right hand offend thee, cut it off and cast it from thee. For it is profitable for thee that one of thy members should perish, and not that thy whole body should be cast into hell.

*Exodus 20:13
§No source

*Senseless; vain; empty-headed

*Exodus 20:14

"It hath been said, 'Whosoever shall put away his wife, let him give her a writing of divorcement.'* But I say unto you, that whosoever shall put away his wife, saving for the cause of fornication, causeth her to commit adultery. And whosoever shall marry her that is divorced commiteth adultery.

"Again ye have heard that it hath been said by them of old time, 'Thou shalt not forswear thyself, but shalt perform unto the Lord thine oaths.'§ But I say unto you, swear not at all, neither by heaven, for it is God's throne, nor by the earth, for it is his footstool, neither by Jerusalem, for it is the city of the great King. Neither shalt thou swear by thy head, because thou canst not make one hair white or black. But let your communication be, 'Yea, yea,' 'Nay, nay,' for whatsoever is more than these cometh of evil.

"Ye have heard that it hath been said, 'An eye for an eye, and a tooth for a tooth.'* But I say unto you, that ye resist not evil, but whosoever shall smite thee on thy right cheek, turn to him the other also. And if any man will sue thee at the law and take away thy coat, let him have thy cloak also. And whosoever shall compel thee to go a mile, go with him twain. Give to him that asketh thee, and from him that would borrow of thee turn thou not away.

"Ye have heard that it hath been said, 'Thou shalt love thy neighbor,* and hate thine enemy.'§ But I say unto you, love your enemies, bless them that curse you, do good to them that hate you, and pray for them which despitefully use you and persecute you, that ye may be the children of your Father which is in heaven.

"For he maketh his sun to rise on the evil and on the good, and sendeth rain on the just and on the unjust. For if ye love them which love you, what reward have ye? Do not even the publicans the same? And if ye salute your brethren only, what do ye more than others? Do not even the publicans so?

"And if ye do good to them which do good to you, what thank have ye? For sinners also do even the same. And if ye lend to them of whom ye hope to receive, what thank have ye? For sinners also lend to sinners, to receive as much again.

"But love ye your enemies, and do good, and lend, hoping for nothing again, and your reward shall be great.

**Deuteronomy 24:1*

§*Leviticus 19:12*

**Exodus 21:24; Leviticus 24:20; Deuteronomy 19:21*

**Leviticus 19:18*
§*Deuteronomy 23:6*

Luke 6:33-36

Ye shall be the children of the Highest. For he is kind unto the unthankful and to the evil.

"Be ye therefore merciful, as your Father also is merciful. Be ye therefore perfect, even as your Father which is in heaven is perfect.

"Take heed that ye do not your alms before men to be seen of them, otherwise ye have no reward of your Father which is in heaven. Therefore when thou doest thine alms, do not sound a trumpet before thee as the hypocrites do in the synagogues and in the streets, that they may have glory of men. Verily I say unto you, they have their reward. But when thou doest alms, let not thy left hand know what thy right hand doeth, that thine alms may be in secret, and thy Father which seeth in secret himself shall reward thee openly.

"When thou prayest, thou shalt not be as the hypocrites are. For they love to pray standing in the synagogues and in the corners of the streets that they may be seen of men. Verily I say unto you, they have their reward. But thou, when thou prayest, enter into thy closet, and when thou hast shut thy door, pray to thy Father which is in secret, and thy Father which seeth in secret shall reward thee openly.

"But when ye pray, use not vain repetitions as the heathen do, for they think that they shall be heard for their much speaking. Be not ye therefore like unto them, for your Father knoweth what things ye have need of before ye ask him.

"After this manner therefore pray ye:

"Our Father which art in heaven, Hallowed be thy name. Thy kingdom come. Thy will be done in earth as it is in heaven. Give us this day our daily bread, and forgive us our debts as we forgive our debtors. Lead us not into temptation, but deliver us from evil. For thine is the kingdom and the power and the glory forever. Amen.

"For if ye forgive men their trespasses, your heavenly Father will also forgive you. But if ye forgive not men their trespasses, neither will your Father forgive your trespasses.

"Moreover when ye fast, be not as the hypocrites, of a sad countenance. For they disfigure their faces that they may appear unto men to fast. Verily I say unto you, they have their reward. But thou, when thou fastest, anoint

Matthew 5:48

Matthew 6:1-34

thine head and wash thy face; that thou appear not unto men to fast, but unto thy Father which is in secret. And thy Father which seeth in secret shall reward thee openly.

"Lay not up for yourselves treasures upon earth where moth and rust doth corrupt and where thieves break through and steal. But lay up for yourselves treasures in heaven where neither moth nor rust doth corrupt, and where thieves do not break through nor steal. For where your treasure is, there will your heart be also.

"The light of the body is the eye. If therefore thine eye be single, thy whole body shall be full of light. But if thine eye be evil, thy whole body shall be full of darkness. If therefore the light that is in thee be darkness, how great is that darkness!

"No man can serve two masters, for either he will hate the one and love the other, or else he will hold to the one and despise the other. Ye cannot serve God and mammon.

"Therefore I say unto you, take no thought for your life, what ye shall eat, or what ye shall drink, nor yet for your body, what ye shall put on. Is not the life more than meat, and the body than raiment?

"Behold the fouls of the air. For they sow not, neither do they reap, nor gather into barns. Yet your heavenly Father feedeth them. Are ye not much better than they?

"Which of you by taking thought can add one cubit unto his stature?

"And why take ye thought for raiment? Consider the lilies of the field, how they grow. They toil not, neither do they spin. Yet I say unto you, that even Solomon in all his glory was not arrayed like one of these. Wherefore, if God so clothe the grass of the field, which today is and tomorrow is cast into the oven, shall he not much more clothe you, O ye of little faith?

"Therefore take no thought, saying, 'What shall we eat?' or 'What shall we drink?' or 'Wherewithal shall we be clothed?' For after all these things do the Gentiles seek. For your heavenly Father knoweth that ye have need of all these things. But seek ye first the kingdom of God and his righteousness, and all these things shall be added unto you.

"Take therefore no thought for the morrow, for the morrow shall take thought for the things of itself.

Sufficient unto the day is the evil thereof.

"Judge not, and ye shall not be judged. Condemn not, and ye shall not be condemned. Forgive, and ye shall be forgiven. Give, and it shall be given unto you, good measure, pressed down, shaken together, and running over shall men give into your bosom. For with what judgment ye judge, ye shall be judged, and with what measure ye mete, it shall be measured to you again. | Luke 6:37

Matthew 7:2/
Luke 6:38

"Why beholdest thou the mote that is in thy brother's eye, but perceivest not the beam that is in thine own eye? Or how canst thou say to thy brother, 'Let me pull out the mote that is in thine eye,' when thou thyself beholdest not the beam that is in thine own eye? Thou hypocrite, first cast out the beam out of thine own eye, and then shalt thou see clearly to pull out the mote that is in thy brother's eye." | Luke 6:41

Matthew 7:4-5/
Luke 6:42

He spake a parable unto them. "Can the blind lead the blind? Shall they not both fall into the ditch? The disciple is not above his master, but everyone that is perfect shall be as his master. | Luke 6:39-40

"Give not that which is holy unto the dogs, neither cast ye your pearls before swine, lest they trample them under their feet and turn again and rend you. | Matthew 7:6-11

"Ask and it shall be given you. Seek and ye shall find. Knock and it shall be opened unto you. For everyone that asketh receiveth, and he that seeketh findeth, and to him that knocketh it shall be opened.

"Or what man is there of you, whom if his son ask bread, will he give him a stone? Or if he ask a fish, will he give him a serpent? If ye then, being evil, know how to give good gifts unto your children, how much more shall your Father which is in heaven give good things to them that ask him?

"Therefore as ye would that men should do to you, do ye also to them likewise. For this *is* the law and the prophets. | Matthew 7:12/
Luke 6:31

"Enter ye in at the strait gate, for wide is the gate and broad is the way that leadeth to destruction, and many there be which go in thereat. Because strait is the gate and narrow is the way which leadeth unto life, and few there be that find it. | Matthew 7:13-19

"Beware of false prophets which come to you in sheep's clothing, but inwardly they are ravening wolves.

Ye shall know them by their fruits. Do men gather grapes of thorns or figs of thistles? Even so, every good tree bringeth forth good fruit, but a corrupt tree bringeth forth evil fruit. A good tree cannot bring forth evil fruit, neither can a corrupt tree bring forth good fruit. Every tree that bringeth not forth good fruit is hewn down and cast into the fire.

"A good man out of the good treasure of his heart bringeth forth that which is good, and an evil man out of the evil treasure of his heart bringeth forth that which is evil. For of the abundance of the heart his mouth speaketh. Wherefore by their fruits ye shall know them. — Luke 6:45 / Matthew 7:20-22

"Not everyone that saith unto me, 'Lord, Lord,' shall enter into the kingdom of heaven, but he that doeth the will of my Father which is in heaven. Many will say to me in that day, 'Lord, Lord, have we not prophesied in thy name? And in thy name have cast out devils? And in thy name done many wonderful works?'

"Then will I profess unto them, 'Why call ye me, 'Lord, Lord,' and do not the things which I say? I never knew you. Depart from me, ye that work iniquity.' — Matthew 7:23 / Luke 6:46

"Therefore whosoever cometh to me and heareth these sayings of mine and doeth them, I will liken him unto a wise man which built a house, and digged deep, and laid the foundation on a rock. And the rain descended, and the floods came, and the winds blew, and beat vehemently upon that house, and could not shake it. It fell not, for it was founded upon a rock. — Matthew 7:24-25 / Luke 6:47-48

"Everyone that heareth these sayings of mine and doeth them not shall be likened unto a foolish man, that without a foundation built his house upon the sand. And the rain descended, and the floods came, and the winds blew, and beat vehemently upon that house, Immediately it fell, and great was the fall of it." — Matthew 7:26-27 / Luke 6:49

It came to pass, when Jesus had ended these sayings, the people were astonished at his doctrine. For he taught them as one having authority, and not as the scribes. — Matthew 7:28-29

4

When Jesus had ended all his sayings in the audience of the people, he was come down from the mountain and entered into Capernaum. Great multitudes followed him. — Matthew 8:1,5 / Luke 7:1

A certain centurion's servant who was dear unto him was sick and ready to die. When he heard of Jesus, he sent unto him the elders of the Jews, beseeching him that he would come and heal his servant, saying, "Lord, my servant lieth at home sick of the palsy, grievously tormented."	Luke 7:2 Matthew 8:6/ Luke 7:3
When they came to Jesus, they besought him instantly, saying that he was worthy for whom he should do this. "For he loveth our nation, and he hath built us a synagogue."	Luke 7:4-5
Jesus said unto them, "I will come and heal him."	
Then Jesus went with them. When he was now not far from the house, the centurion sent friends to him, saying unto him, "Lord, trouble not thyself. For I am not worthy that thou shouldest enter under my roof. Wherefore neither thought I myself worthy to come unto thee. But speak the word only, and my servant shall be healed. For I am a man set under authority, having soldiers under me. I say unto one, go, and he goeth, and to another, come, and he cometh, and to my servant, do this, and he doeth it."	Matthew 8:7 Luke 7:6 Matthew 8:8/ Luke 7:7 Matthew 8:9/ Luke 7:8
When Jesus heard these things, he marvelled, and turned and said to the people that followed him, "Verily I say unto you, I have not found so great faith, no, not in Israel. I say unto you that many shall come from the east and west and shall sit down with Abraham, and Isaac, and Jacob in the kingdom of heaven. But the children of the kingdom shall be cast out into outer darkness. There shall be weeping and gnashing of teeth."	Matthew 8:10/ Luke 7:9 Matthew 8:11-12
Jesus said, "Go thy way, and as thou hast believed, so be it done." They that were sent, returning to the house, found the servant that had been sick was healed in the selfsame hour.	Matthew 8:13/ Luke 7:10
It came to pass the day after, that he went into a city called Nain. Many of his disciples went with him, and much people. Now when he came nigh to the gate of the city, behold, there was a dead man carried out, the only son of his mother. She was a widow, and much people of the city was with her.	Luke 7:11-17
When the Lord saw her, he had compassion on her and said unto her, "Weep not." He came and touched the bier. They that bare him stood still.	
He said, "Young man, I say unto thee, arise."	

He that was dead sat up and began to speak, and he delivered him to his mother.

There came a fear on all, and they glorified God, saying, "A great prophet is risen up among us," and, "God hath visited his people." This rumor of him went forth throughout all Judea and throughout all the region round about.

Now when John had heard in the prison the works of Christ, he sent two of his disciples to Jesus. When the men were come unto him, they said, "John Baptist hath sent us unto thee, saying, 'Art thou he that should come, or do we look for another?'" | Matthew 11:2/ Luke 7:19
Matthew 11:3/ Luke 7:20

In that same hour he cured many of their infirmities and plagues, and of evil spirits, and unto many that were blind he gave sight. | Luke 7:21

Then Jesus answered and said unto them, "Go your way and tell John what things ye have seen and heard, how the blind receive their sight, and the lame walk, the lepers are cleansed, and the deaf hear, the dead are raised up, and the poor have the gospel preached to them. Blessed is he whosoever shall not be offended in me." | Matthew 11:4-5 Luke 7:22

Matthew 11:6

When the messengers of John were departed, Jesus began to say unto the people concerning John, "What went ye out into the wilderness for to see? A reed shaken with the wind? But what went ye out for to see? A man clothed in soft raiment? Behold, they that wear soft clothing, they which are gorgeously apparelled and live delicately, are in kings' courts. | Matthew 11:7/ Luke 7:24

Matthew 11:8/ Luke 7:25

"But what went ye out for to see? A prophet? Yea, I say unto you, and much more than a prophet. For this is he of whom it is written, 'Behold, I send my messenger before thy face, which shall prepare thy way before thee.'* | Luke 7:26 Matthew 11:10

*Malachi 3:1

"Verily I say unto you, among those that are born of women there hath not risen a greater prophet than John the Baptist. Notwithstanding he that is least in the kingdom of heaven is greater than he. | Matthew 11:11/ Luke 7:28

"From the days of John the Baptist until now the kingdom of heaven suffereth violence, and the violent take it by force. For all the prophets and the law prophesied until John. And if ye will receive it, this is Elijah, which was for to come. He that hath ears to hear, let him hear." | Matthew 11:12-15

All the people that heard him, and the publicans, justified God, being baptized with the baptism of John. | Luke 7:29-31

But the Pharisees and lawyers rejected the counsel of God against themselves, being not baptized of him.

The Lord said, "Whereunto shall I liken the men of this generation? And to what are they like? They are like unto children sitting in the marketplace and calling one to another, and saying, 'We have piped unto you, and ye have not danced. We have mourned unto you, and ye have not lamented.' | Matthew 11:17/ Luke 7:32

"'For John the Baptist came neither eating bread nor drinking wine, and ye say, 'He hath a devil.' The Son of man came eating and drinking, and ye say, 'Behold a gluttonous man and a winebibber, a friend of publicans and sinners!' | Luke 7:33 Matthew 11:19/ Luke 7:34

"But wisdom is justified of all her children." | Luke 7:35

Then began he to upbraid the cities wherein most of his mighty works were done because they repented not. | Matthew 11:20-30

"Woe unto thee, Chorazin! Woe unto thee, Bethsaida! For if the mighty works which were done in you had been done in Tyre and Sidon, they would have repented long ago in sackcloth and ashes. But I say unto you, it shall be more tolerable for Tyre and Sidon at the day of judgment, than for you.

"And thou, Capernaum, which art exalted unto heaven, shalt be brought down to hell. For if the mighty works which have been done in thee had been done in Sodom, it would have remained unto this day. But I say unto you, that it shall be more tolerable for the land of Sodom in the day of judgment, than for thee."

At that time Jesus answered and said, "I thank thee, O Father, Lord of heaven and earth, because thou hast hid these things from the wise and prudent and hast revealed them unto babes. Even so, Father, for so it seemed good in thy sight.

"All things are delivered unto me of my Father. No man knoweth the Son, but the Father, neither knoweth any man the Father, save the Son, and he to whomsoever the Son will reveal him.

"Come unto me, all ye that labor and are heavy laden, and I will give you rest. Take my yoke upon you and learn of me. For I am meek and lowly in heart, and ye shall find rest unto your souls. For my yoke is easy and my burden is light."

5

One of the Pharisees desired him that he would eat with him. He went into the Pharisee's house and sat down to meat.

Behold, a woman in the city which was a sinner, when she knew that Jesus sat at meat in the Pharisee's house, brought an alabaster box of ointment and stood at his feet behind him weeping, and began to wash his feet with tears, and did wipe them with the hairs of her head, and kissed his feet, and anointed them with the ointment.

Now when the Pharisee which had bidden him saw it, he spake within himself, saying, "This man, if he were a prophet, would have known who and what manner of woman this is that toucheth him, for she is a sinner."

Jesus answering said unto him, "Simon, I have somewhat to say unto thee."

He said, "Master, say on."

"There was a certain creditor which had two debtors. The one owed five hundred pence and the other fifty. When they had nothing to pay, he frankly forgave them both. Tell me therefore, which of them will love him most?"

Simon answered and said, "I suppose that he to whom he forgave most."

He said unto him, "Thou hast rightly judged."

He turned to the woman and said unto Simon, "Seest thou this woman? I entered into thine house. Thou gavest me no water for my feet. But she hath washed my feet with tears and wiped them with the hairs of her head.

"Thou gavest me no kiss. But this woman since the time I came in hath not ceased to kiss my feet.

"My head with oil thou didst not anoint. But this woman hath anointed my feet with ointment.

'Wherefore I say unto thee, her sins, which are many, are forgiven, for she loved much. But to whom little is forgiven, the same loveth little."

He said unto her, "Thy sins are forgiven."

They that sat at meat with him began to say within themselves, "Who is this that forgiveth sins also?"

He said to the woman, "Thy faith had saved thee. Go in peace."

Luke 7:36-50

It came to pass afterward, that he went throughout every city and village, preaching and shewing the glad tidings of the kingdom of God. The twelve were with him, and certain women which had been healed of evil spirits and infirmities, Mary called Magdalene, out of whom Jesus had cast seven devils, and Joanna the wife of Chuza, Herod's steward, and Susanna, and many others which ministered unto him of their substance. | Mark 16:9/ Luke 8:1-3

The multitude came together again, so that they could not so much as eat bread. When his friends heard of it, they went out to lay hold on him, for they said, "He is beside himself." | Mark 3:20-21

Then was brought unto him one possessed with a devil, blind and dumb. He healed him insomuch that the blind and dumb both spake and saw. All the people were amazed and said, "Is not this the son of David?" | Matthew 12:22-23

But when the Pharisees and the scribes which came down from Jerusalem heard it, they said, "This fellow doth not cast out devils, but by Beelzebub the prince of the devils." | Matthew 12:24/ Mark 3:22

Jesus knew their thoughts and called them unto him, and said unto them in parables, "How can Satan cast out Satan? Every kingdom divided against itself is brought to desolation, and every city or house divided against itself shall not stand. | Matthew 12:25/ Mark 3:23

"If Satan rise up against himself and be divided, how shall then his kingdom stand? And if I by Beelzebub cast out devils, by whom do your children cast them out? Therefore they shall be your judges. But if I cast out devils by the Spirit of God, then the kingdom of God is come unto you. | Matthew 12:26/ Mark 3:26
Matthew 12:27-30

"Or else how can one enter into a strong man's house and spoil his goods, except he first bind the strong man? Then he will spoil his house.

"He that is not with me is against me, and he that gathereth not with me scattereth abroad.

"Verily I say unto you, all manner of sin and blasphemy shall be forgiven unto men, but he that shall blaspheme against the Holy Ghost shall not be forgiven, but is in danger of eternal damnation. | Matthew 12:31/ Mark 3:28-29

"And whosoever speaketh a word against the Son of man, it shall be forgiven him. But whosoever speaketh | Matthew 12:32-45 against the Holy Ghost, it shall not be forgiven him, neither in this world, neither in the world to come.

"Either make the tree good and his fruit good, or else make the tree corrupt and his fruit corrupt. For the tree is known by his fruit.

"O generation of vipers, how can ye, being evil, speak good things? For out of the abundance of the heart the mouth speaketh. A good man out of the good treasure of the heart bringeth forth good things, and an evil man out of the evil treasure bringeth forth evil things. But I say unto you that every idle word that men shall speak, they shall give an account thereof in the day of judgment. For by thy words thou shalt be justified, and by thy words thou shalt be condemned."

Then certain of the scribes and of the Pharisees answered, saying, "Master, we would see a sign from thee."

But he answered and said unto them, "An evil and adulterous generation seeketh after a sign. There shall no sign be given to it, but the sign of the prophet Jonah. For as Jonah was three days and three nights in the whale's belly,* so shall the Son of man be three days and three nights in the heart of the earth.

Jonah 1:1-17; 2:1-10

"The men of Nineveh shall rise in judgment with this generation and shall condemn it, because they repented at the preaching of Jonah, and behold, a greater than Jonah is here.

"The queen of the south shall rise up in the judgment with this generation and shall condemn it, for she came from the uttermost parts of the earth to hear the wisdom of Solomon, and behold, a greater than Solomon is here.

"When the unclean spirit is gone out of a man, he walketh through dry places, seeking rest and findeth none. Then he saith, 'I will return into my house from whence I came out.'

"When he is come, he findeth it empty, swept, and garnished. Then goeth he and taketh with himself seven other spirits more wicked than himself, and they enter in and dwell there. And the last state of that man is worse than the first. Even so shall it be also unto this wicked generation."

While he yet talked to the people, there came to him his mother and his brethren, and standing without for the press, sent unto him, desiring to speak with him. The multitude sat about him.

Matthew 12:46/
Mark 3:31-32/
Luke 8:19

Then one said unto him, "Behold, thy mother and thy brethren stand without, desiring to speak with thee."

But he answered and said unto him that told him, "Who is my mother? And who are my brethren?"

He stretched forth his hand toward his disciples which sat about him and said, "Behold my mother and my brethren! For whosoever shall hear the word of God and do the will of my Father which is in heaven, the same is my brother and my sister and mother."

6

The same day went Jesus out of the house and sat by the seaside. When there was gathered a great multitude come to him out of every city, he entered into a ship and sat in the sea.

The whole multitude stood on the shore.

He taught them many things by parables, and said unto them in his doctrine, "Behold, a sower went forth to sow his seed. It came to pass, as he sowed, some seeds fell by the wayside, and it was trodden down, and the fowls of the air came and devoured them up.

"Some fell on stony ground where they had not much earth, and immediately they sprang up because they had no depth of earth. When the sun was up, they were scorched. Because they had no root and lacked moisture, they withered away.

"Some fell among thorns, and the thorns grew up and choked them, and it yielded no fruit.

"But other fell on good ground, and sprang up, and brought forth fruit, some a hundredfold, some sixtyfold, some thirtyfold."

When he had said these things, he cried, "He that hath ears to hear, let him hear."

When he was alone, they that were about him with the twelve asked him, "Why speakest thou unto them in parables?"

He answered and said unto them, "Because it is given unto you to know the mysteries of the kingdom of heaven, but unto them that are without it is not given. For whosoever hath, to him shall be given, and he shall have more abundance.

"But whosoever hath not, from him shall be taken away even that he hath.

"Therefore speak I to them in parables, because they seeing see not, and hearing they hear not, neither do they understand, lest at any time they should be converted, and their sins should be forgiven them. | Matthew 13:13/ Mark 4:12

"In them is fulfilled the prophecy of Isaiah, which saith, 'By hearing ye shall hear and shall not understand, and seeing ye shall see and shall not perceive. For this people's heart is waxed gross, and their ears are dull of hearing, and their eyes they have closed, lest at any time they should see with their eyes, and hear with their ears, and should understand with their heart, and should be converted, and I should heal them.'* | Matthew 13:14-17

Isaiah 6:9-10

"But blessed are your eyes, for they see, and your ears, for they hear. For verily I say unto you, that many prophets and righteous men have desired to see those things which ye see and have not seen them, and to hear those things which ye hear and have not heard them."

His disciples asked him, saying, "What might this parable be?" | Luke 8:9

He said unto them, "Know ye not this parable? How then will ye know all parables? Here ye therefore the parable of the sower: | Mark 4:13 / Matthew 13:18/ Luke 8:11

"The seed is the word of God. The sower soweth the word. When anyone heareth the word of the kingdom and understandeth it not, then Satan cometh immediately and taketh away the word that was sown in their hearts, lest they should believe and be saved. This is he which received seed by the wayside. | Mark 4:14 / Matthew 13:19/ Mark 4:15/ Luke 8:12

"But he that received the seed on stony ground, the same is he that heareth the word and immediately receive it with joy. Yet hath he not root in himself, and so endure for a while. Afterward when tribulation or persecution ariseth because of the word, immediately he is offended and in time of temptation fall away. | Matthew 13:20/ Mark 4:16 / Matthew 13:21/ Mark 4:17/ Luke 8:13

"He also that received seed among the thorns is he that heareth the word, and the cares of this world, and the deceitfulness of riches, and the lusts and pleasures of this life choke the word, and it becometh unfruitful. | Matthew 13:22/ Mark 4:19/ Luke 8:14

"But these that are sown on good ground are they which, in an honest and good heart, having heard the word, keep it, and understandeth it, and bring forth fruit | Matthew 13:23/ Mark 4:20/ Luke 8:15

with patience, some thirtyfold, some sixty, and some a hundredfold."

He said unto them, "No man, when he hath lighted a candle, covereth it with a vessel, or putteth it under a bushel, or under a bed, but setteth it on a candlestick, that they which enter in may see the light. For there is nothing hid that shall not be made manifest, neither anything kept secret that shall not be known and come abroad.

"If any man have ears to hear, let him hear.

"Take heed therefore what ye hear. With what measure ye mete, it shall be measured to you, and unto you that hear shall more be given. For he that hath, to him shall be given. And he that hath not, from him shall be taken even that which he seemeth to have."

He said, "So is the kingdom of God as if a man should cast seed into the ground, and should sleep, and rise night and day, and the seed should spring and grow up, he knoweth not how. For the earth bringeth forth fruit of herself, first the blade, then the ear, after that the full corn in the ear. But when the fruit is brought forth, immediately he putteth in the sickle, because the harvest is come."

Another parable put he forth unto them, saying, "The kingdom of heaven is likened unto a man which sowed good seed in his field. But while men slept, his enemy came and sowed tares among the wheat and went his way. But when the blade was sprung up and brought forth fruit, then appeared the tares also.

"So the servants of the householder came and said unto him, 'Sir, didst not thou sow good seed in thy field? From whence then hath it tares?'

"He said unto them, 'An enemy hath done this.'

"The servants said unto him, 'Wilt thou then that we go and gather them up?'

"But he said, 'Nay; lest while ye gather up the tares, ye root up also the wheat with them. Let both grow together until the harvest, and in the time of harvest I will say to the reapers, "Gather ye together first the tares and bind them in bundles to burn them, but gather the wheat into my barn".'"

Another parable put he forth unto them, saying, "Whereunto shall we liken the kingdom of God? Or with what comparison shall we compare it? It is

Mark 4:21/
Luke 8:16

Mark 4:22/
Luke 8:17

Mark 4:23
Mark 4:24-25/
Luke 8:18

Mark 4:26-29

Matthew 13:24-30

Matthew 13:31/
Mark 4:30
Matthew 13:32/

like a grain of mustard seed which, when it is sown in the earth, is the least of all seeds. But when it is grown, it is the greatest among herbs, and becometh a tree, and shooteth out great branches so that the birds of the air come and lodge in the branches thereof." | Mark 4:31-32

Another parable spake he unto them. "The kingdom of heaven is like unto leaven, which a woman took and hid in three measures of meal till the whole was leavened." | Matthew 13:33

All these things spake Jesus unto the multitude in parables. With many such parables spake he the word unto them as they were able to hear it. Without a parable spake he not unto them, that it might be fulfilled which was spoken by the prophet, saying, "I will open my mouth in parables. I will utter things which have been kept secret from the foundation of the world."* | Matthew 13:34/ Mark 4:33

Matthew 13:35

*Psalm 78:2

Then Jesus sent the multitude away and went into the house. When they were alone, his disciples came unto him, saying, "Declare unto us the parable of the tares of the field." | Matthew 13:36/ Mark 4:34

He answered and said unto them, "He that soweth the good seed is the Son of man. The field is the world. The good seed are the children of the kingdom, but the tares are the children of the wicked one. The enemy that soweth them is the devil. The harvest is the end of the world; and the reapers are the angels. | Matthew 13:37-53

"As therefore the tares are gathered and burned in the fire, so shall it be in the end of this world. The Son of man shall send forth his angels, and they shall gather out of his kingdom all things that offend and them which do iniquity, and shall cast them into a furnace of fire. There shall be wailing and gnashing of teeth. Then shall the righteous shine forth as the sun in the kingdom of their Father. Who hath ears to hear, let him hear.

"Again, the kingdom of heaven is like unto treasure hid in a field, the which when a man hath found, he hideth, and for joy thereof goeth and selleth all that he hath and buyeth that field.

"Again, the kingdom of heaven is like unto a merchant man seeking goodly pearls, who when he had found one pearl of great price, went and sold all that he had and bought it.

"Again, the kingdom of heaven is like unto a net that was cast into the sea and gathered of every kind, which when it was full, they drew to shore and sat down and gathered the good into vessels, but cast the bad away.

"So shall it be at the end of the world. The angels shall come forth and sever the wicked from among the just and shall cast them into the furnace of fire.

"There shall be wailing and gnashing of teeth."

Jesus said unto them, "Have ye understood all these things?"

They said unto him, "Yea, Lord."

Then said he unto them, "Therefore every scribe which is instructed unto the kingdom of heaven is like unto a man that is a householder, which bringeth forth out of his treasure things new and old."

And it came to pass, that when Jesus had finished these parables, he departed thence.

7

The same day, when the even was come, Jesus saw great multitudes about him. He said, "Let us pass over unto the other side."	Matthew 8:18/ Mark 4:35
It came to pass that, as they went in the way, a certain scribe came and said unto him, "Master, I will follow thee whithersoever thou goest."	Matthew 8:19/ Luke 9:57
Jesus said unto him, "The foxes have holes, and the birds of the air have nests, but the Son of man hath not where to lay his head."	Matthew 8:20/ Luke 9:58
He said unto another of his disciples, "Follow me." But he said, "Lord, suffer me first to go and bury my father."	Matthew 8:21/ Luke 9:59
Jesus said unto him, "Let the dead bury their dead. But go thou and preach the kingdom of God." Another also said, "Lord, I will follow thee. But let me first go bid them farewell which are at home at my house." Jesus said unto him, "No man having put his hand to the plow and looking back is fit for the kingdom of God."	Luke 9:60-62
When they had sent away the multitude, they entered into a ship. There were also with him other little ships with his disciples. He said unto them, "Let us go over unto the other side of the lake." They launched forth.	Matthew 8:23/ Mark 4:36/ Luke 8:22
But as they sailed, he fell asleep on a pillow in the hinder part of the ship. There arose a great storm of wind	Mark 4:38,37/ Luke 8:23

on the lake, and the waves beat into the ship so that it was filled with water. They were in jeopardy.

His disciples came to him and awoke him, saying, "Master, master, carest thou not that we perish?" | Matthew 8:25-26/ Mark 4:38-39/ Luke 8:24

Then he arose and rebuked the winds, and said unto the raging sea, "Peace, be still." The wind ceased, and there was a great calm.

He said unto them, "Why are ye so fearful? How is it that ye have no faith?" | Mark 4:40

They feared exceedingly and marvelled, saying one to another, "What manner of man is this! For he commandeth even the winds and the sea, and they obey him!" | Matthew 8:27/ Mark 4:41/ Luke 8:25

They came over unto the other side of the sea and arrived at the country of the Gadarenes, which is over against Galilee. | Mark 5:1/ Luke 8:26

When he was come out of the ship and went forth to land, immediately there met him two possessed with devils, exceeding fierce, coming out of the tombs, so that no man might pass by that way. | Matthew 8:28/ Mark 5:2-3/ Luke 8:27

A certain man had devils long time and ware no clothes, neither abode in any house, but had his dwelling among the tombs. No man could bind him, no, not with chains, because that he had been often bound with fetters and chains, and the chains had been plucked asunder by him, and the fetters broken in pieces. Neither could any man tame him. Always, night and day, he was in the mountains and in the tombs crying and cutting himself with stones. | Mark 5:4-5

But when he saw Jesus afar off, he ran and fell down before him and worshipped him. | Mark 5:6/ Luke 8:28

He said unto him, "Come out of the man, thou unclean spirit." | Mark 5:8

He cried out with a loud voice, and said, "What have I to do with thee, Jesus, thou Son of the most high God? Art thou come hither to torment me before the time? I adjure thee by God that thou torment me not." | Matthew 8:29/ Mark 5:7/ Luke 8:28

Jesus asked him, "What is thy name?" | Mark 5:9/ Luke 8:30

He answered, saying, "My name is Legion, for we are many." They besought him much that he would not command them to go out into the deep. | Mark 5:10/ Luke 8:31

Now there was a good way off nigh unto the mountains a great herd of swine feeding, about two thousand. So all the devils besought him, saying, "If thou cast us | Matthew 8:30/ Mark 5:11,13 Matthew 8:31/

out, send us into the swine that we may enter into them."	Mark 5:12
Jesus said unto them, "Go."	Mattew 8:32/
Then the unclean spirits went out of the man and entered into the swine. The whole herd of swine ran violently down a steep place into the sea and perished in the waters.	Mark 5:13/ Luke 8:33
When they that fed the swine saw what was done, they fled and told everything in the city and in the country. The whole city came out to meet Jesus and to see what it was that was done.	Matthew 8:33-34/ Mark 5:14/ Luke 8:34
They found the man that was possessed with devils and had the legion sitting at the feet of Jesus, clothed and in his right mind, and they were afraid. They that saw it told them how he that was possessed of the devils was healed, and also concerning the swine.	Mark 5:15/ Luke 8:35 Mark 5:16/ Luke 8:36
Then the whole multitude of the country of the Gadarenes round about besought him to depart out of their coasts, for they were taken with great fear.	Mark 5:17/ Luke 8:37
When he was come into the ship, he that had been possessed with devils besought him that he might be with him. Howbeit Jesus suffered him not, but sent him away, saying, "Return to thine own house and to thy friends, and tell them how great things the Lord hath done for thee, and hath had compassion on thee."	Mark 5:18-19/ Luke 8:38-39
He departed, and began to publish in Decapolis how great things Jesus had done for him, and all men did marvel.	Mark 5:20
When Jesus was passed over again by ship unto the other side into his own city, much people gathered unto him, and he was nigh unto the sea. The people gladly received him, for they were all waiting for him.	Matthew 9:1/ Mark 5:21/ Luke 8:40
Behold, there came a certain one of the rulers of the synagogue, Jairus by name. When he saw him, he fell down at Jesus' feet and besought him greatly, saying, "My little daughter lieth at the point of death. I pray thee, come and lay thy hands on her that she may be healed, and she shall live." For he had only one daughter, about twelve years of age.	Matthew 9:18/ Mark 5:22/ Luke 8:41 Mark 5:23 Matthew 9:19/ Mark 5:24/ Luke 8:42
Jesus arose and went with him, and so did his disciples. Much people followed him and thronged him as he went.	
A certain woman which was diseased with an issue of blood twelve years and had suffered many things of many	Matthew 9:20-21/ Mark 5:25-27

physicians, had spent all that she had and was nothing bettered but rather grew worse, when she had heard of Jesus, came in the press behind and touched the hem of his garment. For she said within herself, "If I may but touch his clothes, I shall be whole."

Straightway the fountain of her blood was dried up, and she felt in her body that she was healed of that plague. | Mark 5:29

Jesus, immediately knowing in himself that virtue had gone out of him, turned him about in the press and said, "Who touched me?" | Mark 5:30-31/ Luke 8:45

When all denied, Peter and they that were with him said unto him, "Master, the multitude throng thee and press thee, and sayest thou, 'Who touched me?'"

Jesus said, "Somebody hath touched me, for I perceive that virtue is gone out of me." He looked round about to see her that had done this thing. | Luke 8:46 / Mark 5:32

When the woman saw that she was not hid, she came fearing and trembling, knowing what was done in her, and falling down before him, she declared unto him before all the people for what cause she had touched him and how she was healed immediately. | Mark 5:33/ Luke 8:47

He said unto her, "Daughter, be of good comfort. Thy faith hath made thee whole. Go in peace and be whole of thy plague." | Mark 5:34/ Luke 8:48

While he yet spake, there came one from the ruler of the synagogue's house, saying to him, "Thy daughter is dead. Why troublest thou the master any further?" | Mark 5:35/ Luke 8:49

As soon as Jesus heard the word that was spoken, he said unto the ruler of the synagogue, "Be not afraid. Only believe, and she shall be made whole." | Mark 5:36/ Luke 8:50

He came into the house of the ruler of the synagogue and saw the tumult, and the minstrels and the people making a noise, and them that wept and wailed greatly. He said unto them, "Why make ye this ado and weep? Give place, for the maid is not dead, but sleepeth." | Matthew 9:23/ Mark 5:38 / Matthew 9:24/ Mark 5:39

They laughed him to scorn, knowing that she was dead. He put them all out. | Luke 8:53-54

When he came in where the damsel was lying, he suffered no man to go in, save Peter and James and John and the father and the mother of the maiden. He took the damsel by the hand and said unto her, "Talitha cumi;" which is, being interpreted, "Damsel, I say unto thee, arise." | Mark 5:40/ Luke 8:51 / Mark 5:41

Her spirit came again, and straightway she arose and walked, for she was of the age of twelve years. Her parents were astonished with a great astonishment.	Matthew 9:26/ Mark 5:42-43/ Luke 8:55-56
He commanded that something should be given her to eat, and charged them straitly that they should tell no man what was done.	
But the fame hereof went abroad into all that land.	
When Jesus departed thence, two blind men followed him crying and saying, "Thou son of David, have mercy on us."	Matthew 9:27-34
When he was come into the house, the blind men came to him, and Jesus said unto them, "Believe ye that I am able to do this?"	
They said unto him, "Yea, Lord."	
Then touched he their eyes, saying, "According to your faith be it unto you."	
Their eyes were opened, and Jesus straitly charged them, saying, "See that no man know it."	
But they, when they were departed, spread abroad his fame in all that country.	
As they went out, behold, they brought to him a dumb man possessed with a devil. When the devil was cast out, the dumb spake, and the multitudes marvelled, saying, "It was never so seen in Israel."	
But the Pharisees said, "He casteth out devils through the prince of the devils."	
He went out from thence and came into his own country, and his disciples followed him. When the sabbath day was come, he began to teach in the synagogue. Many hearing him were astonished, saying, "From whence hath this man these things? What wisdom is this which is given unto him, that even such mighty works are wrought by his hands?	Mark 6:1-2
"Is not this the carpenter's son? Is not his mother called Mary? And his brethren James and Joses and Simon and Judas? Are not his sisters here with us? Whence then hath this man all these things?"	Matthew 13:55 Matthew 13:56/ Mark 6:3
And they were offended at him.	
But Jesus said unto them, "A prophet is not without honor, save in his own country, and among his own kin, and in his own house."	Matthew 13:57/ Mark 6:4
He could do no mighty works there because of their unbelief, save that he laid his hands upon a few sick folk, and healed them. He marveled because of their unbelief.	Matthew 13:58/ Mark 6:5-6

8

Jesus went about all the cities and villages, teaching in their synagogues, and preaching the gospel of the kingdom, healing every sickness and every disease among the people.	Matthew 9:35-38
But when he saw the multitudes, he was moved with compassion on them, because they fainted and were scattered abroad as sheep having no shepherd. Then said he unto his disciples, "The harvest truly is plenteous, but the laborers are few. Pray ye therefore the Lord of the harvest, that he will send forth laborers into his harvest."	
Then he called his twelve disciples together and gave them power and authority over all devils to cast them out, and to heal all manner of sickness and all manner of disease. He sent them forth by two and two to preach the kingdom of God and to heal the sick.	Matthew 10:1/ Luke 9:1 Mark 6:7/ Luke 9:2
He commanded them, saying, "Go not into the way of the Gentiles, and into any city of the Samaritans enter ye not. But go rather to the lost sheep of the house of Israel.	Matthew 10:5/ Luke 9:3 Matthew 10:6-8
"As ye go, preach, saying, 'The kingdom of heaven is at hand.' Heal the sick, cleanse the lepers, raise the dead, cast out devils. Freely ye have received, freely give.	
"Provide nothing for your journey, save a staff only. No gold, nor silver, nor brass in your purses, nor scrip, neither bread, neither two coats, neither shoes, but be shod with sandals. For the workman is worthy of his meat.	Matthew 10:9-10/ Mark 6:8-9/ Luke 9:3
"Into whatsoever city or town ye shall enter, inquire who in it is worthy, and there abide till ye depart from that place.	Matthew 10:11/ Mark 6:10
"When ye come into a house, salute it. If the house be worthy, let your peace come upon it. But if it be not worthy, let your peace return to you.	Matthew 10:12-13
"Whosoever shall not receive you nor hear your words, when ye depart out of that house or city, shake off the very dust from your feet for a testimony against them. Verily I say unto you, it shall be more tolerable for the land of Sodom and Gomorrah in the day of judgment than for that city.	Matthew 10:14/ Luke 9:5 Matthew 10:15-42
"Behold, I send you forth as sheep in the midst of wolves. Be ye therefore wise as serpents and harmless as doves. But beware of men, for they will deliver you up	

to the councils, and they will scourge you in their synagogues. Ye shall be brought before governors and kings for my sake for a testimony against them and the Gentiles.

"But when they deliver you up, take no thought how or what ye shall speak. For it shall be given you in that same hour what ye shall speak. For it is not ye that speak, but the Spirit of your Father which speaketh in you.

"The brother shall deliver up the brother to death, and the father the child. The children shall rise up against their parents and cause them to be put to death. Ye shall be hated of all men for my name's sake, but he that endureth to the end shall be saved.

"But when they persecute you in this city, flee ye into another. For verily I say unto you, ye shall not have gone over the cities of Israel till the Son of man be come. The disciple is not above his master, nor the servant above his lord. It is enough for the disciple that he be as his master and the servant as his lord. If they have called the master of the house Beelzebub, how much more shall they call them of his household?

"Fear them not therefore, for there is nothing covered that shall not be revealed, and hid that shall not be made known. What I tell you in darkness, that speak ye in light. What ye hear in the ear, that preach ye upon the housetops.

"Fear not them which kill the body, but are not able to kill the soul. But rather fear him which is able to destroy both soul and body in hell. Are not two sparrows sold for a farthing? And one of them shall not fall on the ground without your Father. But the very hairs of your head are all numbered. Fear ye not therefore. Ye are of more value than many sparrows.

"Whosoever therefore shall confess me before men, him will I confess also before my Father which is in heaven. But whosoever shall deny me before men, him will I also deny before my Father which is in heaven.

"Think not that I am come to send peace on earth. I came not to send peace, but a sword. For I am come to set a man at variance against his father, and the daughter against her mother, and the daughter-in-law against her mother-in-law.

"A man's foes shall be they of his own household. He that loveth father or mother more than me is not worthy of me, and he that loveth son or daughter more than me is not worthy of me.

"He that taketh not his cross and followeth after me is not worthy of me. He that findeth his life shall lose it, and he that loseth his life for my sake shall find it.

"He that receiveth you receiveth me, and he that receiveth me receiveth him that sent me. He that receiveth a prophet in the name of a prophet shall receive a prophet's reward, and he that receiveth a righteous man in the name of a righteous man shall receive a righteous man's reward. Whosoever shall give to drink unto one of these little ones a cup of cold water only in the name of a disciple, verily I say unto you, he shall in no wise lose his reward."

It came to pass, when Jesus had made an end of commanding his twelve disciples, he departed thence to teach and to preach in their cities. | Matthew 11:1

They departed and went through the towns, preaching the gospel and that men should repent. Everywhere they cast out many devils, and anointed with oil many that were sick, and healed them. | Mark 6:12-13/ Luke 9:6

At that time Herod the tetrarch heard of the fame of Jesus, of all that was done by him, for his name was spread abroad. He was perplexed and said, "John have I beheaded, but who is this of whom I hear such things?" And he desired to see him. | Matthew 14:1 Mark 6:14/ Luke 9:7,9

It was said of some that John was risen from the dead. Others said that Elijah had appeared. And others said that one of the old prophets was risen again. | Mark 6:15/ Luke 9:7-8

But when Herod heard thereof, he said unto his servants, "This is John the Baptist whom I beheaded. He is risen from the dead, and therefore mighty works do shew forth themselves in him." | Matthew 14:2/ Mark 6:16

For Herod himself had sent forth and laid hold upon John and bound him, and put him in prison for Herodias' sake, his brother Philip's wife, for he had married her. For John had said unto Herod, "It is not lawful for thee to have thy brother's wife." | Matthew 14:3/ Mark 6:17 Mark 6:18

Therefore Herodias had a quarrel against him and would have put him to death, but she could not. For Herod feared John, knowing that he was a just man and holy, and observed him. When he heard him, he did many things and heard him gladly. And he feared the multitude, because they counted him as a prophet. | Matthew 14:5/ Mark 6:19-20

But when a convenient day was come when Herod's birthday was kept, that Herod made a supper to his lords, high captains, and chief estates of Galilee. When the daughter of Herodias came in and danced before them, and pleased Herod and them that sat with him, the king sware unto the damsel with an oath, "Whatsoever thou shalt ask of me, I will give it thee, unto the half of my kingdom."	Matthew 14:6/ Mark 6:21-23
She went forth and said unto her mother, "What shall I ask?"	Mark 6:24
She said, "The head of John the Baptist."	
She came in straightway with haste unto the king and asked, saying, "I will that thou give me the head of John the Baptist in a charger."	Matthew 14:8/ Mark 6:25
The king was exceeding sorry. Yet for his oath's sake, and for their sakes which sat with him at meat, he would not reject her. Immediately the king sent an executioner and commanded his head to be brought, and he went and beheaded John in the prison.	Matthew 14:9/ Mark 6:26 Matthew 14:10/ Mark 6:27
His head was brought in a charger and given to the damsel. She brought it to her mother.	Matthew 14:11
When his disciples heard of it, they came and took up his corpse and laid it in a tomb, and went and told Jesus.	Matthew 14:12/ Mark 6:29

9

The apostles, when they were returned, gathered themselves together unto Jesus and told him all things, both what they had done and what they had taught.	Mark 6:30/ Luke 9:10
He said unto them, "Come ye yourselves apart into a desert place and rest a while." For there were many coming and going, and they had no leisure so much as to eat.	Mark 6:31
He took them and departed thence by ship over the sea of Galilee, which is the sea of Tiberias. They went aside privately into a desert place belonging to the city called Bethsaida. The people saw them departing, and many knew him and ran on foot out of all the cities and outwent them, and came together unto him because they saw his miracles which he did on them that were diseased.	Matthew 14:13/ Mark 6:32/ Luke 9:10/ John 6:1 Matthew 14:13/ Mark 6:33/ John 6:2
Jesus, when he came out, saw a great multitude and was moved with compassion toward them, because they were as sheep not having a shepherd. Jesus went up into	Matthew 14:14/ Mark 6:34 John 6:3

a mountain, and there he sat with his disciples. He began to teach them many things of the kingdom of God and healed them that had need of healing. | Mark 6:34/ Luke 9:11

When the day began to wear away, then came the twelve unto him and said, "This is a desert place, and now the time is far passed. Send the multitude away, that they may go into the towns and villages and country round about and lodge, and buy themselves bread, for they have nothing to eat." | Matthew 14:15/ Mark 6:35-36/ Luke 9:12

But Jesus said unto them, "They need not depart. Give ye them to eat." | Matthew 14:16/ Mark 6:37

They said unto him, "Shall we go and buy two hundred pennyworth of bread and give them to eat?"

Jesus then saith unto Philip, "Whence shall we buy bread, that these may eat?" This he said to prove him, for he himself knew what he would do. | John 6:5-7

Philip answered him, "Two hundred pennyworth of bread is not sufficient for them, that everyone of them may take a little."

He said unto them, "How many loaves have ye? Go and see." | Mark 6:38

Andrew, Simon Peter's brother, said unto him, "There is a lad here which hath five barley loaves and two small fishes. But what are they among so many?" | John 6:8-9

He said, "Bring them hither to me." | Matthew 14:18

Now there was much green grass in the place. Jesus commanded them, "Make them sit down in ranks by hundreds and by fifties." They did so and made them all sit down. | Mark 6:39-40/ Luke 9:14-15/ John 6:10

Then he took the five loaves and the two fishes and, looking up to heaven, he blessed them and brake and distributed them to his disciples to set before the multitude. And they did all eat. | Mark 6:41/ Luke 9:16/ John 6:11 Mark 6:42

When they were filled, he said unto his disciples, "Gather up the fragments that remain, that nothing be lost." | John 6:12

Therefore they gathered them together of the fragments of the five barley loaves and of the fishes, twelve baskets full which remained over and above unto them that had eaten. They that had eaten were about five thousand men, beside women and children. | Mark 6:43/ John 6:13 Matthew 14:21

Then those men, when they had seen the miracle that Jesus did, said, "This is of a truth that prophet that should come into the world."* | John 6:14

When Jesus therefore perceived that they would come and take him by force to make him a king, he constrained his disciples to get into the ship and to go before him unto the other side toward Capernaum while he sent the multitudes away.	Mathew 14:22/ Mark 6:45/ John 6:15,17
When he had sent them away, he went up into a mountain apart to pray.	Matthew 14:23/ Mark 6:46-47
When the evening was come, the ship was in the midst of the sea, and he was alone on the land.	
The sea arose by reason of a great wind that blew.	John 6:18
In the fourth watch of the night Jesus saw them toiling in rowing, tossed with waves, for the wind was contrary unto them. So he came unto them, walking upon the sea, and would have passed by them.	Matthew 14:24-25/ Mark 6:48/ John 6:19
When the disciples had rowed about five and twenty or thirty furlongs, they saw Jesus walking on the sea and drawing nigh unto the ship. They were troubled, saying, "It is a spirit." And they cried out for fear.	Matthew 14:26-27/ Mark 6:50/ John 6:19
But immediately Jesus talked with them, saying, "Be of good cheer. It is I. Be not afraid."	
Peter answered him and said, "Lord, if it be thou, bid me come unto thee on the water."	Matthew 14:28-31
He said, "Come."	
When Peter was come down out of the ship, he walked on the water to go to Jesus. But when he saw the wind boisterous, he was afraid, and beginning to sink, he cried, saying, "Lord, save me!"	
Immediately Jesus stretched forth his hand and caught him, and said unto him, "O thou of little faith, wherefore didst thou doubt?"	
When they were come into the ship, the wind ceased. They were sore amazed in themselves beyond measure and wondered. For they considered not the miracle of the loaves, for their heart was hardened. Then they worshipped him, saying, "Of a truth thou art the Son of God."	Matthew 14:32/ Mark 6:51 Mark 6:52 Matthew 14:33
The day following when they had passed over, they came into the land of Gennesaret and drew to the shore. When they were come out of the ship, straightway the men of that place knew him and ran through that whole region round about, and began to carry about in beds those that were sick, and brought unto him all that were diseased, where they heard he was.	Mark 6:53/ John 6:22 Matthew 14:35-36/ Mark 6:54-56

Whithersoever he entered, into villages or cities or country, they laid the sick in the streets and besought him that they might only touch the hem of his garment. As many as touched him were made perfectly whole.

When the people which stood on the other side of the sea saw that there was none other boat there, save that one whereinto his disciples were entered, and that Jesus went not with his disciples into the boat, but that his disciples were gone away alone—howbeit there came other boats from Tiberias nigh unto the place where they did eat bread, after that the Lord had given thanks. When the people therefore saw that Jesus was not there, neither his disciples, they also took shipping and came to Capernaum, seeking for Jesus.   John 6:22-24

When they had found him on the other side of the sea as he taught in the synagogue in Capernaum, they said unto him, "Rabbi, when camest thou hither?"   John 6:25-58

Jesus answered them and said, "Verily, verily, I say unto you, ye seek me—not because ye saw the miracles—but because ye did eat of the loaves and were filled. Labor not for the meat which perisheth, but for that meat which endureth unto everlasting life, which the Son of man shall give unto you. For him hath God the Father sealed."

Then said they unto him, "What shall we do that we might work the works of God?"

Jesus answered and said unto them, "This is the work of God, that ye believe on him whom he hath sent."

They said therefore unto him, "What sign shewest thou then, that we may see and believe thee? What dost thou work? Our fathers did eat manna in the desert. As it is written, 'He gave them bread from heaven to eat'."*   *Nehemiah 9:15/ Psalm 78:24-25

Then Jesus said unto them, "Verily, verily, I say unto you, Moses gave you not that bread from heaven, but my Father giveth you the true bread from heaven. For the bread of God is he which cometh down from heaven and giveth life unto the world."

Then said they unto him, "Lord, evermore give us this bread."

Jesus said unto them, "I am the bread of life. He that cometh to me shall never hunger, and he that believeth on me shall never thirst.

"But I said unto you that ye also have seen me and believe not. All that the Father giveth me shall come to me, and him that cometh to me I will in no wise cast out.

"For I came down from heaven, not to do mine own will, but the will of him that sent me. This is the Father's will which hath sent me, that of all which he hath given me I should lose nothing, but should raise it up again at the last day. This is the will of him that sent me, that everyone which seeth the Son and believeth on him may have everlasting life, and I will raise him up at the last day."

The Jews then murmured at him because he said, "I am the bread which came down from heaven." They said, "Is not this Jesus, the son of Joseph, whose father and mother we know? How is it then that he saith, 'I came down from heaven'?"

Jesus therefore answered and said unto them, "Murmur not among yourselves. No man can come to me, except the Father which hath sent me draw him, and I will raise him up at the last day. It is written in the prophets, 'And they shall be all taught of God.'*

*Isaiah 54:13

"Every man therefore that hath heard and hath learned of the Father cometh unto me. Not that any man hath seen the Father, save he which is of God—he hath seen the Father.

"Verily, verily, I say unto you, he that believeth on me hath everlasting life. I am that bread of life. Your fathers did eat manna in the wilderness and are dead. This is the bread which cometh down from heaven, that a man may eat thereof and not die. I am the living bread which came down from heaven. If any man eat of this bread, he shall live forever.

"The bread that I will give is my flesh, which I will give for the life of the world."

The Jews therefore strove among themselves, saying, "How can this man give us his flesh to eat?"

Then Jesus said unto them, "Verily, verily, I say unto you, except ye eat the flesh of the Son of man and drink his blood, ye have no life in you. Whoso eateth my flesh and drinketh my blood hath eternal life, and I will raise him up at the last day.

"For my flesh is meat indeed, and my blood is drink indeed. He that eateth my flesh and drinketh my blood dwelleth in me, and I in him. As the living Father hath sent me and I live by the Father, so he that eateth me, even he shall live by me.

"This is that bread which came down from heaven. Not as your fathers did eat manna and are dead. He that eateth of this bread shall live forever."

Many therefore of his disciples, when they had heard this, said, "This is a hard saying. Who can hear it?"

When Jesus knew in himself that his disciples murmured at it, he said unto them, "Doth this offend you? What and if ye shall see the Son of man ascend up to where he was before? It is the spirit that quickeneth. The flesh profiteth nothing. The words that I speak unto you—they are spirit, and they are life. But there are some of you that believe not."

For Jesus knew from the beginning who they were that believed not, and who should betray him.

He said, "Therefore said I unto you, that no man can come unto me except it were given unto him of my Father."

These things said he in the synagogue as he taught in Capernaum. From that time many of his disciples went back and walked no more with him.

Then said Jesus unto the twelve, "Will ye also go away?"

Simon Peter answered him, "Lord, to whom shall we go? Thou hast the words of eternal life. We believe and are sure that thou art that Christ, the Son of the living God."

Jesus answered them, "Have not I chosen you twelve, and one of you is a devil?"

He spake of Judas Iscariot, the son of Simon, for he it was that should betray him, being one of the twelve.

Sidenotes:
- John 6:60-65
- John 6:59
- John 6:66-71

THE THIRD YEAR OF THE MINISTRY

1

The passover, a feast of the Jews, was nigh. Then came together unto Jesus the Pharisees and certain of the scribes which came from Jerusalem.	John 6:4 Matthew 15:1/ Mark 7:1
When they saw some of his disciples eat bread with defiled—that is to say, with unwashen hands—they found fault.	Mark 7:2-4
For the Pharisees and all the Jews, except they wash their hands oft, eat not, holding the tradition of the elders. When they come from the market, except they wash, they eat not. Many other things there be which they have received to hold, as the washing of cups and pots, brazen vessels, and of tables.	
Then the Pharisees and scribes asked him, "Why do thy disciples transgress the tradition of the elders? For they wash not their hands when they eat bread."	Matthew 15:2/ Mark 7:5
But he answered and said unto them, "Why do ye also transgress the commandment of God by your tradition? Ye hypocrites, well did Isaiah prophesy of you, saying, 'This people draweth nigh unto me with their mouth and honoreth me with their lips, but their heart is far from me. Howbeit in vain do they worship me, teaching for doctrines the commandments of men.'*	Matthew 15:3,7-8 Mark 7:7-9 *Isaiah 29:13*
"For laying aside the commandment of God, ye hold the tradition of men, as the washing of pots and cups. And many other such like things ye do."	
He said unto them, "Full well ye reject the commandment of God, that ye may keep your own tradition. For God commanded, saying, 'Honor thy father and mother;'* and, 'He that curseth father or mother, let him die the death.'§	Matthew 15:4 *Exodus 20:12* §*Exodus 21:17* Mark 7:11-12
"But ye say, 'If a man shall say to his father or mother, "It is Corban—that is to say, a gift—by whatsoever thou mightest be profited by me," he shall be free.' And ye suffer him no more to do ought for his father or his mother.	

"Thus have ye made the commandment of God of none effect by your tradition which ye have delivered. And many such like things do ye." | Matthew 15:6/ Mark 7:13

When he had called all the people unto him, he said unto them, "Hearken unto me everyone of you and understand. There is nothing from without a man that, entering into the mouth, can defile him. But the things which come out of the mouth, those are they that defile the man. If any man have ears to hear, let him hear." | Mark 7:14

Matthew 15:11/ Mark 7:15

Mark 7:16

When he was entered into the house from the people, his disciples came and said unto him, "Knowest thou that the Pharisees were offended after they heard this saying?" | Matthew 15:12/ Mark 7:17

But he answered and said, "Every plant which my heavenly Father hath not planted shall be rooted up. Let them alone—they be blind leaders of the blind. And if the blind lead the blind, both shall fall into the ditch." | Matthew 15:13-16

Then answered Peter and said unto him, "Declare unto us this parable."

Jesus said, "Are ye also yet without understanding? Do ye not perceive that whatsoever thing from without entereth into the man, it cannot defile him? Because whatsoever entereth in at the mouth goeth not into his heart, but into the belly, and is cast out into the draught, purging all meats. | Mark 7:18
Matthew 15:17/ Mark 7:19

"But those things which proceed out of the mouth of the man, they defile the man. For from within out of the heart of men proceed evil thoughts—adulteries, fornications, murders, thefts, false witness, covetousness, wickedness, deceit, lasciviousness, an evil eye, blasphemies, pride, foolishness. All these evil things come from within and are the things which defile a man. But to eat with unwashen hands defileth not a man." | Matthew 15:18/ Mark 7:20-21

Matthew 15:19-20/ Mark 7:22-23

After these things Jesus walked in Galilee, for he would not walk in Jewry because the Jews sought to kill him. | John 7:1

From thence he arose and went into the borders of Tyre and Sidon and entered into a house, and would have no man know it. But he could not be hid. | Mark 7:24

A certain woman of Canaan whose young daughter had an unclean spirit heard of him. The woman was a Greek, a Syro-phoenician by nation. She came and fell at his feet and cried unto him, saying, "Have mercy on me, O Lord, thou Son of David. My daughter is grievously vexed with a devil." | Matthew 15:22/ Mark 7:25-26

But he answered her not a word. | Matthew 15:23-25

His disciples came and besought him, saying, "Send her away, for she crieth after us."

But he answered and said, "I am not sent but unto the lost sheep of the house of Israel."

Then came she and worshipped him, saying, "Lord, help me."

But Jesus said unto her, "Let the children first be filled, for it is not meet to take the children's bread and to cast it unto the dogs." | Mark 7:27

She answered and said unto him, "Yes, Lord. Yet the dogs under the table eat of the children's crumbs which fall from their masters' table." | Matthew 15:27/ Mark 7:28

Then Jesus answered and said unto her, "O woman, great is thy faith. For this saying go thy way. Be it unto thee even as thou wilt. The devil is gone out of thy daughter." | Matthew 15:28/ Mark 7:29-30

When she was come to her house, she found the devil gone out and her daughter laid upon the bed, made whole from that very hour.

Jesus departed from the coasts of Tyre and Sidon and came nigh unto the sea of Galilee, through the midst of the coasts of Decapolis, and went up into a mountain and sat down there. | Matthew 15:29/ Mark 7:31

Great multitudes came unto him, having with them those that were lame, blind, dumb, maimed, and many others, and cast them down at Jesus' feet. He healed them, insomuch that the multitude wondered when they saw the dumb to speak, the maimed to be whole, the lame to walk, and the blind to see. They glorified the God of Israel. | Matthew 15:30-31

They brought unto him one that was deaf and had an impediment in his speech, and they beseeched him to put his hand upon him. | Mark 7:32-37

He took him aside from the multitude and put his fingers into his ears. He spit and touched his tongue and, looking up to heaven, he sighed and said unto him, "Ephphatha," that is, *Be opened.*

Straightway his ears were opened, and the string of his tongue was loosed, and he spake plain.

He charged them that they should tell no man. But the more he charged them, so much the more a great deal they published it, and were beyond measure astonished, saying, "He hath done all things well. He maketh both the deaf to hear and the dumb to speak."

In those days, the multitude being very great and having nothing to eat, Jesus called his disciples unto him and said, "I have compassion on the multitude, because they have now been with me three days and have nothing to eat. I will not send them away fasting to their own houses, lest they faint in the way, for divers of them came from far."	Matthew 15:32/ Mark 8:1-3
His disciples answered him, "From whence should we have so much bread in the wilderness, as to satisfy so great a multitude?"	Matthew 15:33/ Mark 8:4
Jesus asked them, "How many loaves have ye?" They said, "Seven, and a few little fishes."	Matthew 15:34/ Mark 8:5
He commanded the multitude to sit down on the ground. He took the seven loaves and the fishes and blessed and brake them, and gave to his disciples to set before the multitude.	Matthew 15:35 Matthew 15:36/ Mark :6-7
They did all eat and were filled. They took up of the broken meat that was left seven baskets full. They that had eaten were about four thousand men, beside women and children	Matthew 15:37 Matthew 15:38-39/ Mark 8:9-10
He sent the multitude away. Straightway he entered into a ship with his disciples and came into the coasts of Magdala, into the parts of Dalmanutha.	

2

The Pharisees also with the Sadducees came forth and began to question with him, seeking of him a sign from heaven, tempting him.	Matthew 16:1/ Mark 8:11
He answered and said unto them, "When it is evening ye say, 'It will be fair weather, for the sky is red.' And in the morning, 'It will be foul weather today, for the sky is red and lowering.' O ye hypocrites, ye can discern the face of the sky, but can ye not discern the signs of the times?"	Matthew 16:2-3
He sighed deeply in his spirit and said, "Why doth this generation seek after a sign? Verily I say unto you, a wicked and adulterous generation seeketh after a sign. There shall no sign be given unto it but the sign of the prophet Jonah."	Matthew 16:4/ Mark 8:12
He left them, and entering into the ship again departed to the other side.	Mark 8:13-14

Now the disciples had forgotten to take bread, neither had they in the ship with them more than one loaf. Then Jesus charged them, saying, "Take heed and beware of the leaven of the Pharisees and of the Sadducees, and of the leaven of Herod." | Matthew 16:6/ Mark 8:15

They reasoned among themselves, saying, "It is because we have taken no bread." | Matthew 16:7

When Jesus perceived it, he said unto them, "O ye of little faith, why reason ye among yourselves, because ye have brought no bread? Do ye not yet understand? Have ye your heart yet hardened? Having eyes, see ye not? And having ears, hear ye not? | Matthew 16:8-9/ Mark 8:17-18

"Do ye not remember? When I brake the five loaves among five thousand, how many baskets full of fragments took ye up?" | Mark 8:19

They said unto him, "Twelve."

"And the seven loaves among four thousand, how many baskets full of fragments took ye up?" | Matthew 16:10/ Mark 8:20

They said, "Seven."

"How is it that ye do not understand that I spake it not to you concerning bread, that ye should beware of the leaven of the Pharisees and of the Sadducees?" | Matthew 16:11-12

Then understood they how that he bade them not beware of the leaven of bread, but of the doctrine of the Pharisees and of the Sadducees.

He came to Bethsaida, and they brought a blind man unto him and besought him to touch him. He took the blind man by the hand and led him out of the town. When he had spit on his eyes and put his hands upon him, he asked him if he saw ought. | Mark 8:22-26

He looked up and said, "I see men as trees, walking."

After that he put his hands again upon his eyes and made him look up. He was restored and saw every man clearly.

He sent him away to his house, saying, "Neither go into the town, nor tell it to any in the town."

It came to pass, Jesus went out into the towns of Caesarea Philippi, and his disciples were with him. By the way, as he was alone praying, he asked his disciples, saying, "Whom do people say that I the Son of man am?" | Matthew 16:13/ Mark 8:27/ Luke 9:18 Luke 9:19

They answered, "Some say that thou art John the Baptist, but some say Elijah, and others Jeremiah, or that one of the old prophets is risen again." | Matthew 16:14/ Mark 8:28/ Luke 9:19

He said unto them, "But whom say ye that I am?"	Matthew 16:15
Simon Peter answering said, "Thou art the Christ, the Son of the living God."	Matthew 16:16/ Luke 9:20
Jesus answered and said unto him, "Blessed art thou, Simon Bar-Jonah, for flesh and blood hath not revealed it unto thee, but my Father which is in heaven. Upon this rock I will build my church, and the gates of hell shall not prevail against it.	Matthew 16:17-19
"I say also unto thee that thou art Peter, and I will give unto thee the keys of the kingdom of heaven. Whatsoever thou shalt bind on earth shall be bound in heaven, and whatsoever thou shalt loose on earth shall be loosed in heaven."	
Then he straitly charged his disciples and commanded them to tell no man that he was Jesus the Christ.	Matthew 16:20/ Luke 9:21
From that time forth began Jesus to teach his disciples how that he must go unto Jerusalem, saying, "The Son of man must suffer many things and be rejected of the elders and chief priests and scribes, and be killed, and after three days rise again." He spake that saying openly.	Matthew 16:21/ Mark 8:31/ Luke 9:22 Mark 8:32
Then Peter took him and began to rebuke him, saying, "Be it far from thee, Lord! This shall not be unto thee."	Matthew 16:22
But when he had turned about and looked on his disciples, he rebuked Peter, saying, "Get thee behind me, Satan. Thou art an offence unto me, for thou savorest not the things that be of God, but the things that be of men."	Matthew 16:23/ Mark 8:33
When he had called the people unto him with his disciples also, he said to them all, "If any man will come after me, let him deny himself and take up his cross daily and follow me. For whosoever will save his life shall lose it. But whosoever will lose his life for my sake and the gospel's shall find it.	Mark 8:34/ Luke 9:23 Matthew 16:25/ Mark 8:35
"For what shall it profit a man if he shall gain the whole world and lose his own soul? Or what shall a man give in exchange for his soul?	Mark 8:36-37
"Whosoever therefore shall be ashamed of me and of my words in this adulterous and sinful generation, of him also shall the Son of man be ashamed when he cometh with the holy angels in his own glory and in the glory of his Father, and reward every man according to his works.	Matthew 16:27/ Mark 8:38/ Luke 9:26
"Verily I say unto you, there be some standing here which shall not taste of death till they have seen the Son of man coming in power with the kingdom of God."	Matthew 16:28/ Mark 9:1

3

After six days Jesus took with him Peter, James, and John, and went up into a high mountain apart by themselves to pray. As he prayed, he was transfigured before them.	Matthew 17:1/ Mark 9:2/ Luke 9:28-29
The fashion of his countenance was altered, and his face did shine as the sun, and his raiment became shining and glistering, exceeding white as snow so as no fuller on earth can white them.	Matthew 17:2/ Mark 9:3-4/ Luke 9:29
There appeared unto them Moses and Elijah, who appeared in glory and spake with Jesus of his decease which he should accomplish at Jerusalem.	Mark 9:4/ Luke 9:30-31
But Peter and they that were with him were heavy with sleep. When they were awake, they saw his glory and the two men that stood with him.	Luke 9:32
It came to pass as they departed from him, Peter said unto Jesus, "Master, it is good for us to be here. If thou wilt, let us make here three tabernacles, one for thee, and one for Moses, and one for Elijah." For he wist not what to say, for they were sore afraid.	Matthew 17:4/ Luke 9:33 Mark 9:6
While he yet spake, there came a bright cloud that overshadowed them, and they feared as they entered into the cloud. There came a voice out of the cloud, saying, "This is my beloved Son in whom I am well pleased. Hear ye him."	Matthew 17:5/ Mark 9:7/ Luke 9:34-35
When the disciples heard it, they fell on their face and were sore afraid. Jesus came and touched them and said, "Arise and be not afraid."	Matthew 17:6-9
When they had lifted up their eyes, they saw no man save Jesus only.	
As they came down from the mountain, Jesus charged them, saying, "Tell the vision to no man until the Son of man be risen again from the dead."	
They kept that saying with themselves, questioning one with another what the rising from the dead should mean.	Mark 9:10
His disciples asked him, saying, "Why then say the scribes that Elijah must first come?"	Matthew 17:10-11
Jesus answered and said unto them, "Elijah truly shall first come and restore all things. But I say unto you that Elijah is come already, and they knew him not, but have done unto him whatsoever they listed, as it is written of him.	Matthew 17:12/ Mark 9:12-13

"Likewise it is written of the Son of man, that he must suffer many things of them and be set at nought." | Matthew 17:13

Then the disciples understood that he spake unto them of John the Baptist.

4

It came to pass that on the next day when he came to his disciples, he saw a great multitude about them, and the scribes questioning with them. Straightway all the people when they beheld him were greatly amazed and, running to him, saluted him. | Mark 9:14-16/ Luke 9:37

He asked the scribes, "What question ye with them?"

A certain man, one of the multitude, came kneeling down to him and said, "Master, I have brought unto thee my son which hath a dumb spirit. Lord, I beseech thee, have mercy on my son, for he is mine only child. | Matthew 17:14-15/ Mark 9:17-18/ Luke 9:38-39

"He is lunatic and sore vexed. Wheresoever he taketh him, he suddenly crieth out, and it teareth him that he foameth again, and gnasheth with his teeth, and pineth away, and bruising him hardly departeth from him.

"I brought him to thy disciples and besought that they should cast him out, and they could not cure him." | Matthew 17:16-17/ Mark 9:18-19/ Luke 9:40-41

Then Jesus answered and said, "O faithless and perverse generation, how long shall I be with you? How long shall I suffer you? Bring thy son unto me."

They brought him unto him. When he saw him as he was yet a coming, straightway the spirit threw him down on the ground and tare him, and he wallowed foaming. | Mark 9:20/ Luke 9:42

He asked his father, "How long is it ago since this came unto him?" | Mark 9:21-24

He said, "Of a child. And ofttimes it hath cast him into the fire and into the waters to destroy him. But if thou canst do anything, have compassion on us and help us."

Jesus said unto him, "If thou canst believe, all things are possible to him that believeth."

Straightway the father of the child cried out and said with tears, "Lord, I believe! Help thou mine unbelief."

When Jesus saw that the people came running together, he rebuked the unclean spirit, saying unto him, "Thou dumb and deaf spirit, I charge thee, come out of him and enter no more into him." | Mark 9:25/ Luke 9:42

The spirit cried and rent him sore and came out of him. He was as one dead, insomuch that many said, "He is dead."

But Jesus took him by the hand and lifted him up, and he arose. Jesus delivered him again to his father, and they were all amazed at the mighty power of God.

When Jesus came into the house, his disciples asked him privately, "Why could not we cast him out?"

Jesus said unto them, "Because of your unbelief. For verily I say unto you, if ye have faith as a grain of mustard seed, ye shall say unto this mountain, 'Remove hence to yonder place,' and it shall remove. Nothing shall be impossible unto you.

"Howbeit this kind goeth not out but by prayer and fasting."

They departed thence and passed through Galilee, and he would not that any man should know it. While they abode in Galilee, Jesus taught his disciples and said unto them, "Let these sayings sink down into your ears. The Son of man shall be betrayed into the hands of men, and they shall kill him. After that he is killed, he shall rise the third day."

But they understood not this saying. It was hid from them, that they perceived it not. They were afraid to ask him, and they were exceeding sorry.

When they came to Capernaum, they that received tribute money came to Peter and said, "Doth not your master pay tribute?"

He said, "Yes."

When he was come into the house, Jesus prevented him, saying, "What thinkest thou, Simon? Of whom do the kings of the earth take custom or tribute? Of their own children or of strangers?"

Peter said unto him, "Of strangers."

Jesus said unto him, "Then are the children free. Notwithstanding, lest we should offend them, go thou to the sea and cast a hook. Take up the fish that first cometh up. When thou hast opened his mouth, thou shalt find a piece of money. That take and give unto them for me and thee."

Being in the house, he called the twelve and asked them, "What was it that ye disputed among yourselves by the way?"

But they held their peace, for by the way they had disputed among themselves who should be the greatest in the kingdom of heaven.	Matthew 18:1/ Mark 9:34
Jesus, perceiving the thought of their heart, sat down and said unto them, "If any man desire to be first, the same shall be last of all and servant of all."	Mark 9:35/ Luke 9:47
He called a little child unto him and set him in the midst of them. When he had taken him in his arms, he said unto them, "Verily I say unto you, except ye be converted and become as little children, ye shall not enter into the kingdom of heaven. Whosoever therefore shall humble himself as this little child, the same is greatest in the kingdom of heaven. For he that is least among you all, the same shall be great.	Matthew 18:2/ Mark 9:36 Matthew 18:3-4/ Luke 9:48
"Whosoever shall receive one such little child in my name receiveth me. And whosoever shall receive me, receiveth not me, but him that sent me.	Matthew 18:5/ Mark 9:37
"But whosoever shall offend one of these little ones that believe in me, it were better for him that a millstone were hanged about his neck and he were drowned in the depth of the sea.	Matthew 18:6/ Mark 9:42
"Woe unto the world because of offences! For it must needs be that offences come, but woe to that man by whom the offence cometh! Wherefore if thy hand offend thee, cut it off and cast [it] from thee. It is better for thee to enter into life maimed than having two hands to go into hell, into the everlasting fire that never shall be quenched, where their worm dieth not, and the fire is not quenched.	Matthew 18:7 Matthew 18:8/ Mark 9:43 Mark 9:44-46
"And if thy foot offend thee, cut it off. It is better for thee to enter halt into life than having two feet to be cast into hell, into the fire that never shall be quenched, where their worm dieth not, and the fire is not quenched.	
"And if thine eye offend thee, pluck it out and cast it from thee. It is better for thee to enter into life with one eye than having two eyes to be cast into hell fire, where their worm dieth not, and the fire is not quenched.	Matthew 18:9/ Mark 9:47-48
"Take heed that ye despise not one of these little ones. For I say unto you that in heaven their angels do always behold the face of my Father which is in heaven. For the Son of man is come to save that which was lost.	Matthew 18:10-14
"How think ye? If a man have a hundred sheep, and one of them be gone astray, doth he not leave the ninety	

and nine and goeth into the mountains and seeketh that which is gone astray?

"And if it so be that he find it, verily I say unto you, he rejoiceth more of that sheep than of the ninety and nine which went not astray. Even so it is not the will of your Father which is in heaven, that one of these little ones should perish."

John answered and said, "Master, we saw one casting out devils in thy name, and we forbad him because he followeth not with us." | Luke 9:49

But Jesus said, "Forbid him not, for there is no man which shall do a miracle in my name that can lightly speak evil of me. | Mark 9:39/ Luke 9:50

"He that is not against us is for us. For whomsoever shall give you a cup of water to drink in my name, because ye belong to Christ, verily I say unto you, he shall not lose his reward. | Mark 9:41

"Moreover if thy brother shall trespass against thee, go and tell him his fault between thee and him alone. If he shall hear thee, thou hast gained thy brother. But if he will not hear thee, then take with thee one or two more, that in the mouth of two or three witnesses every word may be established. | Matthew 18:15-35

'If he shall neglect to hear them, tell it unto the church. If he neglect to hear the church, let him be unto thee as a heathen man and a publican.

"Verily I say unto you, whatsoever ye shall bind on earth shall be bound in heaven, and whatsoever ye shall loose on earth shall be loosed in heaven. Again I say unto you, that if two of you shall agree on earth as touching anything that they shall ask, it shall be done for them of my Father which is in heaven. For where two or three are gathered together in my name, there am I in the midst of them."

Then came Peter to him and said, "Lord, how oft shall my brother sin against me, and I forgive him? Till seven times?"

Jesus said unto him, "I say not unto thee, until seven times, but until seventy times seven.

"Therefore is the kingdom of heaven likened unto a certain king which would take account of his servants. When he had begun to reckon, one was brought unto him which owed him ten thousand talents. But forasmuch as he had not to pay, his lord commanded him to be sold, and his wife and children, and all that he had, and payment to be made.

"The servant therefore fell down and worshipped him, saying, 'Lord, have patience with me, and I will pay thee all.'

"Then the lord of that servant was moved with compassion, and loosed him and forgave him the debt.

"But the same servant went out and found one of his fellow servants which owed him a hundred pence. He laid hands on him and took him by the throat, saying, 'Pay me that thou owest.'

"His fellow servant fell down at his feet and besought him, saying, 'Have patience with me, and I will pay thee all.'

"And he would not, but went and cast him into prison till he should pay the debt.

"So when his fellow servants saw what was done, they were very sorry and came and told unto their lord all that was done. Then his lord, after that he had called him, said unto him, 'O thou wicked servant! I forgave thee all that debt because thou desiredst me. Shouldest not thou also have had compassion on thy fellow servant, even as I had pity on thee?'

"His lord was wroth and delivered him to the tormentors till he should pay all that was due unto him. So likewise shall my heavenly Father do also unto you, if ye from your hearts forgive not everyone his brother their trespasses.

"For everyone shall be salted with fire, and every sacrifice shall be salted with salt. Salt is good, but if the salt have lost his saltness, wherewith will ye season it? Have salt in yourselves, and have peace one with another." | Mark 9:49-50

After these things the Lord appointed other seventy also and sent them two and two before his face into every city and place whither he himself would come. | Luke 10:1-16

Therefore said he unto them, "The harvest truly is great, but the laborers are few. Pray ye therefore the Lord of the harvest that he would send forth laborers into his harvest.

"Go your ways. Behold, I send you forth as lambs among wolves. Carry neither purse nor scrip nor shoes, and salute no man by the way. Into whatsoever house ye enter, first say, 'Peace be to this house.' If the son of peace be there, your peace shall rest upon it. If not, it shall turn to you again.

"In the same house remain, eating and drinking such things as they give. For the laborer is worthy of his hire. Go not from house to house.

"Into whatsoever city ye enter, and they receive you, eat such things as are set before you and heal the sick that are therein. Say unto them, 'The kingdom of God is come nigh unto you.'

"But into whatsoever city ye enter, and they receive you not, go your ways out into the streets of the same and say, 'Even the very dust of your city which cleaveth on us, we do wipe off against you. Notwithstanding be ye sure of this, that the kingdom of God is come nigh unto you.'

"But I say unto you, that it shall be more tolerable in that day for Sodom than for that city.

"Woe unto thee, Chorazin! Woe unto thee, Bethsaida! For if the mighty works had been done in Tyre and Sidon which have been done in you, they had a great while ago repented, sitting in sackcloth and ashes. But it shall be more tolerable for Tyre and Sidon at the judgment than for you.

"And thou, Capernaum, which art exalted to heaven, shalt be thrust down to hell.

"He that heareth you heareth me, and he that despiseth you despiseth me. He that despiseth me despiseth him that sent me."

5

The Jews' feast of tabernacles was at hand. His brethren therefore said unto him, "Depart hence and go into Judea, that thy disciples also may see the works that thou doest. For there is no man that doeth anything in secret, and he himself seeketh to be known openly. If thou doest these things, shew thyself to the world."

For neither did his brethren believe in him.

Then Jesus said unto them, "My time is not yet come, but your time is always ready. The world cannot hate you, but me it hateth because I testify of it, that the works

John 7:2-9

thereof are evil. Go ye up unto this feast. I go not up yet unto this feast, for my time is not yet full come."

When he had said these words unto them, he abode still in Galilee.

It came to pass, when the time was come that he should be received up, he steadfastly set his face to go to Jerusalem unto the feast, not openly, but as it were in secret, and sent messengers before his face. | Luke 9:51-52/ John 7:10

They went and entered into a village of the Samaritans to make ready for him. They did not receive him because his face was as though he would go to Jerusalem. | Luke 9:52-56

When his disciples James and John saw this, they said, "Lord, wilt thou that we command fire to come down from heaven and consume them, even as Elijah did?"

But he turned and rebuked them and said, "Ye know not what manner or spirit ye are of. For the Son of man is not come to destroy men's lives, but to save them."

They went to another village. Then the Jews sought him at the feast and said, "Where is he?" | John 7:11-53

There was much murmuring among the people concerning him, for some said, "He is a good man." Others said, "Nay, but he deceiveth the people." Howbeit no man spake openly of him for fear of the Jews.

Now about the midst of the feast Jesus went up into the temple and taught. The Jews marvelled, saying, "How knoweth this man letters, having never learned?"

Jesus answered them and said, "My doctrine is not mine, but his that sent me. If any man will do his will, he shall know of the doctrine, whether it be of God or whether I speak of myself. He that speaketh of himself seeketh his own glory, but he that seeketh his glory that sent him, the same is true, and no unrighteousness is in him.

"Did not Moses give you the law, and yet none of you keepeth the law? Why go ye about to kill me?"

The people answered and said, "Thou hast a devil. Who goeth about to kill thee?"

Jesus answered and said unto them, "I have done one work and ye all marvel. Moses therefore gave unto you circumcision—not because it is of Moses, but of the fathers—and ye on the sabbath day circumcise a man. If a man on the sabbath day receive circumcision that the law of Moses should not be broken, are ye angry at me because I have made a man every whit whole on the sabbath day?

"Judge not according to the appearance, but judge righteous judgment."

Then said some of them of Jerusalem, "Is not this he whom they seek to kill? But lo, he speaketh boldly, and they say nothing unto him."

"Do the rulers know indeed that this is the very Christ?"

"Howbeit we know this man whence he is. But when Christ cometh, no man knoweth whence he is."

Then cried Jesus in the temple as he taught, saying, "Ye both know me, and ye know whence I am. I am not come of myself, but he that sent me is true, whom ye know not. But I know him, for I am from him, and he hath sent me."

Then they sought to take him. But no man laid hands on him because his hour was not yet come.

Many of the people believed on him and said, "When Christ cometh, will he do more miracles than these which this man hath done?"

The Pharisees heard that the people murmured such things concerning him, and the Pharisees and the chief priests sent officers to take him.

Then said Jesus unto them, "Yet a little while am I with you, then I go unto him that sent me. Ye shall seek me and shall not find me, and where I am, thither ye cannot come."

Then said the Jews among themselves, "Whither will he go, that we shall not find him?"

"Will he go unto the dispersed among the Gentiles and teach the Gentiles?"

"What manner of saying is this that he said, 'Ye shall seek me and shall not find me. And where I am, thither ye cannot come'?"

In the last day, that great day of the feast, Jesus stood and cried, saying, "If any man thirst, let him come unto me and drink. He that believeth on me, as the scripture hath said, 'Out of his belly shall flow rivers of living water.'"*

*No reference

But this spake he of the Spirit which they that believe on him should receive. For the Holy Ghost was not yet given because that Jesus was not yet glorified.

Many of the people therefore, when they heard this saying, said, "Of a truth this is the Prophet."* **Deuteronomy 18:15,18*

Others said, "This is the Christ."

But some said, "Shall Christ come out of Galilee? Hath not the scriptures said that Christ cometh of the seed of David§ and out of the town of Bethlehem where David was?"*   So there was a division among the people because of him. Some of them would have taken him, but no man laid hands on him. *§Psalm 132:11; Isaiah 11:1; Jeremiah 23:5-6 *Micah 5:2*

Then came the officers to the chief priests and Pharisees, and they said unto them, "Why have ye not brought him?"

The officers answered, "Never man spake like this man."

Then answered them the Pharisees, "Are ye also deceived? Have any of the rulers or of the Pharisees believed on him? But this people who knoweth not the law are cursed."

Nicodemus—he that came to Jesus by night, being one of them—said unto them, "Doth our law judge any man before it hear him and know what he doeth?"

They answered and said unto him, "Art thou also of Galilee? Search and look, for out of Galilee ariseth no prophet." And every man went unto his own house.

6

Jesus went unto the mount of Olives. Early in the morning he came again into the temple, and all the people came unto him. He sat down and taught them. John 8:1-59

The scribes and Pharisees brought unto him a woman taken in adultery. When they had set her in the midst, they said unto him, "Master, this woman was taken in adultery, in the very act. Now Moses in the law commanded us that such should be stoned. But what sayest thou?"

This they said, tempting him, that they might have to accuse him. But Jesus stooped down and with his finger wrote on the ground as though he heard them not.

So when they continued asking him, he lifted up himself and said unto them, "He that is without sin among you, let him first cast a stone at her." Again he stooped down and wrote on the ground.

They which heard it, being convicted by their own conscience, went out one by one, beginning at the eldest even unto the last. Jesus was left alone, and the woman standing in the midst.

When Jesus had lifted up himself and saw none but the woman, he said unto her, "Woman, where are those thine accusers? Hath no man condemned thee?"

She said, "No man, Lord."

Jesus said unto her, "Neither do I condemn thee. Go and sin no more."

Then spake Jesus again unto them, saying, "I am the light of the world. He that followeth me shall not walk in darkness, but shall have the light of life."

The Pharisees therefore said unto him, "Thou bearest record of thyself. Thy record is not true."

Jesus answered and said unto them, "Though I bear record of myself, yet my record is true. For I know whence I came and whither I go, but ye cannot tell whence I come and whither I go. Ye judge after the flesh. I judge no man. And yet if I judge, my judgment is true. For I am not alone, but I and the Father that sent me.

"It is also written in your law that the testimony of two men is true. I am one that bear witness of myself, and the Father that sent me beareth witness of me."

Then said they unto him, "Where is thy Father?"

Jesus answered, "Ye neither know me nor my Father. If ye had known me, ye should have known my Father also."

These words spake Jesus in the treasury as he taught in the temple. No man laid hands on him, for his hour was not yet come.

Then said Jesus again unto them, "I go my way, and ye shall seek me and shall die in your sins. Whither I go, ye cannot come."

Then said the Jews, "Will he kill himself?" Because he said, "Whither I go, ye cannot come."

He said unto them, "Ye are from beneath. I am from above. Ye are of this world. I am not of this world. I said therefore unto you that ye shall die in yours sins, for if ye believe not that I am he, ye shall die in your sins."

Then said they unto him, "*Who* art thou?"

Jesus said unto them, "Even the same that I said unto you from the beginning. I have many things to say and to judge of you. But he that sent me is true, and I speak to the world those things which I have heard of him."

They understood not that he spake to them of the Father.

Then said Jesus unto them, "When ye have lifted up the Son of man, then shall ye know that I am he and that I do nothing of myself. But as my Father hath taught me, I speak these things. He that sent me is with me. The Father hath not left me alone, for I do always those things that please him."

As he spake these words, many believed on him.

Then said Jesus to those Jews which believed on him, "If ye continue in my word, then are ye my disciples indeed. Ye shall know the truth, and the truth shall make you free."

They answered him, "We be Abraham's seed and were never in bondage to any man. How sayest thou, 'Ye shall be made free'?"

Jesus answered them, "Verily, verily, I say unto you, whosoever commiteth sin is the servant of sin. The servant abideth not in the house forever, but the Son abideth ever. If the Son therefore shall make you free, ye shall be free indeed.

"I know that ye are Abraham's seed. But ye seek to kill me because my word hath no place in you. I speak that which I have seen with my Father. Ye do that which ye have seen with your father."

They answered and said unto him, "Abraham is our father."

Jesus said unto them, "If ye were Abraham's children, ye would do the works of Abraham. But now ye seek to kill me, a man that hath told you the truth which I have heard of God. This did not Abraham. Ye do the deeds of your father."

Then they said to him, "We be not born of fornication. We have one father, even God."

Jesus said unto them, "If God were your father, ye would love me, for I proceeded forth and came from God. Neither came I of myself, but he sent me. Why do ye not understand my speech? Even because ye cannot hear my word.

"Ye are of your father the devil, and the lusts of your father ye will do. He was a murderer from the beginning and abode not in the truth because there is no truth in him. When he speaketh a lie, he speaketh of his own, for he is a liar and the father of it.

"Because I tell you the truth, ye believe me not. Which of you convinceth me of sin? If I say the truth, why do ye not believe me? He that is of God heareth God's words. Ye therefore hear them not because ye are not of God."

Then answered the Jews and said unto him, "Say we not well that thou art a Samaritan and hast a devil?"

Jesus answered, "I have not a devil. But I honor my Father, and ye do dishonor me. I seek not mine own glory. There is one that seeketh and judgeth. Verily, verily, I say unto you, if a man keep my saying, he shall never see death."

Then said the Jews unto him, "Now we know that thou hast a devil. Abraham is dead, and the prophets. And thou sayest, 'If a man keep my saying, he shall never taste of death'? Art thou greater than our father Abraham, which is dead? And the prophets are dead. Whom makest thou thyself?"

Jesus answered, "If I honor myself, my honor is nothing. It is my Father that honoreth me, of whom ye say that he is your God. Yet ye have not known him. But I know him, and if I should say I know him not, I shall be a liar like unto you. But I know him and keep his saying. Your father Abraham rejoiced to see my day, and he saw it and was glad."

Then said the Jews unto him, "Thou art not yet fifty years old, and hast thou seen Abraham?"

Jesus said unto them, "Verily, verily, I say unto you, before Abraham was I Am."* *Exodus 3:14*

Then took they up stones to cast at him, but Jesus hid himself and went out of the temple, going through the midst of them, and so passed by.

7

As Jesus passed by, he saw a man which was blind from his birth. His disciples asked him, saying, "Master, who did sin, this man or his parents, that he was born blind?" John 9:1-7

Jesus answered, "Neither hath this man sinned nor his parents, but that the works of God should be made manifest in him. I must work the works of him that sent me while it is day. The night cometh when no man can work. As long as I am in the world, I am the light of the world."

When he had thus spoken, he spat on the ground and made clay of the spittle, and he anointed the eyes of the blind man with the clay and said unto him, "Go, wash in the pool of Siloam." Which is by interpretation, *Sent*.

He went his way therefore and washed and came seeing. And it was the sabbath day.

John 9:14

The neighbors therefore, and they which before had seen him that was blind, said, "Is not this he that sat and begged?"

John 9:8-13

Some said, "This is he."

Others said, "He is like him."

But he said, "I am he."

Therefore said they unto him, "How were thine eyes opened?"

He answered and said, "A man that is called Jesus made clay and anointed mine eyes and said unto me, 'Go to the pool of Siloam and wash.' I went and washed, and I received sight."

Then said they unto him, "Where is he?"

He said, "I know not."

They brought to the Pharisees him that aforetime was blind. Then again the Pharisees also asked him how he had received his sight. He said unto them, "He put clay upon mine eyes, and I washed and do see."

John 9:15-22

Therefore said some of the Pharisees, "This man is not of God because he keepeth not the sabbath day."

Others said, "How can a man that is a sinner do such miracles?" And there was a division among them.

They said unto the blind man again, "What sayest thou of him that he hath opened thine eyes?"

He said, "He is a prophet."

But the Jews did not believe concerning him that he had been blind and received his sight, until they called the parents of him that had received his sight. They asked them, saying, "Is this your son who ye say was born blind? How then doth he now see?"

His parents answered them and said, "We know that this is our son and that he was born blind. But by what means he now seeth, we know not. Or who hath opened his eyes, we know not. He is of age—ask him. He shall speak for himself."

These words spake his parents because they feared the Jews. For the Jews had agreed already that if any man did confess that he was Christ, he should be put out of the synagogue.

Then again called they the man that was blind and said unto him, "Give God the praise. We know that this man is a sinner."

John 9:24-41

He answered and said, "Whether he be a sinner or no, I know not. One thing I know, that whereas I was blind, now I see."

Then said they to him again, "What did he to thee? How opened he thine eyes?"

He answered them, "I have told you already, and ye did not hear. Wherefore would ye hear it again? Will ye also be his disciples?"

Then they reviled him and said, "*Thou* art his disciple, but we are Moses' disciples. We know that God spake unto Moses. As for this fellow, we know not from whence he is."

The man answered and said unto them, "Why, herein is a marvelous thing, that ye know not from whence he is! And yet he hath opened mine eyes. Now we know that God heareth not sinners, but if any man be a worshipper of God and doeth his will, him he heareth. Since the world began was it not heard that any man opened the eyes of one that was born blind. If this man were not of God, he could do nothing."

They answered and said unto him, "Thou wast altogether born in sins, and dost thou teach us?"

They cast him out.

Jesus heard that they had cast him out, and when he had found him, he said unto him, "Dost thou believe on the Son of God?"

He answered and said, "Who is he, Lord, that I might believe on him?"

Jesus said unto him, "Thou hast both seen him, and it is he that talketh with thee."

He said, "Lord, I believe." And he worshipped him.

Jesus said, "For judgment I am come into this world, that they which see not might see, and that they which see might be made blind."

Some of the Pharisees which were with him heard these words and said unto him, "Are we blind also?"

Jesus said unto them, "If ye were blind, ye should have no sin. But now ye say, 'We see,' therefore your sin remaineth.

"Verily, verily, I say unto you, he that entereth not by the door into the sheepfold, but climbeth up some other way, the same is a thief and a robber.

"But he that entereth in by the door is the shepherd of the sheep. To him the porter openeth, and the sheep hear his voice. He calleth his own sheep by name and leadeth them out. When he putteth forth his own sheep, he goeth before them, and the sheep follow him, for they know his voice. A stranger will they not follow, but will flee from him, for they know not the voice of strangers."

This parable spake Jesus unto them, but they understood not what things they were which he spake unto them.

Then said Jesus unto them again, "Verily, verily, I say unto you, I am the door of the sheep. All that ever came before me are thieves and robbers, but the sheep did not hear them. I am the door. By me if any man enter in, he shall be saved and shall go in and out and find pasture. The thief cometh not but for to steal and to kill and to destroy. I am come that they might have life, and that they might have it more abundantly.

"I am the good shepherd. The good shepherd giveth his life for the sheep. But he that is a hireling and not the shepherd, whose own the sheep are not, seeth the wolf coming and leaveth the sheep and fleeth, and the wolf catcheth them and scattereth the sheep. The hireling fleeth because he is a hireling and careth not for the sheep. I am the good shepherd and know my sheep and am known of mine. As the Father knoweth me, even so know I the Father, and I lay down my life for the sheep.

"Other sheep I have which are not of this fold. Them also I must bring, and they shall hear my voice. There shall be one fold and one shepherd.

"Therefore doth my Father love me, because I lay down my life that I might take it again. No man taketh it from me, but I lay it down of myself. I have power to lay it down, and I have power to take it again. This commandment have I received of my Father."

John 10:1-21

There was a division therefore again among the Jews for these sayings. Many of them said, "He hath a devil and is mad. Why hear ye him?"

Others said, "These are not the words of him that hath a devil. Can a devil open the eyes of the blind?"

8

The seventy returned again with joy, saying, "Lord, even the devils are subject unto us through thy name." *Luke 10:17-42*

He said unto them, "I beheld Satan as lightning fall from heaven. Behold, I give unto you power to tread on serpents and scorpions and over all the power of the enemy. Nothing shall by any means hurt you. Notwithstanding in this rejoice not, that the spirits are subject unto you, but rather rejoice because your names are written in heaven."

In that hour Jesus rejoiced in spirit and said, "I thank thee, O Father, Lord of heaven and earth, that thou hast hid these things from the wise and prudent and hast revealed them unto babes. Even so, Father, for so it seemed good in thy sight.

"All things are delivered to me of my Father. No man knoweth who the Son is but the Father, and who the Father is but the Son, and he to whom the Son will reveal him."

He turned him unto his disciples and said privately, "Blessed are the eyes which see the things that ye see. For I tell you that many prophets and kings have desired to see those things which ye see and have not seen them, and to hear those things which ye hear, and have not heard them."

Behold, a certain lawyer stood up and tempted him, saying, "Master, what shall I do to inherit eternal life?"

He said unto him, "What is written in the law? How readest thou?"

He answering said, "Thou shalt love the Lord thy God with all thy heart, and with all thy soul, and with all thy strength, and with all thy mind, and thy neighbor as thyself."* **Deuteronomy 6:5; Leviticus 19:18*

He said unto him, "Thou hast answered right. This do and thou shalt live."

But he, willing to justify himself, said unto Jesus, "And who is my neighbor?"

Jesus answering said, "A certain man went down from Jerusalem to Jericho and fell among thieves, which stripped him of his raiment and wounded him and departed, leaving him half dead.

"By chance there came down a certain priest that way. When he saw him, he passed by on the other side. Likewise a Levite, when he was at the place, came and looked on him and passed by on the other side.

"But a certain Samaritan, as he journeyed, came where he was. When he saw him, he had compassion on him and went to him and bound up his wounds, pouring in oil and wine, and set him on his own beast, and brought him to an inn and took care of him.

"On the morrow when he departed, he took out two pence and gave them to the host and said unto him, 'Take care of him. Whatsoever thou spendest more, when I come again I will repay thee.'

"Which now of these three, thinkest thou, was neighbor unto him that fell among the thieves?"

He said, "He that shewed mercy on him."

Then said Jesus unto him, "Go and do thou likewise."

Now it came to pass as they went that he entered into a certain village. A certain woman named Martha received him into her house. She had a sister called Mary, which also sat at Jesus' feet and heard his word. But Martha was cumbered about much serving, and came to him and said, "Lord, dost thou not care that my sister hath left me to serve alone? Bid her therefore that she help me."

Jesus answered and said unto her, "Martha, Martha, thou art careful and troubled about many things. But one thing is needful, and Mary hath chosen that good part, which shall not be taken away from her."

It came to pass that, as he was praying in a certain place, when he ceased, one of his disciples said unto him, "Lord, teach us to pray as John also taught his disciples."

He said unto them, "When ye pray say, 'Our Father which art in heaven, Hallowed be thy name. Thy kingdom come. Thy will be done as in heaven so in earth. Give us day by day our daily bread. Forgive us our sins, for we also forgive everyone that is indebted to us. Lead us not into temptation, but deliver us from evil.'"

Luke 11:1-15

He said unto them, "Which of you shall have a friend and shall go unto him at midnight and say unto him, "Friend, lend me three loaves. For a friend of mine in his journey is come to me, and I have nothing to set before him'?

"And he from within shall answer and say, 'Trouble me not. The door is now shut, and my children are with me in bed. I cannot rise and give thee.'

"I say unto you, though he will not rise and give him because he is his friend, yet because of his importunity he will rise and give him as many as he needeth.

"I say unto you, ask and it shall be given you, seek and ye shall find, knock and it shall be opened unto you. For everyone that asketh receiveth; and he that seeketh findeth, and to him that knocketh it shall be opened.

"If a son shall ask bread of any of you that is a father, will he give him a stone? Or if he ask a fish, will he for a fish give him a serpent? Or if he shall ask an egg, will he offer him a scorpion? If ye then, being evil, know how to give good gifts unto your children, how much more shall your heavenly Father give the Holy Spirit to them that ask him?"

He was casting out a devil, and it was dumb. It came to pass, when the devil was gone out, the dumb spake, and the people wondered. But some of them said, "He casteth out devils through Beelzebub the chief of the devils."

But he, knowing their thoughts, said unto them, "Every kingdom divided against itself is brought to desolation, and a house divided against a house falleth. If Satan also be divided against himself, how shall his kingdom stand? Because ye say that I cast out devils through Beelzebub. | Luke 11:17-26

"And if I by Beelzebub cast out devils, by whom do your sons cast them out? Therefore shall they be your judges. But if I with the finger of God cast out devils, no doubt the kingdom of God is come upon you.

"When a strong man armed keepeth his palace, his goods are in peace. But when a stronger than he shall come upon him and overcome him, he taketh from him all his armor wherein he trusted and divideth his spoils.

"He that is not with me is against me, and he that gathereth not with me scattereth.

"When the unclean spirit is gone out of a man, he walketh through dry places seeking rest, and finding none, he saith, 'I will return unto my house whence I came out.' When he cometh, he findeth it swept and garnished. Then goeth he and taketh to him seven other spirits more wicked than himself. They enter in and dwell there, and the last state of that man is worse than the first."

Others, tempting him, sought of him a sign from heaven. | Luke 11:16

When the people were gathered thick together, he began to say, "This is an evil generation. They seek a sign, and there shall no sign be given it, but the sign of Jonah the prophet.* For as Jonah was a sign unto the Ninevites, so shall also the Son of man be to this generation. | Luke 11:29-32

*Jonah 1-3

"The queen of the south shall rise up in the judgment with the men of this generation and condemn them. For she came from the utmost parts of the earth to hear the wisdom of Solomon,§ and behold, a greater than Solomon is here. | §Queen of Sheba; 1 Kings 10:1-13; 2 Chronicles 9:1-13

"The men of Nineveh shall rise up in the judgment with this generation and shall condemn it. For they repented at the preaching of Jonah,* and behold, a greater than Jonah is here." | *Jonah 3

It came to pass, as he spake these things, a certain woman of the company lifted up her voice and said unto him, "Blessed is the womb that bare thee and the paps which thou hast sucked." | Luke 11:27-28

But he said, "Yea rather, blessed are they that hear the word of God and keep it. | Luke 11:33-54

"No man when he hath lighted a candle putteth it in a secret place, neither under a bushel, but on a candlestick, that they which come in may see the light.

"The light of the body is the eye. Therefore when thine eye is single, thy whole body also is full of light. But when thine eye is evil, thy body also is full of darkness. Take heed therefore that the light which is in thee be not darkness. If thy whole body therefore be full of light, having no part dark, the whole shall be full of light as when the bright shining of a candle doth give thee light."

As he spake, a certain Pharisee besought him to dine with him. He went in and sat down to meat. When the

Pharisee saw it, he marvelled that he had not first washed before dinner.

The Lord said unto him, "Now do ye Pharisees make clean the outside of the cup and the platter, but your inward part is full of ravening and wickedness. Ye fools, did not he that made that which is without make that which is within also? But rather give alms of such things as ye have, and behold, all things are clean unto you.

"But woe unto you, Pharisees! For ye tithe mint and rue and all manner of herbs, and pass over judgment and the love of God. These things ought ye to have done and not to leave the other undone.

"Woe unto you, Pharisees! For ye love the uppermost seats in the synagogues and greetings in the markets.

"Woe unto you, scribes and Pharisees, hypocrites! For ye are as graves which appear not, and the men that walk over them are not aware of them."

Then answered one of the lawyers and said unto him, "Master, thus saying thou reproachest us also."

He said, "Woe unto you also, ye lawyers! For ye lade men with burdens grievous to be borne, and ye yourselves touch not the burdens with one of your fingers. Woe unto you! For ye build the sepulchers of the prophets, and your fathers killed them. Truly ye bear witness that ye allow the deeds of your fathers. For they indeed killed them and ye build their sepulchres.

"Therefore also said the wisdom of God, 'I will send them prophets and apostles, and some of them they shall slay and persecute that the blood of all the prophets which was shed from the foundation of the world may be required of this generation, from the blood of Abel* unto the blood of Zechariah which perished between the altar and the temple.§ Verily I say unto you, it shall be required of this generation.

"Woe unto you, lawyers! For ye have taken away the key of knowledge. Ye entered not in yourselves, and them that were entering in ye hindered."

As he said these things unto them, the scribes and the Pharisees began to urge him vehemently and to provoke him to speak of many things, laying wait for him, seeking to catch something out of his mouth that they might accuse him.

Genesis 4:8

§*2 Chron 24:20-22*

9

In the meantime, when there were gathered together an innumerable multitude of people, insomuch that they trode one upon another, he began to say unto his disciples first of all, "Beware ye of the leaven of the Pharisees, which is hypocrisy.

"For there is nothing covered that shall not be revealed, neither hid that shall not be known. Therefore whatsoever ye have spoken in darkness shall be heard in the light, and that which ye have spoken in the ear in closets shall be proclaimed upon the housetops.

"I say unto you my friends, be not afraid of them that kill the body, and after that have no more that they can do. But I will forewarn you whom ye shall fear. Fear him which, after he hath killed, hath power to cast into hell. Yea, I say unto you, fear him.

"Are not five sparrows sold for two farthings, and not one of them is forgotten before God? But even the very hairs of your head are all numbered. Fear not therefore. Ye are of more value than many sparrows.

"Also I say unto you, whosoever shall confess me before men, him shall the Son of man also confess before the angels of God. But he that denieth me before men shall be denied before the angels of God.

"Whosoever shall speak a word against the Son of man, it shall be forgiven him. But unto him that blasphemeth against the Holy Ghost it shall not be forgiven.

"When they bring you unto the synagogues and unto magistrates and powers, take ye no thought how or what thing ye shall answer or what ye shall say. For the Holy Ghost shall teach you in the same hour what ye ought to say."

One of the company said unto him, "Master, speak to my brother, that he divide the inheritance with me."

He said unto him, "Man, who made me a judge or a divider over you? Take heed and beware of covetousness. For a man's life consisteth not in the abundance of the things which he possesseth."

He spake a parable unto them, saying, "The ground of a certain rich man brought forth plentifully. He thought within himself, saying, 'What shall I do, because I have no room where to bestow my fruits?'

Luke 12:1-59

"And he said, 'This will I do. I will pull down my barns and build greater, and there will I bestow all my fruits and my goods. I will say to my soul, "Soul, thou hast much goods laid up for many years. Take thine ease. Eat, drink, and be merry."'

"But God said unto him, 'Thou fool, this night shall thy soul be required of thee. Then whose shall those things be which thou hast provided?'

"So is he that layeth up treasure for himself and is not rich toward God."

He said unto his disciples, "Therefore I say unto you, take no thought for your life, what ye shall eat, neither for the body, what ye shall put on. The life is more than meat, and the body is more than raiment.

"Consider the ravens, for they neither sow nor reap, which neither have storehouse nor barn. And God feedeth them. How much more are ye better than the fowls?

"Which of you with taking thought can add to his stature one cubit? If ye then be not able to do that which is least, why take ye thought for the rest?

"Consider the lilies how they grow. They toil not. They spin not. Yet I say unto you that Solomon in all his glory was not arrayed like one of these. If then God so clothe the grass, which is today in the field and tomorrow is cast into the oven, how much more will he clothe you, O ye of little faith?

"Seek not ye what ye shall eat, or what ye shall drink, neither be ye of doubtful mind. For all these things do the nations of the world seek after, and your Father knoweth that ye have need of these things. But rather seek ye the kingdom of God, and all these things shall be added unto you.

"Fear not, little flock, for it is your Father's good pleasure to give you the kingdom. Sell that ye have and give alms. Provide yourselves bags which wax not old, a treasure in the heavens that faileth not, where no thief approacheth, neither moth corrupteth. For where your treasure is, there will your heart be also.

"Let your loins be girded about, and your lights burning, and ye yourselves like unto men that wait for their lord, when he will return from the wedding, that when he cometh and knocketh, they may open unto him immediately. Blessed are those servants whom the lord when he cometh shall find watching. Verily I say unto you, that he shall gird himself and make them to sit down to meat, and will come forth and serve them. If he shall come in the second watch, or come in the third watch, and find them so, blessed are those servants.

"This know, that if the goodman of the house had known what hour the thief would come, he would have watched and not have suffered his house to be broken through. Be ye therefore ready also, for the Son of man cometh at an hour when ye think not."

Then Peter said unto him, "Lord, speakest thou this parable unto us, or even to all?"

The Lord said, "Who then is that faithful and wise steward, whom his lord shall make ruler over his household to give them their portion of meat in due season? Blessed is that servant whom his lord when he cometh shall find so doing. Of a truth I say unto you that he will make him ruler over all that he hath.

"But and if that servant say in his heart, 'My lord delayeth his coming,' and shall begin to beat the menservants and maidens, and to eat and drink, and to be drunken, the lord of that servant will come in a day when he looketh not for him, and at an hour when he is not aware, and will cut him in sunder, and will appoint him his portion with the unbelievers.

"That servant which knew his lord's will and prepared not himself, neither did according to his will, shall be beaten with many stripes. But he that knew not, and did commit things worthy of stripes, shall be beaten with few stripes. For unto whomsoever much is given, of him shall be much required. To whom men have committed much, of him they will ask the more.

"I am come to send fire on the earth, and what will I, if it be already kindled? But I have a baptism to be baptized with, and how am I straitened till it be accomplished!

"Suppose ye that I am come to give peace on earth? I tell you, nay, but rather division. For from henceforth there shall be five in one house divided, three against two, and two against three.

"The father shall be divided against the son, and the son against the father, the mother against the daughter, and the daughter against the mother, the mother-in-law against her daughter-in-law, and the daughter-in-law against her mother-in-law."

He said also to the people, "When ye see a cloud rise out of the west, straightway ye say, 'There cometh a shower.' And so it is. And when ye see the south wind blow, ye say, 'There will be heat.' And it cometh to pass. Ye hypocrites, ye can discern the face of the sky and of the earth, but how is it that ye do not discern this time? Yea, and why even of yourselves judge ye not what is right?

"When thou goest with thine adversary to the magistrate, as thou art in the way, give diligence that thou mayest be delivered from him lest he hale thee to the judge, and the judge deliver thee to the officer, and the officer cast thee into prison. I tell thee, thou shalt not depart thence, till thou hast paid the very last mite."

There were present at that season some that told him of the Galileans whose blood Pilate had mingled with their sacrifices. | Luke 13:1-9

Jesus answering said unto them, "Suppose ye that these Galileans were sinners above all the Galileans because they suffered such things? I tell you, nay. But except ye repent, ye shall all likewise perish.

"Or those eighteen upon whom the tower in Siloam fell and slew them, think ye that they were sinners above all men that dwelt in Jerusalem? I tell you, nay. But except ye repent, ye shall all likewise perish."

He spake also this parable: "A certain man had a fig tree planted in his vineyard. He came and sought fruit thereon and found none. Then said he unto the dresser of his vineyard, 'Behold, these three years I come seeking fruit on this fig tree and find none. Cut it down. Why cumbereth it the ground?'

"He answering said unto him, 'Lord, let it alone this year also till I shall dig about it and dung it. If it bear fruit, well. And if not, then after that thou shalt cut it down.'"

10

It was at Jerusalem the feast of the dedication, and it was winter. Jesus walked in the temple in Solomon's porch. | John 10:22-42

Then came the Jews round about him and said unto

him, "How long dost thou make us to doubt? If thou be the Christ, tell us plainly."

Jesus answered them, "I told you and ye believed not. The works that I do in my Father's name, they bear witness of me. But ye believe not because ye are not of my sheep, as I said unto you. My sheep hear my voice, and I know them, and they follow me. I give unto them eternal life, and they shall never perish, neither shall any man pluck them out of my hand. My Father which gave them me is greater than all. No man is able to pluck them out of my Father's hand.

"I and my Father are one."

Then the Jews took up stones again to stone him.

Jesus answered them, "Many good works have I shewed you from my Father. For which of those works do ye stone me?"

The Jews answered him, saying, "For a good work we stone thee not, but for blasphemy, and because that thou, being a man, makest thyself God."

Jesus answered them, "Is it not written in your law, 'I said, ye are gods'?* If he called them gods unto whom the word of God came, and the scriptures cannot be broken, say ye of him whom the Father hath sanctified and sent into the world, 'Thou blasphemest,' because I said I am the Son of God? If I do not the works of my Father, believe me not. But if I do, though ye believe not me, believe the works, that ye may know and believe that the Father is in me, and I in him."

Psalm 82:6

Therefore they sought again to take him.

But he escaped out of their hand and went away again beyond Jordan into the place where John at first baptized, and there he abode. Many resorted unto him and said, "John did no miracle, but all things that John spake of this man were true." And many believed on him there.

He was teaching in one of the synagogues on the sabbath. Behold, there was a woman which had a spirit of infirmity eighteen years and was bowed together, and could in no wise lift up herself. When Jesus saw her, he called her to him and said unto her, "Woman, thou art loosed from thine infirmity."

Luke 13:10-35

He laid his hands on her, and immediately she was made straight, and glorified God.

The ruler of the synagogue answered with indignation because that Jesus had healed on the sabbath day, and said unto the people, "There are six days in which men ought to work. In them therefore come and be healed and not on the sabbath day."

The Lord then answered him and said, "Thou hypocrite! Doth not each one of you on the sabbath loose his ox or his ass from the stall and lead him away to watering? Ought not this woman, being a daughter of Abraham whom Satan hath bound, lo, these eighteen years, be loosed from this bond on the sabbath day?"

When he had said these things, all his adversaries were ashamed, and all the people rejoiced for all the glorious things that were done by him.

Then said he, "Unto what is the kingdom of God like? And whereunto shall I resemble it? It is like a grain of mustard seed which a man took and cast into his garden. It grew and waxed a great tree, and the fowls of the air lodged in the branches of it."

Again he said, "Whereunto shall I liken the kingdom of God? It is like leaven which a woman took and hid in three measures of meal till the whole was leavened."

He went through the cities and villages teaching, and journeying toward Jerusalem. Then said one unto him, "Lord, are there few that be saved?"

He said unto them, "Strive to enter in at the strait gate. For many, I say unto you, will seek to enter in and shall not be able.

"When once the master of the house is risen up and hath shut to the door, and ye begin to stand without and to knock at the door, saying, 'Lord, Lord, open to us,' and he shall answer and say unto you, 'I know you not whence ye are,' then shall ye begin to say, 'We have eaten and drunk in thy presence, and thou hast taught in our streets.'

"But he shall say, 'I tell you, I know you not whence ye are. Depart from me, all ye workers of iniquity.'

"There shall be weeping and gnashing of teeth when ye shall see Abraham and Isaac and Jacob and all the prophets in the kingdom of God, and you yourselves thrust out.

"They shall come from the east, and from the west, and from the north, and from the south, and shall sit down in the kingdom of God. Behold, there are last which shall be first, and there are first which shall be last."

The same day there came certain of the Pharisees, saying unto him, "Get thee out and depart hence, for Herod will kill thee."

He said unto them, "Go ye and tell that fox, behold, I cast out devils, and I do cures today and tomorrow, and the third day I shall be perfected. Nevertheless I must walk today and tomorrow and the day following, for it cannot be that a prophet perish out of Jerusalem.

"O Jerusalem, Jerusalem, which killest the prophets and stonest them that are sent unto thee. How often would I have gathered thy children together as a hen doth gather her brood under her wings, and ye would not! Behold, your house is left unto you desolate. Verily I say unto you, ye shall not see me until the time come when ye shall say, 'Blessed is he that cometh in the name of the Lord.'"

11

It came to pass, as he went into the house of one of the chief Pharisees to eat bread on the sabbath day, that they watched him. Behold, there was a certain man before him which had the dropsy. Jesus answering spake unto the lawyers and Pharisees, saying, "Is it lawful to heal on the sabbath day?" Luke 14:1-35

They held their peace.

He took him and healed him and let him go, and answered them, saying, "Which of you shall have an ass or an ox fallen into a pit, and will not straightway pull him out on the sabbath day?"

They could not answer him again to these things.

He put forth a parable to those which were bidden, when he marked how they chose out the chief rooms, saying unto them, "When thou art bidden of any man to a wedding, sit not down in the highest room lest a more honorable man than thou be bidden of him, and he that bade thee and him come and say to thee, 'Give this man place.' And thou begin with shame to take the lowest room.

"But when thou art bidden, go and sit down in the lowest room, that when he that bade thee cometh, he may say unto thee, 'Friend, go up higher.' Then shalt thou have worship in the presence of them that sit at meat with thee. For whosoever exalteth himself shall be abased, and he that humbleth himself shall be exalted."

Then said he also to him that bade him, "When thou makest a dinner or a supper, call not thy friends nor thy brethren, neither thy kinsmen nor thy rich neighbors, lest they also bid thee again, and a recompense be made thee. But when thou makest a feast, call the poor, the maimed, the lame, the blind, and thou shalt be blessed. For they cannot recompense thee. For thou shalt be recompensed at the resurrection of the just."

When one of them that sat at meat with him heard these things, he said unto him, "Blessed is he that shall eat bread in the kingdom of God."

Then he said unto him, "A certain man made a great supper and bade many, and sent his servant at supper time to say to them that were bidden, 'Come, for all things are now ready.'

"They all with one consent began to make excuse. The first said unto him, 'I have bought a piece of ground, and I must needs go and see it. I pray thee have me excused.'

Another said, 'I have bought five yoke of oxen, and I go to prove them. I pray thee have me excused.'

And another said, 'I have married a wife, and therefore I cannot come.'

"So that servant came and shewed his lord these things. Then the master of the house being angry said to his servant, 'Go out quickly into the streets and lanes of the city and bring in hither the poor, and the maimed, and the halt, and the blind.'

"The servant said, 'Lord, it is done as thou hast commanded, and yet there is room.'

"The lord said unto the servant, 'Go out into the highways and hedges and compel them to come in, that my house may be filled. For I say unto you that none of those men which were bidden shall taste of my supper.'"

There were great multitudes with him. He turned and said unto them, "If any man come to me and hate not his father, and mother, and wife, and children, and brethren, and sisters, yea, and his own life also, he cannot be my disciple. And whosoever doth not bear his cross and come after me cannot be my disciple.

"For which of you intending to build a tower sitteth not down first and counteth the cost, whether he have sufficient to finish it? Lest haply, after he hath laid the foundation and is not able to finish it, all that behold it begin to mock him, saying, 'This man began to build, and was not able to finish.'

"Or what king going to make war against another king sitteth not down first and consulteth whether he be able with ten thousand to meet him that cometh against him with twenty thousand? Or else, while the other is yet a great way off, he sendeth an ambassage and desireth conditions of peace. So likewise, whosoever he be of you that forsaketh not all that he hath, he cannot be my disciple.

"Salt is good, but if the salt have lost his savor, wherewith shall it be seasoned? It is neither fit for the land, nor yet for the dunghill, but men cast it out. He that hath ears to hear, let him hear."

Then drew near unto him all the publicans and sinners for to hear him. The Pharisees and scribes murmured, saying, "This man receiveth sinners and eateth with them."

Luke 15:1-32

He spake this parable unto them, saying, "What man of you having a hundred sheep, if he lose one of them, doth not leave the ninety and nine in the wilderness and go after that which is lost until he find it?

"And when he hath found it, he layeth it on his shoulders, rejoicing. When he cometh home, he calleth together his friends and neighbors, saying unto them, 'Rejoice with me, for I have found my sheep which was lost.' I say unto you that likewise joy shall be in heaven over one sinner that repenteth, more than over ninety and nine just persons which need no repentance.

"Either what woman having ten pieces of silver, if she lose one piece, doth not light a candle and sweep the house, and seek diligently till she find it?

"And when she hath found it, she calleth her friends and her neighbors together, saying, 'Rejoice with me, for I have found the piece which I had lost.' Likewise I say unto you, there is joy in the presence of the angels of God over one sinner that repenteth."

And he said, "A certain man had two sons. The younger of them said to his father, 'Father, give me the portion of goods that falleth to me.'

"He divided unto them his living.

"Not many days after the younger son gathered all together and took his journey into a far country and there wasted his substance with riotous living.

When he had spent all, there arose a mighty famine in that land, and he began to be in want. He went and joined himself to a citizen of that country. He sent him into his fields to feed swine. He would fain have filled his belly with the husks that the swine did eat, and no man gave unto him.

"When he came to himself, he said, 'How many hired servants of my father's have bread enough and to spare, and I perish with hunger! I will arise and go to my father and will say unto him, "Father, I have sinned against heaven and before thee and am no more worthy to be called thy son. Make me as one of thy hired servants."'

"He arose and came to his father. But when he was yet a great way off, his father saw him and had compassion, and ran and fell on his neck and kissed him. The son said unto him, 'Father, I have sinned against heaven and in thy sight and am no more worthy to be called thy son.'

"But the father said to his servants, 'Bring forth the best robe and put it on him. Put a ring on his hand and shoes on his feet. Bring hither the fatted calf and kill it. Let us eat and be merry. For this my son was dead and is alive again. He was lost and is found.' And they began to be merry.

"Now his elder son was in the field. As he came and drew nigh to the house, he heard music and dancing. He called one of the servants and asked what these things meant.

"He said unto him, 'Thy brother is come, and thy father hath killed the fatted calf because he hath received him safe and sound.'

"He was angry and would not go in. Therefore came his father out and entreated him.

"He answering said to his father, 'Lo, these many years do I serve thee, neither transgressed I at any time thy commandment. Yet thou never gavest me a kid, that I might make merry with my friends. But as soon as this thy son was come, which hath devoured thy living with harlots, thou hast killed for him the fatted calf.'

"He said unto him, 'Son, thou art ever with me, and

all that I have is thine. It was meet that we should make merry and be glad, for this thy brother was dead and is alive again, and was lost and is found.'"

He said also unto his disciples, "There was a certain rich man which had a steward. The same was accused unto him that he had wasted his goods. He called him and said unto him, 'How is it that I hear this of thee? Give an account of thy stewardship, for thou mayest be no longer steward.'

Luke 16:1-31

"Then the steward said within himself, 'What shall I do? For my lord taketh away from me the stewardship. I cannot dig. To beg I am ashamed.

"'I am resolved what to do, that when I am put out of the stewardship, they may receive me into their houses.'

"He called everyone of his lord's debtors unto him and said unto the first, 'How much owest thou unto my lord?'

"He said, 'A hundred measures of oil.'

"He said unto him, 'Take thy bill and sit down quickly and write fifty.'

"Then said he to another, 'How much owest thou?'

"And he said, 'A hundred measures of wheat.' And he said unto him, 'Take thy bill and write fourscore.'

"The lord commended the unjust steward because he had done wisely, for the children of this world are in their generation wiser than the children of light. I say unto you, make to yourselves friends of the mammon of unrighteousness, that when ye fail, they may receive you into everlasting habitations.

"He that is faithful in that which is least is faithful also in much, and he that is unjust in the least is unjust also in much. If therefore ye have not been faithful in the unrighteous mammon, who will commit to your trust the true riches? If ye have not been faithful in that which is another man's, who shall give you that which is your own?

"No servant can serve two masters, for either he will hate the one and love the other, or else he will hold to the one and despise the other. Ye cannot serve God and mammon."

The Pharisees also who were covetous heard all these things, and they derided him. He said unto them, "Ye are they which justify yourselves before men. But God knoweth your hearts, for that which is highly esteemed among men is abomination in the sight of God.

"The law and the prophets were until John. Since that time the kingdom of God is preached, and every man presseth into it. It is easier for heaven and earth to pass than one tittle of the law to fail.

"Whosoever putteth away his wife and marrieth another committeth adultery, and whosoever marrieth her that is put away from her husband committeth adultery.

"There was a certain rich man which was clothed in purple and fine linen and fared sumptuously everyday. And there was a certain beggar named Lazarus which was laid at his gate full of sores, desiring to be fed with the crumbs which fell from the rich man's table. Moreover the dogs came and licked his sores.

"It came to pass that the beggar died and was carried by the angels into Abraham's bosom.

"The rich man also died and was buried. In hell he lift up his eyes, being in torments, and saw Abraham afar off and Lazarus in his bosom. He cried and said, 'Father Abraham, have mercy on me and send Lazarus, that he may dip the tip of his finger in water and cool my tongue, for I am tormented in this flame.'

"But Abraham said, 'Son, remember that thou in thy lifetime receivedst thy good things, and likewise Lazarus evil things. But now he is comforted and thou art tormented. Beside all this, between us and you there is a great gulf fixed, so that they which would pass from hence to you cannot, neither can they pass to us that would come from thence.'

"Then he said, 'I pray thee therefore, Father, that thou wouldest send him to my father's house, for I have five brethren, that he may testify unto them lest they also come into this place of torment.'

"Abraham said unto him, 'They have Moses and the prophets. Let them hear them.'

"He said, 'Nay, Father Abraham, but if one went unto them from the dead, they will repent.'

"He said unto him, 'If they hear not Moses and the prophets, neither will they be persuaded, though one rose from the dead.'"

Then said he unto the disciples, 'It is impossible but that offenses will come, but woe unto him through whom they come! It were better for him that a millstone were hanged about his neck and he cast into the sea, than that

Luke 17:1-10

he should offend one of these little ones.

"Take heed to yourselves. If thy brother trespass against thee, rebuke him, and if he repent, forgive him. If he trespass against thee seven times in a day, and seven times in a day turn again to thee, saying, 'I repent,' thou shalt forgive him."

The apostles said unto the Lord, "Increase our faith."

The Lord said, "If ye had faith as a grain of mustard seed, ye might say unto this sycamine tree, 'Be thou plucked up by the root, and be thou planted in the sea,' and it should obey you.

"But which of you having a servant plowing or feeding cattle will say unto him by and by, when he is come from the field, 'Go and sit down to meat'? And will not rather say unto him, 'Make ready wherewith I may sup, and gird thyself and serve me till I have eaten and drunken, and afterward thou shalt eat and drink'?

"Doth he thank that servant because he did the things that were commanded him? I trow not. So likewise ye, when ye shall have done all those things which are commanded you, say, 'We are unprofitable servants. We have done that which was our duty to do.'"

12

A certain man was sick named Lazarus of Bethany, the town of Mary and her sister Martha. It was that Mary which anointed the Lord with ointment and wiped his feet with her hair whose brother Lazarus was sick. Therefore his sisters sent unto him, saying, "Lord, behold, he whom thou lovest is sick." *John 11:1-12*

When Jesus heard that, he said, "This sickness is not unto death, but for the glory of God, that the Son of God might be glorified thereby."

Now Jesus loved Martha and her sister and Lazarus. When he had heard therefore that he was sick, he abode two days still in the same place where he was. Then after that said he to his disciples, "Let us go into Judea again."

His disciples said unto him, "Master, the Jews of late sought to stone thee, and goest thou thither again?"

Jesus answered, "Are there not twelve hours in the day? If any man walk in the day, he stumbleth not because he seeth the light of this world. But if a man walk in the night, he stumbleth because there is no light in him."

These things said he, and after that he said unto them, "Our friend Lazarus sleepeth. But I go that I may awake him out of sleep."

Then said his disciples, "Lord, if he sleep he shall do well."

Then said Jesus unto them plainly, "Lazarus is dead. And I am glad for your sakes that I was not there, to the intent ye may believe. Nevertheless let us go unto him." | John 11:14-16

Then said Thomas which is called Didymus unto his fellow disciples, "Let us also go, that we may die with him."

Now Bethany was nigh unto Jerusalem about fifteen furlongs off, and many of the Jews came to Martha and Mary to comfort them concerning their brother. Martha, as soon as she heard that Jesus was coming, went and met him. But Mary sat still in the house. | John 11:18-20

When Jesus came, he found that he had lain in the grave four days already. | John 11:17

Then said Martha unto Jesus, "Lord, if thou hadst been here, my brother had not died. But I know that, even now, whatsoever thou wilt ask of God, God will give it thee." | John 11:21-54

Jesus said unto her, "Thy brother shall rise again."

Martha said unto him, "I know that he shall rise again in the resurrection at the last day."

Jesus said unto her, "*I* am the resurrection and the life. He that believeth in me, though he were dead, yet shall he live. Whosoever liveth and believeth in me shall never die. Believest thou this?"

She said unto him, "Yea, Lord. I believe that thou art the Christ, the Son of God, which should come into the world."

When she had so said, she went her way and called Mary her sister secretly, saying, "The Master is come and calleth for thee."

As soon as she heard that, she arose quickly, and came unto him.

Now Jesus was not yet come into the town, but was in that place where Martha met him. The Jews then which were with her in the house and comforted her, when they saw Mary, that she rose up hastily and went out, followed her, saying, "She goeth unto the grave to weep there."

Then when Mary was come where Jesus was and saw him, she fell down at his feet, saying unto him, "Lord, if thou hadst been here, my brother had not died."

When Jesus therefore saw her weeping, and the Jews also weeping which came with her, he groaned in the spirit and was troubled, and said, "Where have ye laid him?"

They said unto him, "Lord, come and see."

Jesus wept.

Then said the Jews, "Behold how he loved him!"

Some of them said, "Could not this man which opened the eyes of the blind have caused that even this man should not have died?"

Jesus therefore again groaning in himself came to the grave. It was a cave, and a stone lay upon it. Jesus said, "Take ye away the stone."

Martha, the sister of him that was dead, said unto him, "Lord, by this time he stinketh, for he hath been dead four days."

Jesus said unto her, "Said I not unto thee that if thou wouldest believe, thou shouldest see the glory of God?"

They took away the stone from the place where the dead was laid. Jesus lifted up his eyes and said, "Father, I thank thee that thou hast heard me. I knew that thou hearest me always, but because of the people which stand by I said it, that they may believe that thou hast sent me."

When he had thus spoken, he cried with a loud voice, "Lazarus, come forth."

He that was dead came forth, bound hand and foot with graveclothes, and his face was bound about with a napkin.

Jesus said unto them, "Loose him and let him go."

Then many of the Jews which came to Mary and had seen the things which Jesus did believed on him. But some of them went their ways to the Pharisees and told them what things Jesus had done.

Then gathered the chief priests and the Pharisees a council and said, "What do we? For this man doeth many miracles. If we let him thus alone, all men will believe on him, and the Romans shall come and take away both our place and nation."

One of them named Caiaphas, being the high priest that same year, said unto them, "Ye know nothing at all, nor consider that it is expedient for us that one man should die for the people, that the whole nation perish not."

This spake he not of himself, but being high priest that year, he prophesied that Jesus should die for that nation. And not for that nation only, but that also he should gather together in one the children of God that were scattered abroad.

From that day forth they took counsel together for to put him to death. Jesus therefore walked no more openly among the Jews, but went thence unto a country near to the wilderness, into a city called Ephraim, and there continued with his disciples.

THE FINAL JOURNEY TO JERUSALEM

1

The Jews' passover was nigh at hand. Many went out of the country up to Jerusalem before the passover to purify themselves. Then sought they for Jesus, and spake among themselves as they stood in the temple, "What think ye, that he will not come to the feast?"

Now both the chief priests and the Pharisees had given a commandment that, if any man knew where he were, he should shew it that they might take him. | John 11:55-57

It came to pass, as he went to Jerusalem, that he passed through the midst of Samaria and Galilee. As he entered into a certain village, there met him ten men that were lepers which stood afar off. They lifted up their voices and said, "Jesus, Master, have mercy on us." | Luke 17:11-37

When he saw them, he said unto them, "Go shew yourselves unto the priests."

It came to pass that, as they went, they were cleansed. One of them when he saw that he was healed turned back, and with a loud voice glorified God and fell on his face at his feet, giving him thanks. He was a Samaritan.

Jesus answering said, "Were there not ten cleansed? But where are the nine? There are not found that returned to give glory to God save this stranger." He said unto him, "Arise, go thy way. Thy faith hath made thee whole."

When he was demanded of the Pharisees, when the kingdom of God should come, he answered them and said, "The kingdom of God cometh not with observation. Neither shall they say, 'Lo here!' or, 'Lo there!' For behold, the kingdom of God is within you."

He said unto the disciples, "The days will come when ye shall desire to see one of the days of the Son of man, and ye shall not see it. They shall say to you 'See here' or 'See there.' Go not after them nor follow them. For as the lightning that lighteneth out of the one part under heaven shineth unto the other part under heaven, so shall also the

Son of man be in his day. But first must he suffer many things and be rejected of this generation.

"As it was in the days of Noah, so shall it be also in the days of the Son of man. They did eat, they drank, they married wives, they were given in marriage, until the day that Noah entered into the ark, and the flood came and destroyed them all.*

*Genesis 6:3-5; Genesis 7:7,19-21

"Likewise also as it was in the days of Lot. They did eat, they drank, they bought, they sold, they planted, they builded; but the same day that Lot went out of Sodom, it rained fire and brimstone from heaven and destroyed them all.§

§Genesis 19:15-16; Genesis 19:24

"Even thus shall it be in the day when the Son of man is revealed. In that day, he which shall be upon the housetop and his stuff in the house, let him not come down to take it away. And he that is in the field, let him likewise not return back. Remember Lot's wife.*

*Genesis 19:26

"Whosoever shall seek to save his life shall lose it, and whosoever shall lose his life shall preserve it.

"I tell you, in that night there shall be two men in one bed. The one shall be taken and the other shall be left. Two women shall be grinding together. The one shall be taken and the other left. Two men shall be in the field. The one shall be taken and the other left."

They answered and said unto him, "Where, Lord?"

He said unto them, "Wheresoever the body is, thither will the eagles be gathered together."

He spake a parable unto them to this end, that men ought always to pray and not to faint, saying, "There was in a city a judge which feared not God, neither regarded man. And there was a widow in that city. She came unto him, saying, 'Avenge me of mine adversary.'

Luke 18:1-14

He would not for a while, but afterward he said within himself, 'Though I fear not God nor regard man, yet because this widow troubleth me I will avenge her, lest by her continual coming she weary me.'"

The Lord said, "Hear what the unjust judge said. Shall not God avenge his own elect which cry day and night unto him, though he bear long with them? I tell you that he will avenge them speedily. Nevertheless when the Son of man cometh, shall he find faith on earth?"

He spake this parable unto certain which trusted in themselves that they were righteous, and despised others.

"Two men went up into the temple to pray, the one a Pharisee and the other a publican. The Pharisee stood and prayed thus with himself, 'God, I thank thee that I am not as other men are—extortioners, unjust, adulterers, or even as this publican. I fast twice in the week. I give tithes of all that I possess.'

"The publican, standing afar off, would not lift up so much as his eyes unto heaven, but smote upon his breast, saying, 'God be merciful to me a sinner.'

"I tell you, this man went down to his house justified rather than the other, for everyone that exalteth himself shall be abased, and he that humbleth himself shall be exalted."

2

It came to pass that, when Jesus had finished these sayings, he departed from Galilee and came into the coasts of Judea beyond Jordan. Great multitudes followed him, and as he was wont, he healed them there and taught them again.	Matthew 19:1 Matthew 19:2/ Mark 10:1
The Pharisees also came unto him, tempting him, and saying unto him, "Is it lawful for a man to put away his wife for every cause?"	Matthew 19:3
He answered and said unto them, "Have ye not read that from the beginning of the creation God made them male and female, and said, 'For this cause shall a man leave his father and mother and shall cleave to his wife, and they twain shall be one flesh'?* Wherefore they are no more twain, but one flesh. What therefore God hath joined together, let not man put asunder."	Matthew 19:4-5/ Mark 10:6-7 Matthew 19:6 *Genesis 2:24
They said unto him, "Why did Moses then command to write a bill of divorcement and to put her away?"§	Matthew 19:7 §Deuteronomy 24:1
Jesus answered and said unto them, "Moses because of the hardness of your hearts suffered you to put away your wives, but from the beginning it was not so."	Matthew 19:8/ Mark 10:5
In the house his disciples asked him again of the same matter. He said unto them, "Whosoever shall put away his wife, except it be for fornication, and shall marry another commiteth adultery against her. If a woman shall put away her husband and be married to another, she	Mark 10:10 Matthew 19:9/ Mark 10:11-12

committeth adultery. And whoso marrieth her which is put away doth commit adultery."

His disciples said unto him, "If the case of the man be so with his wife, it is not good to marry." | Matthew 19:10-12

But he said unto them, "All men cannot receive this saying, save they to whom it is given. For there are some eunuchs which were so born from their mother's womb. And there are some eunuchs which were made eunuchs of men. And there be eunuchs which have made themselves eunuchs for the kingdom of heaven's sake. He that is able to receive it, let him receive it."

Then were brought little children unto him, that he should put his hands on them and pray. When his disciples saw it, they rebuked those that brought them. | Matthew 19:13/ Mark 10:13/ Luke 18:15

But when Jesus saw it, he was much displeased, and called them unto him and said, "Suffer the little children to come unto me and forbid them not, for of such is the kingdom of God. Verily I say unto you, whosoever shall not receive the kingdom of God as a little child shall in no wise enter therein." | Mark 10:14/ Luke 18:16

Luke 18:17

He took them up in his arms, laid his hands upon them, and blessed them. | Matthew 19:15/ Mark 10:16

When he was gone forth into the way, a certain ruler came running, kneeled to him, and asked him, "Good Master, what shall I do that I may inherit eternal life?" | Mark 10:17/ Luke 18:18

Jesus said unto him, "Why callest thou me good? There is none good but one, that is, God. But if thou wilt enter into life, keep the commandments." | Matthew 19:17/ Mark 10:18

He said unto him, "Which?" | Matthew 19:18-19/ Mark 10:19

Jesus said, "Thou knowest the commandments. Thou shalt do no murder. Thou shalt not commit adultery. Thou shalt not steal. Thou shalt not bear false witness. Defraud not. Honor thy father and thy mother. And, thou shalt love thy neighbor as thyself."

The young man said unto him, "Master, all these things have I kept from my youth. What lack I yet?" | Matthew 19:20/ Mark 10:20

Now when Jesus heard these things, he loved him, and said unto him, "If thou wilt be perfect, one thing thou lackest. Go thy way, sell whatsoever thou hast, and give to the poor. Thou shalt have treasure in heaven. And come, take up the cross and follow me." | Matthew 19:21/ Mark 10:21/ Luke 18:22

But when the young man heard this, he was very sorrowful and went away grieved, for he was very rich. When | Matthew 19:22-23/ Mark 10:22-23/

Jesus saw that he was sorrowful, he looked round about and said unto his disciples, "Verily I say unto you, that a rich man shall hardly enter into the kingdom of heaven." | Luke 18:23-24

The disciples were astonished at his words. But Jesus answereth again and said unto them, "Children, how hard it is for them that trust in riches to enter into the kingdom of God! It is easier for a camel to go through the eye of a needle than for a rich man to enter into the kingdom of God." | Mark 10:24-25

When his disciples heard it, they were exceedingly amazed, saying, "Who then can be saved?" | Matthew 19:25

But Jesus looking upon them said, "With men this is impossible, but not with God. For with God all things are possible." | Matthew 19:26/ Mark 10:27

Then Peter said unto him, "Behold, we have forsaken all and followed thee. What shall we have therefore?" | Matthew 19:27/ Luke 18:28

Jesus said unto them, "Verily I say unto you, that ye which have followed me, in the regeneration when the Son of man shall sit in the throne of his glory, ye also shall sit upon twelve thrones, judging the twelve tribes of Israel. | Matthew 19:28

"Everyone that hath forsaken houses, or brethren, or sisters, or father, or mother, or wife, or children, or lands for my name's sake and the gospel's, shall receive a hundredfold now in this time, houses, and brethren, and sisters, and mothers, and children, and lands—with persecutions—and in the world to come shall inherit eternal life. But many that are first shall be last, and the last shall be first. | Matthew 19:29/ Mark 10:29-30

Matthew 19:30

"For the kingdom of heaven is like unto a man that is a householder, which went out early in the morning to hire laborers into his vineyard. When he had agreed with the laborers for a penny a day, he sent them into his vineyard. | Matthew 20:1-16

"He went out about the third hour and saw others standing idle in the marketplace, and said unto them, 'Go ye also into the vineyard, and whatsoever is right I will give you.' And they went their way.

"Again he went out about the sixth and ninth hour and did likewise. About the eleventh hour he went out and found others standing idle, and said unto them, 'Why stand ye here all the day idle?'

"They said unto him, 'Because no man hath hired us.'

"He said unto them, 'Go ye also into the vineyard, and whatsoever is right, that shall ye receive.'

"So when even was come, the lord of the vineyard said unto his steward, 'Call the laborers and give them their hire, beginning from the last unto the first.'

"When they came that were hired about the eleventh hour, they received every man a penny. But when the first came, they supposed that they should have received more, and they likewise received every man a penny.

"When they had received it, they murmured against the goodman of the house, saying, 'These last have wrought but one hour, and thou hast made them equal to us which have borne the burden and heat of the day.'

"But he answered one of them and said, 'Friend, I do thee no wrong. Didst not thou agree with me for a penny? Take that thine is and go thy way. I will give unto this last even as unto thee. Is it not lawful for me to do what I will with mine own? Is thine eye evil because I am good?'

"So the last shall be first, and the first last. For many be called, but few chosen."

3

They were in the way going up to Jerusalem, and Jesus took the twelve disciples apart and began to tell them what things should happen unto him, saying, "Behold, we go up to Jerusalem, and all things that are written by the prophets concerning the Son of man shall be accomplished. For he shall be betrayed unto the chief priests and unto the scribes, and they shall condemn him to death and shall deliver him to the Gentiles. They shall mock him, scourge him, spit upon him, and shall crucify him. And the third day he shall rise again."	Matthew 20:17/ Mark 10:32 Mark 10:33/ Luke 18:31 Matthew 20:18/ Mark 10:33/ Luke 18:32 Matthew 20:19/ Mark 10:34
They were amazed and understood none of these things. This saying was hid from them, neither knew they the things which were spoken. Jesus went before them. As they followed, they were afraid.	Mark 10:32/ Luke 18:34
Then came to him the mother of James and John, Zebedee's children, with her sons, worshipping him, saying, "Master, we would that thou shouldest do for us whatsoever we shall desire."	Matthew 20:20/ Mark 10:35

He said unto them, "What would ye that I should do for you?"	Mark 10:36
She said unto him, "Grant that these my two sons may sit, the one on thy right hand, and the other on thy left, in thy kingdom."	Matthew 20:21/ Mark 10:37
But Jesus answered and said, "Ye know not what ye ask. Are ye able to drink of the cup that I shall drink of, and to be baptized with the baptism that I am baptized with?"	Matthew 20:22-23/ Mark 10:39-40
They said unto him, "We are able."	
Jesus said unto them, "Ye shall indeed drink of the cup that I drink of and be baptized with the baptism that I am baptized with. But to sit on my right hand and on my left hand is not mine to give. It shall be given to them for whom it is prepared of my Father."	
When the ten heard it, they were moved with indignation against James and John.	Matthew 20:24/ Mark 10:41
But Jesus called them unto him and said, "Ye know that the princes of the Gentiles exercise dominion over them, and they that are great exercise authority upon them.	Matthew 20:25-27
"But it shall not be so among you. Whosoever will be great among you, let him be your minister, and whosoever will be chief among you, let him be your servant. For even the Son of man came not to be ministered unto, but to minister and to give his life a ransom for many."	Mark 10:45
They came to and passed through Jericho. As he went out of Jericho with his disciples and a great number of people, a certain blind man, Bartimaeus the son of Timaeus, sat by the highway side begging. When he heard the multitude pass by, he asked what it meant. They told him that Jesus of Nazareth passeth by.	Mark 10:46/ Luke 19:1; 18:35 Mark 10:47/ Luke 18:36-37
He cried out, saying, "Jesus, thou Son of David, have mercy on me!"	Luke 18:38
Many charged him that he should hold his peace, but he cried so much the more, saying, "Have mercy on me, O Lord, thou Son of David!"	Matthew 20:31/ Mark 10:48/ Luke 18:39
Jesus stood still and commanded him to be brought unto him. They called the blind man, saying unto him, "Be of good comfort. Rise. He calleth thee." Casting away his garment, he rose and came to Jesus.	Mark 10:49/ Luke 18:40 Mark 10:50-51
Jesus answered and said unto him, "What wilt thou that I should do unto thee?"	
The blind man said unto him, "Lord, that I might receive my sight."	

So Jesus had compassion on him and touched his eyes, and said unto him, "Receive thy sight and go thy way. Thy faith hath made thee whole." | Matthew 20:34/ Mark 10:52/ Luke 18:42-43

Immediately he received his sight and followed Jesus in the way, glorifying God. All the people, when they saw it, gave praise unto God.

Behold, there was a man named Zaccheus, which was the chief among the publicans, and he was rich. He sought to see Jesus, who he was, and could not for the press because he was of little stature. | Luke 19:2-28

He ran before and climbed up into a sycamore tree to see him, for he was to pass that way.

When Jesus came to the place, he looked up and saw him and said unto him, "Zaccheus, make haste and come down, for today I must abide at thy house."

He made haste and came down and received him joyfully. When they saw it, they all murmured, saying that he was gone to be a guest with a man that is a sinner.

Zaccheus stood and said unto the Lord, "Behold, Lord, the half of my goods I give to the poor, and if I have taken anything from any man by false accusation, I restore him fourfold."

Jesus said unto him, "This day is salvation come to this house, forasmuch as he also is a son of Abraham. For the Son of man is come to seek and to save that which was lost."

As they heard these things, he added and spake a parable because he was nigh to Jerusalem, and because they thought that the kingdom of God should immediately appear.

He said therefore, "A certain nobleman went into a far country to receive for himself a kingdom and to return. He called his ten servants and delivered them ten pounds, and said unto them, 'Occupy till I come.'

"But his citizens hated him and sent a message after him, saying, 'We will not have this man to reign over us.'

"It came to pass that, when he returned, having received the kingdom, then he commanded these servants to be called unto him to whom he had given the money, that he might know how much every man had gained by trading.

"Then came the first, saying, 'Lord, thy pound hath gained ten pounds.'

"He said unto him, 'Well, thou good servant. Because thou hast been faithful in a very little, have thou authority over ten cities.'

"The second came, saying, 'Lord, thy pound hath gained five pounds.'

"He said likewise to him, 'Be thou also over five cities.'

"Another came, saying, 'Lord, behold, here is thy pound which I have kept laid up in a napkin. For I feared thee because thou art an austere man. Thou takest up that thou layedst not down and reapest that thou didst not sow.'

"He saith unto him, 'Out of thine own mouth will I judge thee, thou wicked servant. Thou knewest that I was an austere man, taking up that I laid not down and reaping that I did not sow. Wherefore then gavest not thou my money into the bank, that at my coming I might have required mine own with usury?'

"He said unto them that stood by, 'Take from him the pound and give it to him that hath ten pounds.'

They said unto him, 'Lord, he hath ten pounds.'

"For I say unto you that unto everyone which hath shall be given, and from him that hath not, even that he hath shall be taken away from him.

"'But those mine enemies which would not that I should reign over them, bring hither and slay them before me.'"

When he had thus spoken, he went before, ascending up to Jerusalem.

Then Jesus, six days before the passover, came to Bethany where Lazarus was whom he raised from the dead. Much people of the Jews therefore knew that he was there, and they came not for Jesus' sake only, but that they might see Lazarus also whom he had raised from the dead.	John 12:1 John 12:9-11
But the chief priests consulted that they might put Lazarus also to death, because that by reason of him many of the Jews went away and believed on Jesus.	
Now when Jesus was in the house of Simon the Leper, they made him a supper. Martha served, but Lazarus was one of them that sat at the table with him.	Matthew 26:6/ John 12:2
Then took Mary an alabaster box of a pound of ointment of spikenard, very costly. She brake the box and	Matthew 26:7/ Mark 14:3/

poured it on the head of Jesus as he sat at meat, and anointed his feet, and wiped his feet with her hair. The house was filled with the odor of the ointment. | John 12:3

Then one of his disciples, Judas Iscariot, Simon's son, which should betray him, had indignation and said, "Why was this waste of the ointment made? For it might have been sold for more than three hundred pence and given to the poor." | Mark 14:4/ John 12:4 Matthew 26:9/ Mark 14:5

This he said, not that he cared for the poor, but because he was a thief and had the bag, and bare what was put therein. | John 12:6

Jesus said, "Let her alone. Why trouble ye her? For ye have the poor with you always, and whensoever ye will, ye may do them good. But me ye have not always. | Mark 14:6-7

"She hath wrought a good work on me. For in that she hath poured this ointment on my body, she hath done what she could. She is come aforehand to anoint my body against the day of my burial. | Matthew 26:12/ Mark 14:8/ John 12:7

"Verily I say unto you, wheresoever this gospel shall be preached throughout the whole world, this also that she hath done shall be spoken of for a memorial of her." | Mark 14:9

THE LAST WEEK

Palm Sunday

On the next day when they drew nigh unto Jerusalem and were come to Bethphage, unto the mount called the mount of Olives, Jesus sent two of his disciples, saying unto them, "Go into the village over against you, and as soon as ye be entered into it, ye shall find an ass tied and a colt with her whereon never man sat. Loose him and bring him unto me.	Matthew 21:1/ Luke 19:29/ John 12:12 Matthew 21:2/ Mark 11:2 Matthew 21:3/ Mark 11:3/ Luke 19:31
"If any man ask you, 'Why do ye loose him?' ye shall say unto him, 'Because the Lord hath need of him,' and straightway they will send him hither."	
The disciples that were sent went their way and found the ass and the colt tied by the door without in a place where two ways met. As they were loosing the colt, the owners that stood there said unto them, "What do ye? Why loose ye the colt?"	Matthew 21:6-7/ Mark 11:4-5/ Luke 19:32-33
They said, "The Lord hath need of him." And they let them go.	Mark 11:6-7/ Luke 19:34-35
They brought the colt to Jesus and cast their garments upon the colt. Jesus sat thereon.	
All this was done that it might be fulfilled which was spoken by the prophet, saying, "Tell ye the daughter of Zion, 'Fear not. Behold, thy King cometh unto thee, meek and sitting upon an ass, and a colt the foal of an ass.'"*	Matthew 21:4-5/ John 12:15
	*Zechariah 9:9
A very great multitude that were come to the feast heard that Jesus was coming to Jerusalem. Many spread their clothes in the way. Others cut down branches from off the palm trees and strawed them in the way.	Matthew 21:8/ Mark 11:8/ Luke 19:36/ John 12:12-13
When he was come nigh, even now at the descent of the mount of Olives, the whole multitude of the disciples that went forth to meet him began to rejoice and praise God with a loud voice for all the mighty works that they had seen, saying, "Hosanna to the Son of David. Blessed is the King of Israel that cometh in the name of the Lord.	Matthew 21:9/ Mark 11:10/ Luke 19:37-38/ John 12:13

Blessed be the kingdom of our father David that cometh in the name of the Lord. Peace and glory in heaven. Hosanna in the highest."

When he was come into Jerusalem, all the city was moved, saying, "Who is this?" | Matthew 21:10-11

The multitude said, "This is Jesus the prophet of Nazareth of Galilee."

Some of the Pharisees from among the multitude said unto him, "Master, rebuke thy disciples." | Luke 19:39-44

He answered and said unto them, "I tell you that, if these should hold their peace, the stones would immediately cry out."

When he was come near, he beheld the city and wept over it, saying, "If thou hadst known, even thou at least in this thy day, the things which belong unto thy peace! But now they are hid from thine eyes.

"For the days shall come upon thee, that thine enemies shall cast a trench about thee and compass thee round, and keep thee in on every side, and shall lay thee even with the ground, and thy children within thee. They shall not leave in thee one stone upon another, because thou knewest not the time of thy visitation."

Jesus entered into Jerusalem, and into the temple. When he had looked round about upon all things, and now the eventide was come, he went out unto Bethany with the twelve. | Mark 11:11

Monday
Cleansing the Temple

In the morning on the morrow, as they returned into the city from Bethany, he was hungry. When he saw a fig tree afar off having leaves, he came to it, if haply he might find anything thereon. When he came to it, he found nothing but leaves, for the time of figs was not yet. | Matthew 21:18/ Mark 11:12
Matthew 21:19/ Mark 11:13-14

Jesus said unto it, "Let no fruit grow on thee henceforward forever." And his disciples heard it.

They came to Jerusalem. Jesus went into the temple of God and began to cast out all them that sold and bought in the temple, and overthrew the tables of the moneychangers and the seats of them that sold doves, and would not suffer that any man should carry any vessel through the temple. | Matthew 21:12/ Mark 11:15

Mark 11:16-17

He taught, saying unto them, "Is it not written, 'My house shall be called of all nations the house of prayer'?* But ye have made it a den of thieves." *Isaiah 56:7*

He taught daily in the temple. The blind and the lame came to him, and he healed them. Matthew 21:14-15/ Luke 19:47

When the chief priests and the scribes and the chief of the people saw the wonderful things that he did, and the children crying in the temple and saying, "Hosanna to the Son of David," they were sore displeased and said unto him, "Hearest thou what these say?" Matthew 21:16

Jesus said unto them, "Yea, have ye never read, 'Out of the mouth of babes and sucklings thou hast perfected praise'?"* *Psalm 8:2*

The chief priests and the scribes and the chief of the people heard it and sought how they might destroy him, but could not find what they might do. For they feared him because all the people were astonished at his doctrine and very attentive to hear him. Mark 11:18 Luke 19:47-48

When even was come, he left them and went out of the city into Bethany, and he lodged there. Matthew 21:17/ Mark 11:19

Tuesday
The End of Days

In the morning as they passed by, they saw the fig tree dried up from the roots. When the disciples saw it, they marvelled. Peter, calling to remembrance, said unto him, "Master, behold how soon the fig tree which thou cursedst is withered away." Mark 11:20 Matthew 21:20/ Mark 11:21

Jesus answered and said unto them, "Have faith in God. For verily I say unto you, if ye have faith and doubt not, ye shall not only do this which is done to the fig tree, but also if ye shall say unto this mountain, 'Be thou removed, and be thou cast into the sea,' it shall be done. Matthew 21:21/ Mark 11:22-23

"Whosoever shall not doubt in his heart, but shall believe that those things which he said shall come to pass, he shall have whatsoever he said.

"Therefore I say unto you, all things whatsoever ye desire, when ye pray, believe that ye receive them and ye shall have them. When ye stand praying, forgive, if ye have ought against any, that your Father also which is in heaven may forgive you your trespasses. But if ye do not Matthew 21:22/ Mark 11:24 Mark 11:25-26 forgive, neither will your Father which is in heaven forgive your trespasses."

They came again to Jerusalem, and he was walking in the temple. It came to pass that the chief priests and the scribes and the elders of the people came unto him as he taught the people in the temple and preached the gospel, and said, "Tell us, by what authority doest thou these things? And who gave thee this authority?" — Matthew 21:23/ Mark 11:27/ Luke 20:1-2

Jesus answered and said unto them, "I will also ask you one question, which if ye answer me, I will tell you by what authority I do these things. The baptism of John— was it from heaven or of men?" — Matthew 21:24/ Mark 11:29 Luke 20:4

They reasoned with themselves, saying, "If we shall say from heaven, he will say, 'Why then did ye not believe him?' But if we shall say of men, we fear all the people will stone us. For they counted John a prophet indeed." — Mark 11:31 Matthew 21:26-27/ Mark 11:32-33/ Luke 20:6-7

They answered Jesus and said, "We cannot tell whence it was."

He said unto them, "Neither do I tell you by what authority I do these things."

He began to speak unto them by parables. "But what think ye? A certain man had two sons. He came to the first and said, 'Son, go work today in my vineyard.' — Mark 12:1 Matthew 21:28-32

"He answered and said, 'I will not.' But afterward he repented and went.

"He came to the second and said likewise. He answered and said, 'I go, sir,' and went not.

"Whether of them twain did the will of his father?"

They said unto him, "The first."

Jesus said unto them, "Verily I say unto you, that the publicans and the harlots go into the kingdom of God before you. For John came unto you in the way of righteousness, and ye believed him not. But the publicans and the harlots believed him. And ye, when ye had seen it, repented not afterward, that ye might believe him.

"Hear another parable. There was a certain householder which planted a vineyard and hedged it round about, digged a winepress in it and built a tower, let it out to husbandmen, and went into a far country for a long time. When the season of the fruit drew near, he sent a servant to the husbandmen that they should give him of the fruit of the vineyard. But the husbandmen caught him, beat him, and sent him away empty. — Matthew 21:33/ Luke 20:9

Matthew 21:34/ Mark 12:3/ Luke 20:10

"Again he sent unto them another servant. At him they cast stones, wounded him in the head, entreated him shamefully, and sent him away empty.

"Again he sent a third. Him they cast out and killed. And many other servants more than the first. They beat one, killed another, and stoned another.

"Then said the lord of the vineyard, 'What shall I do?'

"Having yet therefore one son, his well-beloved, he sent him last of all unto them, saying, 'It may be that they will reverence my son when they see him.'

"But when the husbandmen saw the son, they reasoned among themselves, saying, 'This is the heir. Come, let us kill him, and let us seize on his inheritance.'

"So they caught him and cast him out of the vineyard and killed him. What therefore shall he do unto those husbandmen, when the lord of the vineyard cometh?"

They said unto him, "He will miserably destroy those wicked men and will let out his vineyard unto other husbandmen which shall render him the fruits in their seasons."

Jesus beheld them and said, "Did ye never read in the scriptures, 'The stone which the builders rejected is become the head of the corner. This is the Lord's doing, and it is marvellous in our eyes.'* Therefore I say unto you, the kingdom of God shall be taken from you and given to a nation bringing forth the fruits thereof. Whosoever shall fall on this stone shall be broken, but on whomsoever it shall fall, it will grind him to powder."

Jesus answered and spake unto them again by parables, and said, "The kingdom of heaven is like unto a certain king which made a marriage for his son, and sent forth his servants to call them that were bidden to the wedding.

"They would not come.

"Again he sent forth other servants, saying, 'Tell them which are bidden, 'Behold, I have prepared my dinner. My oxen and my fatlings are killed, and all things are ready. Come unto the marriage.'

"But they made light of it, and went their ways, one to his farm, another to his merchandise. The remnant took his servants, entreated them spitefully, and slew them.

"But when the king heard thereof, he was wroth. He sent forth his armies, destroyed those murderers, and

Mark 12:4/ Luke 20:11	
Matthew 21:35-36/ Mark 12:5/ Luke 20:12	
Matthew 21:37/ Mark 12:6/ Luke 20:13	
Matthew 21:38/ Luke 20:14	
Matthew 21:39-40/ Luke 20:15	
Matthew 21:41 Matthew 21:42/ Mark 12:10 Luke 20:17	
Matthew 21:43-44	
*Psalm 118:22-23	
Matthew 22:1-14	

burned up their city. Then said he to his servants, 'The wedding is ready, but they which were bidden were not worthy. Go ye therefore into the highways, and as many as ye shall find, bid to the marriage.'

"So those servants went out into the highways and gathered together all as many as they found, both bad and good, and the wedding was furnished with guests.

"When the king came in to see the guests, he saw there a man which had not on a wedding garment. He said unto him, 'Friend, how camest thou in hither not having a wedding garment?'

"He was speechless.

"Then said the king to the servants, 'Bind him hand and foot and take him away. Cast him into outer darkness. There shall be weeping and gnashing of teeth.'

"For many are called, but few are chosen."

When the chief priests and the scribes and Pharisees had heard his parables, they perceived that he had spoken against them. But when they sought to lay hands on him, they feared the multitude because they took him for a prophet. They left him and went their way. | Matthew 21:45/ Luke 20:19
Matthew 21:46
Matthew 22:15/ Mark 12:12-14/ Luke 20:20-21

Then the Pharisees took counsel how they might entangle him in his words, so they might deliver him unto the power and authority of the governor. They sent out unto him spies—certain of their disciples with the Pharisees and the Herodians which should feign themselves just men.

When they were come, they asked him, saying, "Master, we know that thou art true and teachest the way of God in truth, neither carest thou for any man, for thou regardest not the person of men. Tell us therefore, what thinkest thou? Is it lawful for us to give tribute unto Caesar, or not?" | Matthew 22:17/ Luke 20:22

But Jesus perceived their craftiness and said unto them, "Why tempt ye me, ye hypocrites? Shew me a penny." | Matthew 22:18-19/ Luke 20:23-24

They brought unto him a penny. | Matthew 22:20

He said unto them, "Whose image and superscription hath it?"

They answered and said, "Caesar's." | Matthew 22:21/ Luke 20:24-25

He said unto them, "Render therefore unto Caesar the things which are Caesar's, and unto God the things that are God's."

When they had heard these words, they marvelled at his answer and could not take hold of his words before the people. They held their peace and went their way.	Matthew 22:22/ Luke 20:26
The same day came to him certain of the Sadducees, which deny that there is any resurrection, and asked him, saying, "Master, Moses wrote unto us, 'If a man having a wife die and leave no children, his brother shall marry his wife and raise up seed unto his brother.'*	Matthew 22:23-24/ Mark 12:19/ Luke 20:27-28
	*Deuteronomy 25:5-6
"Now there were seven brethren. The first took a wife and died without children. The second took her to wife, and he died childless. The third took her in like manner unto the seventh and died, and they left no children. Last of all the woman died also. Therefore in the resurrection when they shall rise, whose wife shall she be of the seven? For they all had her to wife."	Mark 12:20/ Luke 20:29-30 Matthew 22:26/ Luke 20:31-32 Matthew 22:28/ Mark 12:23/ Luke 20:32
Jesus answered and said unto them, "Ye do err because ye know not the scriptures nor the power of God. The children of this world marry and are given in marriage. But they which shall be accounted worthy to obtain that world when they shall rise from the dead neither marry nor are given in marriage, but are as the angels of God in heaven. Neither can they die anymore, for they are equal unto the angels and are the children of God, being the children of the resurrection.	Matt 22:29/ Mark 12:24 Matthew 22:30/ Mark 12:25/ Luke 20:34-35 Luke 20:36
"But as touching the resurrection of the dead, have ye not read that even Moses shewed that the dead are raised, when in the bush God spake unto him, saying, 'I am the God of Abraham, and the God of Isaac, and the God of Jacob'?* God is not the God of the dead, but of the living, for all live unto him. Ye therefore do greatly err."	Matthew 22:31-32/ Mark 12:26*27/ Luke 20:37-38 *Exodus 3:6
When the multitude heard this, they were astonished at his doctrine. Then certain of the scribes answering said, "Master, thou hast well said."	Matthew 22:33 Luke 20:39
But when the Pharisees had heard them reasoning together and that he had put the Sadducees to silence, they were gathered together. One of them which was a lawyer, one of the scribes, came and asked him a question, tempting him and saying, "Master, which is the first commandment of all?"	Matthew 22:34-36/ Mark 12:28
Jesus answered him, "The first of all the commandments is, 'Hear, O Israel! The Lord our God is one Lord, and thou shalt love the Lord thy God with all thy heart, and with all thy soul, and with all thy mind, and with all	Mark 12:29-30

thy strength.'* This is the first and great commandment.

"The second is like unto it, namely this, 'Thou shalt love thy neighbor as thyself.'§ There is none other commandment greater than these. On these two commandments hang all the law and the prophets."

The scribe said unto him, "Well, Master, thou hast said the truth. For there is one God, and there is none other but he. To love him with all the heart, and with all the understanding, and with all the soul, and with all the strength, and to love his neighbor as himself, is more than all whole burnt offerings and sacrifices."

When Jesus saw that he answered discreetly, he said unto him, "Thou art not far from the kingdom of God."

No man after that durst ask him any question.

Jesus, while he taught in the temple, asked the Pharisees gathered together and said, "What think ye of Christ? Whose son is he?"

They said unto him, "The Son of David."

He said unto them, "How then doth David himself by the Holy Ghost call him Lord in the book of Psalms, saying, 'The Lord said unto my Lord, "Sit thou on my right hand till I make thine enemies thy footstool"'?* If David therefore called him Lord, how is he then his son?"

No man was able to answer him a word, neither durst any man from that day forth ask him any more questions at all. And the common people heard him gladly.

Then spake Jesus to the multitude and to his disciples, saying, "The scribes and the Pharisees sit in Moses' seat. All therefore whatsoever they bid you observe, that observe and do. But do not ye after their works, for they say, and do not.

"For they bind heavy burdens, grievous to be borne, and lay them on men's shoulders, but they themselves will not move them with one of their fingers.

"But all their works they do for to be seen of men. They love to walk in long robes, make broad their phylacteries, enlarge the borders of their garments, and love the uppermost rooms at feasts and the chief seats in the synagogues. Love salutations in the marketplaces and to be called of men, 'Rabbi, Rabbi.'

"But be not ye called Rabbi, for one is your Master, even Christ, and all ye are brethren. Call no man your father upon the earth, for one is your Father, which is in

---

Matthew 22:38-40
/Mark 12:31
*Deuteronomy 6:4-5
§Leviticus 19:18

Mark 12:32-34

Matthew 22:41-42/
Mark 12:35

Matthew 22:43-44/
Mark 12:36/
Luke 20:42
Matthew 22:45-46/
Luke 20:44,40
*Psalm 110:1

Mark 12:37
Matthew 23:1-4

Matthew 23:5-7/
Mark 12:38/
Luke 20:46

Matthew 23:8-39

heaven. Neither be ye called masters, for one is your Master, even Christ. But he that is greatest among you shall be your servant.

"Whosoever shall exalt himself shall be abased, and he that shall humble himself shall be exalted.

"But woe unto you, scribes and Pharisees, hypocrites! For ye shut up the kingdom of heaven against men. For ye neither go in yourselves, neither suffer ye them that are entering to go in.

"Woe unto you, scribes and Pharisees, hypocrites! For ye devour widows' houses, and for a pretense make long prayer. Therefore ye shall receive the greater damnation.

"Woe unto you, scribes and Pharisees, hypocrites! For ye compass sea and land to make one proselyte, and when he is made, ye make him twofold more the child of hell than yourselves.

"Woe unto you, ye blind guides which say, 'Whosoever shall swear by the temple, it is nothing. But whosoever shall swear by the gold of the temple, he is a debtor'! Ye fools and blind, for whether is greater, the gold or the temple that sanctifieth the gold?

"And, 'Whosoever shall swear by the altar, it is nothing. But whosoever sweareth by the gift that is upon it, he is guilty.' Ye fools and blind, for whether is greater, the gift, or the altar that sanctifieth the gift?

"Whoso therefore shall swear by the altar, sweareth by it and by all things thereon. And whoso shall swear by the temple, sweareth by it and by him that dwelleth therein. And he that shall swear by heaven, sweareth by the throne of God and by him that sitteth thereon.

"Woe unto you, scribes and Pharisees, hypocrites! For ye pay tithe of mint and anise and cummin, and have omitted the weightier matters of the law—judgment, mercy, and faith. These ought ye to have done and not to leave the other undone. Ye blind guides which strain at a gnat and swallow a camel.

"Woe unto you, scribes and Pharisees, hypocrites! For ye make clean the outside of the cup and of the platter, but within they are full of extortion and excess. Thou blind Pharisee, cleanse first that which is within the cup and platter, that the outside of them may be clean also.

"Woe unto you, scribes and Pharisees, hypocrites! For ye are like unto whited sepulchers which indeed appear beautiful outward, but are within full of dead men's bones and of all uncleanness. Even so ye also outwardly appear righteous unto men, but within ye are full of hypocrisy and iniquity.

"Woe unto you, scribes and Pharisees, hypocrites! Because ye build the tombs of the prophets and garnish the sepulchers of the righteous, and say, 'If we had been in the days of our fathers, we would not have been partakers with them in the blood of the prophets.' Wherefore ye be witnesses unto yourselves, that ye are the children of them which killed the prophets. Fill ye up then the measure of your fathers.

"Ye serpents, ye generation of vipers, how can ye escape the damnation of hell?

"Wherefore, behold, I send unto you prophets and wise men and scribes. Some of them ye shall kill and crucify. Some of them ye shall scourge in your synagogues and persecute them from city to city, that upon you may come all the righteous blood shed upon the earth, from the blood of righteous Abel* unto the blood of Zechariah son of Berechiah, whom ye slew between the temple and the altar.§ Verily I say unto you, all these things shall come upon this generation.

"O Jerusalem, Jerusalem, thou that killest the prophets and stonest them which are sent unto thee, how often would I have gathered thy children together, even as a hen gathereth her chickens under her wings, and ye would not! Behold, your house is left unto you desolate. For I say unto you, ye shall not see me henceforth till ye shall say, 'Blessed is he that cometh in the name of the Lord.'"

Jesus sat over against the treasury and beheld how the people cast money into the treasury. Many that were rich cast in much. There came a certain poor widow, and she threw in two mites, which make a farthing.

He called unto him his disciples and said unto them, "Verily I say unto you, that this poor widow hath cast in more than all they which have cast into the treasury. For all these have cast in of their abundance unto the offerings of God, but she of her want hath cast in all that she had, even all her living."

There were certain Greeks among them that came up to worship at the feast. The same came therefore to Philip, which was of Bethsaida of Galilee, and desired him, saying, "Sir, we would see Jesus."

*Genesis 4:8

§2 Chron 24:20-22

Mark 12:41-42

Mark 12:43-44/ Luke 21:3-4

John 12:20-35

Philip came and told Andrew, and again Andrew and Philip told Jesus.

Jesus answered them, saying, "The hour is come that the Son of man should be glorified. Verily, verily, I say unto you, except a corn of wheat fall into the ground and die, it abideth alone. But if it die, it bringeth forth much fruit. He that loveth his life shall lose it, and he that hateth his life in this world shall keep it unto life eternal.

"If any man serve me, let him follow me, and where I am, there shall also my servant be. If any man serve me, him will my Father honor.

"Now is my soul troubled. What shall I say? 'Father, save me from this hour'? But for this cause came I unto this hour: 'Father, glorify thy name.'"

Then came there a voice from heaven, saying, "I have both glorified it and will glorify it again."

The people therefore that stood by and heard it said that it thundered. Others said, "An angel spake to him."

Jesus answered and said, "This voice came not because of me, but for your sakes. Now is the judgment of this world. Now shall the prince of this world be cast out. And I, if I be lifted up from the earth, will draw all men unto me." This he said, signifying what death he should die.

The people answered him, "We have heard out of the law that Christ abideth forever, and how sayest thou, 'The Son of man must be lifted up'? Who is this Son of man?"

Then Jesus said unto them, "Yet a little while is the light with you. Walk while ye have the light, lest darkness come upon you. For he that walketh in darkness knoweth not whither he goeth. While ye have light, believe in the light, that ye may be the children of light."

These things spake Jesus and departed from the temple, and did hide himself from them. As he went out of the temple, one of his disciples said unto him, "Master, see what manner of buildings are here, adorned with goodly stones and gifts!" *(Matthew 24:1-2/ Mark 13:1-2/ Luke 21:5 John 12:36)*

Jesus said unto them, "See ye these great buildings of the temple? Verily I say unto you, there shall not be left here one stone upon another that shall not be thrown down."

As he sat upon the mount of Olives over against the temple, Peter and James and John and Andrew came unto him privately, saying, "Master, tell us. When shall these *(Matthew 24:3/ Mark 13:3/ Luke 21:7)* things be? What shall be the sign of thy coming and of the end of the world?"

Jesus answered and said unto them, "Take heed that no man deceive you. For many shall come in my name, saying, 'I am Christ, and the time draweth near,' and shall deceive many. Go ye not therefore after them. | Matthew 24:4
Matthew 24:5/
Luke 21:8

"Ye shall hear of wars and rumors of wars and commotions. See that ye be not troubled, for all these things must first come to pass, but the end shall not be yet. For nation shall rise against nation and kingdom against kingdom. There shall be famines and pestilences and great earthquakes in divers places. Fearful sights and great signs shall there be from heaven. All these are the beginning of sorrows. | Matthew 24:6-7/
Mark 13:7-8/
Luke 21:9,11

Matthew 24:8

"But before all these, they shall lay their hands on you and persecute you, delivering you up to councils and into prisons to be afflicted, and in the synagogues ye shall be beaten. Ye shall be brought before rulers and kings for my sake, for a testimony against them. Ye shall be betrayed both by parents and brethren and kinsfolk and friends, and some of you shall they cause to be put to death. But there shall not a hair of your head perish. | Matthew 24:9/
Mark 13:9/
Luke 21:12

Luke 21:16

Luke 21:18

"But when they shall lead you and deliver you up, take no thought beforehand what ye shall speak, neither meditate before what ye shall answer. For I will give you a mouth and wisdom in that hour, which all your adversaries shall not be able to gainsay nor resist. For it is not ye that speak, but the Holy Ghost. | Mark 13:11/
Luke 21:14-15

"Then shall many be offended and shall betray one another and shall hate one another. The brother shall betray the brother to death, and the father the son. Children shall rise up against their parents, and shall cause them to be put to death. | Matthew 24:10
Mark 13:12

"Many false prophets shall rise and shall deceive many. Because iniquity shall abound, the love of many shall wax cold. Ye shall be hated of all men for my name's sake. | Matthew 24:11-12

Luke 21:17

"But he that shall endure unto the end, the same shall be saved. In your patience possess ye your souls. | Matthew 24:13
Luke 21:19

"This gospel of the kingdom shall be preached in all the world for a witness unto all nations, and then shall the end come. | Matthew 24:14

"When ye therefore shall see Jerusalem compassed | Matthew 24:15/

with armies, then stand in the holy place. Know that the abomination of desolation, spoken of by Daniel the prophet, is nigh.* | Luke 21:20
Daniel 9:26-27; 11:31; 12:11

"Then let them which are in Judea flee to the mountains, let them which are in the midst of it depart out, and let not them that are in the countries enter thereinto. | Luke 21:21

"Let him which is on the housetop not come down to take anything out of his house. Neither let him that is in the field return back to take his clothes. | Matthew 24:17-18

"Woe unto them that are with child, and to them that give suck in those days! For there shall be great distress in the land and wrath upon this people. | Matthew 24:19 /Luke 21:23

"Pray ye that your flight be not in the winter, neither on the sabbath day. For in those days shall be great tribulation such as was not since the beginning of the world unto this time, nor ever shall be. For these be the days of vengeance, that all things which are written may be fulfilled. | Matthew 24:20/ Matthew 24:21/ Mark 13:19 Luke 21:22

"They shall fall by the edge of the sword and shall be led away captive into all nations. Jerusalem shall be trodden down of the Gentiles until the times of the Gentiles be fulfilled. And except those days should be shortened, no flesh should be saved. But for the elect's sake whom he hath chosen, those days shall be shortened. | Luke 21:24

Matthew 24:22/ Mark 13:20

"Then if any man shall say unto you, 'Lo, here is Christ,' or, 'Lo, he is there,' believe him not. For false Christs and false prophets shall arise and shall shew great signs and wonders, insomuch that, if it were possible, they shall deceive the very elect. But take ye heed. Behold, I have foretold you all things. | Matthew 24:23-24/ Mark 13:21-22

Mark 13:23

"Wherefore if they shall say unto you, 'Behold, he is in the desert,' go not forth. 'Behold, he is in the secret chambers,' believe it not. For as the lightning cometh out of the east and shineth even unto the west, so shall also the coming of the Son of man be. For wheresoever the carcass is, there will the eagles be gathered together. | Matthew 24:26-28

"Immediately after the tribulation of those days, the powers of heaven shall be shaken. The sun shall be darkened, the moon shall not give her light, and the stars shall fall from heaven. | Matthew 24:29/ Mark 13:24/ Luke 21:25-26

"Upon the earth [shall be] distress of nations with perplexity. The sea and the waves roaring. Men's hearts failing them for fear and for looking after those things which are coming on the earth.

"Then shall appear the sign of the Son of man in heaven. Then shall all the tribes of the earth mourn. They shall see the Son of man coming in the clouds of heaven with great power and glory. He shall send his angels with a great sound of a trumpet, and they shall gather together his elect from the four winds, from the uttermost part of the earth to the uttermost part of heaven. | Matthew 24:30-31/ Mark 13:26-27

"When these things begin to come to pass, then lift up your heads and look, for your redemption draweth nigh. | Luke 21:28

"Now learn a parable of the fig tree. When her branch is yet tender and putteth forth leaves, ye know that summer is near. So likewise ye, when ye see these things come to pass, know that the kingdom of God is near, even at the doors. Verily I say unto you, this generation shall not pass away till all these things be fulfilled. Heaven and earth shall pass away, but my words shall not pass away. | Matthew 24:32/ Mark 13:28 / Matthew 24:33-34/ Luke 21:31-32 / Matthew 24:35

"But of that day and hour knoweth no man, no, not the angels of heaven, neither the Son, but my Father only. But as the days of Noah were,* so shall also the coming of the Son of man be. For as in the days that were before the flood, they were eating and drinking, marrying and giving in marriage, until the day that Noah entered into the ark, and knew not until the flood came and took them all away. So shall also the coming of the Son of man be. | Matthew 24:36/ Mark 13:32 / Matthew 24:37-41 / *Genesis 6:3-5; 7:7,19-21

"Then shall two be in the field. The one shall be taken and the other left. Two women shall be grinding at the mill. The one shall be taken and the other left. Watch and pray therefore, for ye know not what hour your Lord doth come. | Matthew 24:42/ Mark 13:33

"But know this, that if the goodman of the house had known in what watch the thief would come, he would have watched and would not have suffered his house to be broken up. Therefore be ye also ready, for in such an hour as ye think not the Son of man cometh. | Matthew 24:43-44

"For the Son of man is as a man taking a far journey, who left his house and gave authority to his servants, and to every man his work, and commanded the porter to watch. Who then is a faithful and wise servant, whom his lord hath made ruler over his household to give them meat in due season? Blessed is that servant, whom his lord when he cometh shall find so doing. Verily I say unto you, that he shall make him ruler over all his goods. | Mark 13:34 / Matthew 24:45-51

"But and if that evil servant shall say in his heart, 'My

lord delayeth his coming,' and shall begin to smite his fellow servants, and to eat and drink with the drunken, the lord of that servant shall come in a day when he looketh not for him, and in an hour that he is not aware of, and shall cut him asunder and appoint him his portion with the hypocrites. There shall be weeping and gnashing of teeth.

"Watch ye therefore, for ye know not when the master of the house cometh—at even, or at midnight, or at the cockcrowing, or in the morning—lest coming suddenly he find you sleeping. | Mark 13:35-36

"Take heed to yourselves, lest at any time your hearts be overcharged with surfeiting, and drunkenness, and cares of this life, and so that day come upon you unawares. For as a snare shall it come on all them that dwell on the face of the whole earth. Watch ye therefore and pray always, that ye may be accounted worthy to escape all these things that shall come to pass, and to stand before the Son of man. | Luke 21:34-36

"Then shall the kingdom of heaven be likened unto ten virgins which took their lamps and went forth to meet the bridegroom. Five of them were wise and five were foolish. They that were foolish took their lamps and took no oil with them, but the wise took oil in their vessels with their lamps. | Matthew 25:1-1

"While the bridegroom tarried, they all slumbered and slept. At midnight there was a cry made, 'Behold, the bridegroom cometh. Go ye out to meet him.'

"Then all those virgins arose and trimmed their lamps. The foolish said unto the wise, 'Give us of your oil, for our lamps are gone out.'

"But the wise answered, saying, 'Not so, lest there be not enough for us and you. But go ye rather to them that sell and buy for yourselves.'

"While they went to buy, the bridegroom came. They that were ready went in with him to the marriage, and the door was shut.

"Afterward came also the other virgins, saying, 'Lord, Lord, open to us.'

"But he answered and said, 'Verily I say unto you, I know you not.'

"Watch therefore, for ye know neither the day nor the hour wherein the Son of man cometh. 'What I say unto you I say unto all—watch! | Mark 13:37

"For the kingdom of heaven is as a man travelling into a far country, who called his own servants and delivered unto them his goods. Unto one he gave five talents, to another two, and to another one, to every man according to his several ability, and straightway took his journey.

"Then he that had received the five talents went and traded with the same and made them other five talents. Likewise he that had received two—he also gained other two. But he that had received one went and digged in the earth, and hid his lord's money.

"After a long time the lord of those servants came and reckoned with them.

"So he that had received five talents came and brought other five talents, saying, 'Lord, thou deliveredst unto me five talents. Behold, I have gained beside them five talents more.'

"His lord said unto him, 'Well done, thou good and faithful servant. Thou hast been faithful over a few things. I will make thee ruler over many things. Enter thou into the joy of thy lord.'

"He also that had received two talents came and said, 'Lord, thou deliveredst unto me two talents. Behold, I have gained two other talents beside them.'

"His lord said unto him, 'Well done, good and faithful servant. Thou hast been faithful over a few things. I will make thee ruler over many things. Enter thou into the joy of thy lord.'

"Then he which had received the one talent came and said, 'Lord, I knew thee that thou art a hard man, reaping where thou hast not sown, and gathering where thou hast not strawed. I was afraid, and went and hid thy talent in the earth. Lo, there thou hast that is thine.'

"His lord answered and said unto him, 'Thou wicked and slothful servant! Thou knewest that I reap where I sowed not and gather where I have not strawed. Thou oughtest therefore to have put my money to the exchangers, and then at my coming I should have received mine own with usury.

"'Take therefore the talent from him and give it unto him which hath ten talents. For unto everyone that hath shall be given, and he shall have abundance. But from him that hath not shall be taken away even that which he hath.

"'Cast ye the unprofitable servant into outer darkness.

Matthew 25:14-46

There shall be weeping and gnashing of teeth.'

"When the Son of man shall come in his glory and all the holy angels with him, then shall he sit upon the throne of his glory. Before him shall be gathered all nations. He shall separate them one from another as a shepherd divideth his sheep from the goats, and he shall set the sheep on his right hand, but the goats on the left.

"Then shall the King say unto them on his right hand, 'Come, ye blessed of my Father, inherit the kingdom prepared for you from the foundation of the world. For I was an hungred and ye gave me meat. I was thirsty and ye gave me drink. I was a stranger and ye took me in. Naked and ye clothed me. I was sick and ye visited me. I was in prison and ye came unto me.'

"Then shall the righteous answer him, saying, 'Lord, when saw we thee an hungred and fed thee? Or thirsty and gave thee drink? When saw we thee a stranger and took thee in? Or naked and clothed thee? Or when saw we thee sick or in prison and came unto thee?'

"The King shall answer and say unto them, 'Verily I say unto you, inasmuch as ye have done it unto one of the least of these my brethren, ye have done it unto me.'

"Then shall he say also unto them on the left hand, 'Depart from me, ye cursed, into everlasting fire prepared for the devil and his angels. For I was an hungred and ye gave me no meat. I was thirsty and ye gave me no drink. I was a stranger and ye took me not in. Naked and ye clothed me not. Sick and in prison and ye visited me not.'

"Then shall they also answer him, saying, 'Lord, when saw we thee an hungred, or athirst, or a stranger, or naked, or sick, or in prison, and did not minister unto thee?'

"Then he shall answer them, saying, 'Verily I say unto you, inasmuch as ye did it not to one of the least of these, ye did it not to me.'

"These shall go away into everlasting punishment, but the righteous into life eternal."

Let him that readeth understand!   Mark 13:14

It came to pass, when Jesus had finished all these sayings, he said unto his disciples, "Ye know that after two days is the feast of the passover, and the Son of man is betrayed to be crucified."   Matthew 26:1-2

Wednesday
Thirty Pieces of Silver

In the daytime he was teaching in the temple. At night he went out and abode in the mount that is called the mount of Olives. All the people came early in the morning to him in the temple for to hear him. | Luke 21:37-38

But though he had done so many miracles before them, yet they believed not on him, that the saying of Isaiah the prophet might be fulfilled, which he spake, "Lord, who hath believed our report? And to whom hath the arm of the Lord been revealed?"* | John 12:37-50

*Isaiah 53:1

Therefore they could not believe because that Isaiah said again, "He hath blinded their eyes and hardened their heart, that they should not see with their eyes, nor understand with their heart and be converted, and I should heal them."§

§*Isaiah 6:10*

These things said Isaiah when he saw his glory and spake of him.

Nevertheless among the chief rulers also many believed on him. But because of the Pharisees they did not confess him, lest they should be put out of the synagogue, for they loved the praise of men more than the praise of God.

Jesus cried and said, "He that believeth on me, believeth not on me, but on him that sent me. And he that seeth me seeth him that sent me. I am come a light into the world, that whosoever believeth on me should not abide in darkness.

"If any man hear my words and believe not, I judge him not. For I came not to judge the world, but to save the world. He that rejecteth me and receiveth not my words hath one that judgeth him. The word that I have spoken, the same shall judge him in the last day.

"For I have not spoken of myself, but the Father which sent me. He gave me a commandment what I should say and what I should speak. I know that his commandment is life everlasting. Whatsoever I speak therefore, even as the Father said unto me, so I speak."

Now the chief priests, the scribes, and the elders of the people assembled together unto the palace of the high priest, who was called Caiaphas, and consulted how they might take Jesus by subtlety and put him to death. But | Matthew 26:3/ Luke 22:1
Matthew 26:4/ Mark 14:1

they said, "Not on the feast day, lest there be an uproar among the people."

Then entered Satan into Judas Iscariot, one of the twelve. He went unto the chief priests and captains and said unto them, "What will ye give me, and I will deliver him unto you?"

When they heard it, they were glad, and covenanted with him for thirty pieces of silver. From that time he sought opportunity to betray him unto them in the absence of the multitude.

Matthew 26:5

Mark 14:10/
Luke 22:3-4
Matthew 26:15/
Mark 14:11
Matthew 26:16/
Luke 22:6

Thursday
The Last Supper

Then came the first day of the feast of unleavened bread when the passover must be killed. He sent Peter and John, saying, "Go and prepare us the passover, that we may eat."

They said unto him, "Where wilt thou that we go and prepare for thee?"

He said unto them, "Go into the city. There shall a man meet you bearing a pitcher of water. Follow him into the house where he entereth in. Ye shall say unto the goodman of the house, 'The Master said unto thee, "My time is at hand. Where is the guestchamber at thy house where I shall eat the passover with my disciples?"' He will shew you a large upper room furnished and prepared. There make ready for us."

They went forth and came into the city, and found as he had said unto them. They made ready the passover.

In the evening he came with the twelve. When the hour was come, he sat down with the twelve apostles. There was also a strife among them, which of them should be accounted the greatest.

He said unto them, "The kings of the Gentiles exercise lordship over them, and they that exercise authority upon them are called benefactors. But ye shall not be so, but he that is greatest among you, let him be as the younger. And he that is chief, as he that doth serve. For whether is greater, he that sitteth at meat, or he that serveth? Is not he that sitteth at meat? But I am among you as he that serveth.

Matthew 26:17/
Luke 22:7-8

Matthew 26:17-18/
Mark 14:12/
Luke 22:9-11

Mark 14:15

Mark 14:16/
Luke 22:13
Mark 14:17/
Luke 22:14
Luke 22:24-30

"Ye are they which have continued with me in my temptations. I appoint unto you a kingdom, as my Father hath appointed unto me, that ye may eat and drink at my table in my kingdom, and sit on thrones judging the twelve tribes of Israel."

Now when Jesus knew that his hour was come that he should depart out of this world unto the Father, having loved his own which were in the world, he loved them unto the end. John 13:1

He said unto them, "With desire I have desired to eat this passover with you before I suffer. For I say unto you, I will not anymore eat thereof, until it be fulfilled in the kingdom of God." Luke 22:15-16

As they sat and did eat, the devil having now put into the heart of Judas Iscariot, Simon's son, to betray him, Jesus knowing that the Father had given all things into his hands, and that he was come from God and went to God, rose from supper and laid aside his garments, took a towel and girded himself. After that he poured water into a basin and began to wash the disciples' feet and to wipe them with the towel wherewith he was girded. Mark 14:18/
John 13:2
John 13:3-20

Then came he to Simon Peter, and Peter said unto him, "Lord, dost thou wash my feet?"

Jesus answered and said unto him, "What I do thou knowest not now, but thou shalt know hereafter."

Peter said unto him, "Thou shalt never wash my feet."

Jesus answered him, "If I wash thee not, thou hast no part with me."

Simon Peter said unto him, "Lord, not my feet only, but also my hands and my head."

Jesus said to him, "He that is washed needeth not save to wash his feet, but is clean every whit. *Ye* are clean—but not all." For he knew who should betray him.

After he had washed their feet and had taken his garments and was set down again, he said unto them, "Know ye what I have done unto you? Ye call me Master and Lord—and ye say well, for so I am. If I then, your Lord and Master, have washed your feet, ye also ought to wash one another's feet. For I have given you an example, that ye should do as I have done to you.

"Verily, verily, I say unto you, the servant is not greater than his lord, neither he that is sent greater than he that sent him. If ye know these things, happy are ye if ye do them.

"I speak not of you all. I know whom I have chosen, but that the scripture may be fulfilled, 'He that eateth bread with me hath lifted up his heel against me.'* *Psalm 41:9*

"Now I tell you before it come, that when it is come to pass, ye may believe that I am he.

"Verily, verily, I say unto you, he that receiveth whomsoever I send receiveth me, and he that receiveth me receiveth him that sent me."

As they sat and did eat, Jesus was troubled in spirit, and testified, "Verily, verily, I say unto you, that one of you which eateth with me shall betray me." Mark 14:18/ John 13:21

Then the disciples were exceeding sorrowful and looked one on another, doubting of whom he spake. They began every one of them to say unto him one by one, "Lord, is it I?" And another, "Is it I?" Matthew 26:22/ Mark 14:19/ John 13:22

He answered and said unto them, "It is one of the twelve that dippeth with me in the dish. Truly the Son of man goeth as it is written of him, but woe to that man by whom he is betrayed! It had been good for that man if he had never been born." Mark 14:20 Matthew 26:24/ Mark 14:21/ Luke 22:22

Now there was leaning on Jesus' bosom one of his disciples whom Jesus loved.* Simon Peter therefore beckoned to him that he should ask who it should be that should do this thing. John 13:23 Luke 22:23/ John 13:24 *John

He then said unto him, "Lord, who is it?" John 13:25-26

Jesus answered, "He it is, to whom I shall give a sop, when I have dipped it." And when he had dipped the sop, he gave it to Judas Iscariot, the son of Simon.

Then Judas answered and said, "Master, is it I?" Matthew 26:25/

He said unto him, "Thou hast said. That thou doest, do quickly." John 13:27,30

After the sop Satan entered into him. He then went immediately out, and it was night.

Now no man at the table knew for what intent he spake this unto him. For some of them thought because Judas had the bag, that Jesus had said unto him, "Buy those things that we have need of against the feast," or that he should give something to the poor. John 13:28-29

When he was gone out, Jesus said, "Now is the Son of man glorified, and God is glorified in him. If God be John 13:31-32 glorified in him, God shall also glorify him in himself and shall straightway glorify him."

He took bread, blessed it and brake it, gave it to the disciples, and said, "Take, eat. This is my body which is given for you. This do in remembrance of me." | Matthew 26:26/ Luke 22:19

He took the cup, gave thanks, and gave it to them, saying, "Take this and divide it among yourselves. Drink ye all of it. For this is the new testament in my blood which is shed for you for the remission of sins. | Matthew 26:27/ Luke 22:17 Matthew 26:28/ Luke 2:20

"Verily I say unto you, I will drink no more of the fruit of the vine until that day when I drink it new with you in my Father's kingdom. | Matthew 26:29/ Mark 14:25

"Little children, yet a little while I am with you. Ye shall seek me, and as I said unto the Jews, 'Whither I go, ye cannot come,' so now I say to you. | John 13:33-36

"A new commandment I give unto you, that ye love one another. As I have loved you, that ye also love one another. By this shall all men know that ye are my disciples, if ye have love one to another."

Simon Peter said unto him, "Lord, whither goest thou?"

Jesus answered him, "Whither I go, thou canst not follow me now. But thou shalt follow me afterwards."

Peter said unto him, "Lord, why cannot I follow thee now? I am ready to go with thee, both into prison and to death." | Luke 22:33/ John 13:37

The Lord said, "Simon, Simon, behold, Satan hath desired to have you, that he may sift you as wheat. But I have prayed for thee that thy faith fail not, and when thou art converted, strengthen thy brethren. | Luke 22:31-32

"All ye shall be offended because of me this night. For it is written, 'I will smite the shepherd, and the sheep of the flock shall be scattered abroad.'* But after I am risen again, I will go before you into Galilee." | Matthew 26:31-32

Zechariah 13:7

But Peter said unto him, "Though all men shall be offended because of thee, yet will I never be offended. I will lay down my life for thy sake." | Matthew 26:33/ Mark 14:29/ John 13:37

Jesus answered him, "Wilt thou lay down thy life for my sake? I tell thee, Peter, that this night, before the cock crow twice, thou shalt thrice deny that thou knowest me." | Mark 14:30/ Luke 22:34/ John 13:38

But he spake the more vehemently, "Though I should die with thee, I will not deny thee in any wise." | Matthew 26:35/ Mark 14:31

Likewise also said all the disciples.

He said unto them, "When I sent you without purse and scrip and shoes, lacked ye anything?" *Luke 22:35-38*

They said, "Nothing."

Then said he unto them, "But now, he that hath a purse, let him take it, and likewise his scrip. He that hath no sword, let him sell his garment and buy one. For I say unto you that this that is written must yet be accomplished in me, 'And he was reckoned among the transgressors:'* For the things concerning me have an end. **Isaiah 53:12*

They said, "Lord, behold, here are two swords."

He said unto them, "It is enough. Let not your heart be troubled. Ye believe in God. Believe also in me. *John 14:1-31*

"In my Father's house are many mansions. If it were not so, I would have told you. I go to prepare a place for you.

"And if I go and prepare a place for you, I will come again and receive you unto myself, that where I am, there ye may be also. Whither I go ye know, and the way ye know."

Thomas said unto him, "Lord, we know not whither thou goest. How can we know the way?"

Jesus said unto him, "*I* am the way, the truth, and the life. No man cometh unto the Father, but by me. If ye had known me, ye should have known my Father also, and from henceforth ye know him and have seen him."

Philip said unto him, "Lord, shew us the Father, and it sufficeth us."

Jesus said unto him, "Have I been so long time with you, and yet hast thou not known me, Philip? He that hath seen me hath seen the Father. How sayest thou then, shew us the Father? Believest thou not that I am in the Father, and the father in me?

"The words that I speak unto you I speak not of myself. But the Father that dwelleth in me—he doeth the works. Believe me that I am in the Father and the Father in me. Or else believe me for the very works' sake.

"Verily, verily, I say unto you, he that believeth on me, the works that I do shall he do also. And greater works than these shall he do, because I go unto my Father.

"Whatsoever ye shall ask in my name, that will I do, that the Father may be glorified in the Son. If ye shall ask anything in my name, I will do it.

"If ye love me, keep my commandments. I will pray the Father, and he shall give you another Comforter, that he may abide with you forever, even the Spirit of truth whom the world cannot receive because it seeth him not, neither knoweth him. But ye know him, for he dwelleth with you and shall be in you. I will not leave you comfortless. I will come to you.

"Yet a little while, and the world seeth me no more. But ye see me. Because I live, ye shall live also. At that day ye shall know that I am in my Father, and ye in me, and I in you.

"He that hath my commandments and keepeth them—he it is that loveth me. He that loveth me shall be loved of my Father, and I will love him and will manifest myself to him."

Judas said unto him (not Iscariot), "Lord, how is it that thou wilt manifest thyself unto us and not unto the world?"

Jesus answered and said unto him, "If a man love me, he will keep my words. My Father will love him, and we will come unto him and make our abode with him. He that loveth me not keepeth not my sayings.

"The word which ye hear is not mine, but the Father's which sent me. These things have I spoken unto you, being yet present with you. But the Comforter, which is the Holy Ghost whom the Father will send in my name—he shall teach you all things and bring all things to your remembrance whatsoever I have said unto you.

"Peace I leave with you. My peace I give unto you. Not as the world giveth give I unto you. Let not your heart be troubled, neither let it be afraid. Ye have heard how I said unto you I go away and come again unto you. If ye loved me, ye would rejoice because I said I go unto the Father, for my Father is greater than I.

"Now I have told you before it comes to pass, that when it is come to pass ye might believe. Hereafter I will not talk much with you, for the prince of this world cometh and hath nothing in me. But that the world may know that I love the Father, and as the Father gave me commandment, even so I do.

"Arise, let us go hence."

When they had sung a hymn, they went out into the mount of Olives.

Matthew 26:30-31

Then said Jesus unto them, "I am the true vine, and my Father is the husbandman. Every branch in me that beareth not fruit he taketh away, and every branch that beareth fruit he purgeth it, that it may bring forth more fruit.

"Now ye are clean through the word which I have spoken unto you. Abide in me, and I in you. As the branch cannot bear fruit of itself except it abide in the vine, no more can ye except ye abide in me.

"I am the vine. Ye are the branches. He that abideth in me and I in him, the same bringeth forth much fruit, for without me ye can do nothing. If a man abide not in me, he is cast forth as a branch and is withered. Men gather them and cast them into the fire, and they are burned.

"If ye abide in me and my words abide in you, ye shall ask what ye will, and it shall be done unto you. Herein is my Father glorified, that ye bear much fruit. So shall ye be my disciples. As the Father hath loved me, so have I loved you. Continue ye in my love.

"If ye keep my commandments, ye shall abide in my love, even as I have kept my Father's commandments and abide in his love. These things have I spoken unto you, that my joy might remain in you, and that your joy might be full.

"This is my commandment, that ye love one another as I have loved you. Greater love hath no man than this, that a man lay down his life for his friends.

"Ye are my friends if ye do whatsoever I command you. Henceforth I call you not servants, for the servant knoweth not what his lord doeth. But I have called you friends, for all things that I have heard of my Father I have made known unto you.

"Ye have not chosen me, but I have chosen you and ordained you, that ye should go and bring forth fruit, that your fruit should remain, that whatsoever ye shall ask of the Father in my name he may give it you. These things I command you, that ye love one another.

"If the world hate you, ye know that it hated me before it hated you. If ye were of the world, the world would love his own. But because ye are not of the world, but I have chosen you out of the world, therefore the world hateth you.

"Remember the word that I said unto you. The servant is not greater than his lord. If they have persecuted

John 15:1-27

me, they will also persecute you. If they have kept my saying, they will keep yours also. But all these things will they do unto you for my name's sake because they know not him that sent me.

"If I had not come and spoken unto them, they had not had sin. But now they have no cloak for their sin. He that hateth me hateth my Father also.

"If I had not done among them the works which none other man did, they had not had sin. But now have they both seen and hated both me and my Father. But this cometh to pass, that the word might be fulfilled that is written in their law, 'They hated me without a cause.'* *Psalm 35:19; 69:4*

"But when the Comforter is come, whom I will send unto you from the Father, even the Spirit of truth which proceedeth from the Father—he shall testify of me. Ye also shall bear witness, because ye have been with me from the beginning.

"These things have I spoken unto you that ye should not be offended. They shall put you out of the synagogues. Yea, the time cometh that whosoever killeth you will think that he doeth God service. These things will they do unto you because they have not known the Father, nor me. John 16:1-33

"But these things have I told you, that when the time shall come, ye may remember that I told you of them. These things I said not unto you at the beginning because I was with you. But now I go my way to him that sent me; and none of you asketh me, 'Whither goest thou?' Because I have said these things unto you, sorrow hath filled your heart.

"Nevertheless I tell you the truth. It is expedient for you that I go away. For if I go not away, the Comforter will not come unto you. But if I depart, I will send him unto you.

"When he is come, he will reprove the world of sin, of righteousness, and of judgment. Of sin because they believe not on me. Of righteousness because I go to my Father and ye see me no more. Of judgment because the prince of this world is judged.

"I have yet many things to say unto you, but ye cannot bear them now. Howbeit when he, the Spirit of truth, is come, he will guide you into all truth. For he shall not speak of himself, but whatsoever he shall hear, that shall he speak, and he will shew you things to come. He shall glorify me, for he shall receive of mine and shall shew it unto you. All things that the Father hath are mine. Therefore said I that he shall take of mine and shall shew it unto you.

"A little while and ye shall not see me, and again, a little while and ye shall see me, because I go to the Father."

Then said some of his disciples among themselves, "What is this that he said unto us, 'A little while, and ye shall not see me.' And again, 'A little while, and ye shall see me.' And, 'Because I go to the Father'? We cannot tell what he said."

Now Jesus knew that they were desirous to ask him, and said of them, "Do ye inquire among yourselves of that I said, 'A little while, and ye shall not see me,' and again, 'A little while, and ye shall see me'?

"Verily, verily, I say unto you, that ye shall weep and lament, but the world shall rejoice. Ye shall be sorrowful, but your sorrow shall be turned into joy.

"A woman, when she is in travail, hath sorrow because her hour is come. But as soon as she is delivered of the child, she remembereth no more the anguish, for joy that a man is born into the world. Ye now therefore have sorrow, but I will see you again. Your heart shall rejoice, and your joy no man taketh from you.

"In that day ye shall ask me nothing. Verily, verily, I say unto you, whatsoever ye shall ask the Father in my name, he will give it you. Hitherto have ye asked nothing in my name. Ask and ye shall receive, that your joy may be full.

"These things have I spoken unto you in proverbs. But the time cometh when I shall no more speak unto you in proverbs, but I shall shew you plainly of the Father.

"At that day ye shall ask in my name, and I say not unto you that I will pray the Father for you. For the Father himself loveth you because ye have loved me and have believed that I came out from God. I came forth from the Father and am come into the world. Again I leave the world and go to the Father."

His disciples said unto him, "Lo, now speakest thou plainly and speakest no proverb. Now are we sure that thou knowest all things and needest not that any man should ask thee. By this we believe that thou camest forth from God."

Jesus answered them, "Do ye now believe? Behold, the hour cometh—yea, is now come—that ye shall be scattered, every man to his own, and shall leave me alone. And yet I am not alone, because the Father is with me.

"These things I have spoken unto you, that in me ye might have peace. In the world ye shall have tribulation. But be of good cheer. I have overcome the world."

These words spake Jesus, and lifted up his eyes to heaven and said, "Father, the hour is come. Glorify thy Son, that thy Son also may glorify thee. As thou hast given him power over all flesh, that he should give eternal life to as many as thou hast given him.

John 17:1-26

"This is life eternal, that they might know thee the only true God, and Jesus Christ whom thou hast sent.

"I have glorified thee on the earth. I have finished the work which thou gavest me to do. Now O Father, glorify me with thine own self with the glory which I had with thee before the world was.

"I have manifested thy name unto the men which thou gavest me out of the world. Thine they were, and thou gavest them me, and they have kept thy word. Now they have known that all things whatsoever thou hast given me are of thee. For I have given unto them the words which thou gavest me, and they have received them and have known surely that I came out from thee. They have believed that thou didst send me.

"I pray for them. I pray not for the world, but for them which thou hast given me, for they are thine. All mine are thine, and thine are mine, and I am glorified in them.

"Now I am no more in the world, but these are in the world. I come to thee. Holy Father, keep through thine own name those whom thou hast given me, that they may be as one as we are.

"While I was with them in the world, I kept them in thy name. Those that thou gavest me I have kept, and none of them is lost but the son of perdition, that the scripture might be fulfilled. Now come I to thee, and these things I speak in the world, that they might have my joy fulfilled in themselves.

"I have given them thy word, and the world hath hated them because they are not of the world, even as I am not of the world. I pray not that thou shouldest take them out of the world, but that thou shouldest keep them from the evil. They are not of the world, even as I am not of the world.

"Sanctify them through thy truth. Thy word is truth. As thou hast sent me into the world, even so have I also sent them into the world. For their sakes I sanctify myself, that they also might be sanctified through the truth.

"Neither pray I for these alone, but for them also which shall believe on me through their word, that they all may be one as thou, Father, art in me, and I in thee. That they also may be one in us, that the world may believe that thou hast sent me.

"The glory which thou gavest me I have given them, that they may be one even as we are one. I in them and thou in me, that they may be made perfect in one, and that the world may know that thou hast sent me and hast loved them as thou hast loved me.

"Father, I will that they also whom thou hast given me be with me where I am, that they may behold my glory which thou hast given me. For thou lovedst me before the foundation of the world.

"O righteous Father, the world hath not known thee. But I have known thee, and these have known that thou hast sent me. I have declared unto them thy name and will declare it, that the love wherewith thou hast loved me may be in them, and I in them."

When Jesus had spoken these words, he went forth with his disciples over the brook Cedron where was a garden called Gethsemane, into the which he and his disciples entered. Judas also which betrayed him knew the place, for Jesus ofttimes resorted thither with his disciples. | Matthew 26:36/ Mark 14:32/ John 18:1-2

He said to his disciples, "Sit ye here while I go and pray yonder."

He took with him Peter and James and John, and began to be sore amazed, and to be sorrowful and very heavy. Then said he unto them, "My soul is exceeding sorrowful, even unto death. Tarry ye here and watch with me. Pray that ye enter not into temptation." | Matthew 26:37-38/ Mark 14:33 Luke 22:40

He went a little further, about a stone's cast, fell on the ground and prayed, saying, "O my Father, all things are possible unto thee. If it be possible, remove this cup from me. Nevertheless, not my will, but thine be done." | Matthew 26:39/ Mark 14:35/ Luke 22:41-42

He came unto the disciples and found them asleep, and said unto Peter, "Simon, sleepest thou? Couldest thou | Matthew 26:40-41/ Mark 14:37-38 not watch with me one hour? Watch ye and pray, that ye enter not into temptation. The spirit indeed is willing, but the flesh is weak."

He went away again the second time and prayed, saying, "O my Father, if this cup may not pass away from me except I drink it, thy will be done." | Matthew 26:42

When he returned, he found them asleep again, for their eyes were heavy. Neither wist they what to answer him. | Mark 14:40

He left them and went away again, and prayed the third time, saying the same words. Being in an agony, he prayed more earnestly, and his sweat was as it were great drops of blood falling down to the ground. | Matthew 26:44 / Luke 22:44

There appeared an angel unto him from heaven, strengthening him. | Luke 22:43

When he rose up from prayer, he cometh to his disciples the third time and found them sleeping for sorrow, and said unto them, "Sleep on now and take your rest. Behold, the hour is at hand, and the Son of man is betrayed into the hands of sinners." | Matthew 26:45 / Mark 14:41 / Luke 22:45

While he yet spake, Judas then, having received a band of men and officers from the chief priests, scribes, elders, and Pharisees, came thither with lanterns and torches and swords and staves. | Matthew 26:47 / Mark 14:43 / John 18:3

"Rise up. Let us be going. Behold, he that betrayeth me is at hand." | Matthew 26:46 / Mark 14:42

Now Judas had given them a sign, saying, "Whomsoever I shall kiss, that same is he. Take him and hold him fast." As soon as he came, he drew near unto Jesus, and said, "Hail, Master;' and kissed him. | Matthew 26:48-49 / Mark 14:44-45 / Luke 22:47

Jesus said unto him, "Judas, betrayest thou the Son of man with a kiss?" | Matthew 26:50 / Luke 22:48

Jesus therefore, knowing all things that should come upon him, went forth, and said unto them, "Whom seek ye?" And Judas stood with them. | John 18:4-9

They answered him, "Jesus of Nazareth."

Jesus said unto them, "I am he."

As soon then as he had said unto them, "I am he," they went backward and fell to the ground.

Then asked he them again, "Whom seek ye?"

They said, "Jesus of Nazareth."

Jesus answered, "I have told you that I am he. If therefore ye seek me, let these go their way," that the saying might be fulfilled which he spake, "Of them which thou gavest me have I lost none."* | *John 17:12*

When they which were about him saw what would follow, they said unto him, "Lord, shall we smite with the sword?" | Luke 22:49

Then Simon Peter, having a sword, drew it and smote the servant of the high priest, and cut off his right ear. The servant's name was Malchus. | Luke 22:50/ John 18:10

Then said Jesus unto Peter, "Put up thy sword into the sheath. For all they that take the sword shall perish with the sword. Thinkest thou that I cannot now pray to my Father, and he shall presently give me more than twelve legions of angels? But how then shall the scriptures be fulfilled, that thus it must be? Shall I not drink the cup which my Father hath given me? Suffer ye thus far." | Matthew 26:52/ John 18:11 Matthew 26:53-54 Luke 22:51/ John 18:11

He touched his ear and healed him.

Then Jesus said unto the chief priests, captains of the temple, and the elders which were come to him, "Are ye come out as against a thief with swords and staves to take me? I was daily with you in the temple teaching, and ye laid no hands on me. But the scriptures must be fulfilled. This is your hour, and the power of darkness." | Matthew 26:55-56/ Mark 14:48-49/ Luke 22:52-53

Then all the disciples forsook him and fled.

The band and the captain and officers of the Jews took Jesus, bound him, and led him away. | John 18:12-13

There followed him a certain young man, having a linen cloth cast about his naked body. The young men laid hold on him. He left the linen cloth and fled from them naked. | Mark 14:51-52

Friday
The Crucifixion

They led Jesus away to Annas first, for he was father-in-law to Caiaphas, which was the high priest that same year. Annas sent him bound unto Caiaphas, where the scribes and the elders were assembled. Now Caiaphas was he which gave counsel to the Jews, that it was expedient that one man should die for the people. | Mark 14:53/ John 18:13 Matthew 26:57/ John 18:24 John 18:14

Simon Peter followed Jesus afar off, and so did another disciple.* That disciple was known unto the high priest and went in with Jesus into the palace of the high priest. But Peter stood at the door without. | Matthew 26:58/ John 18:15-16 *John

Then went out that other disciple which was known unto the high priest and spake unto her that kept the door, and brought in Peter to see the end.

Caiaphas the high priest then asked Jesus of his disciples and of his doctrine.

Matthew 26:57/
John 18:19

Jesus answered him, "I spake openly to the world. I ever taught in the synagogue and in the temple whither the Jews always resort. In secret have I said nothing. Why askest thou me? Ask them which heard me what I have said unto them. Behold, they know what I said."

John 18:20-23

When he had thus spoken, one of the officers which stood by struck Jesus with the palm of his hand, saying, "Answerest thou the high priest so?"

Jesus answered him, "If I have spoken evil, bear witness of the evil. But if well, why smitest thou me?"

The chief priests and elders and all the council sought for witness against Jesus to put him to death. But though many bare false witness against him, their witness agreed not together. At the last came two and bare false witness against him, saying, "We heard him say, 'I will destroy this temple that is made with hands, and within three days I will build another made without hands.'" But neither so did their witness agree together.

Matthew 26:59-60/
Mark 14:55-57

Mark 14:58-60

The high priest stood up in the midst and asked Jesus, saying, "Answerest thou nothing? What is it which these witness against thee?"

But Jesus held his peace.

Matthew 26:63

The high priest answered and said unto him, "I adjure thee by the living God that thou tell us whether thou be the Christ, the Son of God."

Jesus said, "I am. And I say unto you, hereafter shall ye see the Son of man sitting on the right hand of power and coming in the clouds of heaven."

Matthew 26:64/
Mark 14:62

Then the high priest rent his clothes, saying, "He hath spoken blasphemy. What further need have we of witnesses? Ye have heard the blasphemy. What think ye?"

Matt 26:65-66/
Mark 14:64

They answered and said, "He is guilty of death."

The men that held Jesus mocked him and smote him and buffeted him. Some began to spit in his face. When they had blindfolded him, they struck him on the face with the palms of their hands, saying, "Prophesy unto us, thou Christ, who is it that smote thee?" And many other things blasphemously spake they against him.

Matthew 26:67-68/
Mark 14:65/
Luke 22:63-65

When the servants and officers had kindled a fire of coals in the midst of the hall and were set down together, Peter sat down among them and warmed himself at the fire, for it was cold. | Mark 14:54/ Luke 22:55/ John 18:18

As Peter sat by the fire, the damsel that kept the door earnestly looked upon him and said, "Thou wast with Jesus of Nazareth. Art not thou also one of this man's disciples?" | Mark 14:66-67/ Luke 22:56/ John 18:17

He denied before them all, saying, "Woman, I know him not, neither understand I what thou sayest." | Matthew 26:70/ Mark 14:68/ Luke 22:57

He went out into the porch, and the cock crew.

After about the space of one hour another maid saw him and said unto them that were there, "Of a truth this fellow was also with Jesus of Nazareth." | Matthew 26:71/ Luke 22:58-59

They that stood by said, "Surely thou art one of them, for thou art a Galilean. Thy speech agreeth thereto." | Mark 14:70/

Again he denied with an oath, "I do not know the man." | Matthew 26:72

One of the servants of the high priest, being his kinsman whose ear Peter cut off, said, "Did I not see thee in the garden with him?" | John 18:26

Then he began to curse and to swear, saying, "I know not this man of whom ye speak." | Matthew 26:74/ Mark 14:71-72/ Luke 22:60-62

Immediately, while he yet spake, the cock crew the second time.

The Lord turned and looked upon Peter, and Peter remembered the word that Jesus said unto him, "Before the cock crow twice, thou shalt deny me thrice."

Peter went out and wept bitterly.

When the morning was come, the elders of the people, the chief priests, and the scribes came together and led Jesus into their council, saying, "Art thou the Christ? Tell us." | Matthew 27:1/ Luke 22:66-71

He said unto them, "If I tell you, ye will not believe. If I also ask you, ye will not answer me, nor let me go. Hereafter shall the Son of man sit on the right hand of the power of God."

Then said they all, "Art thou then the Son of God?"

And he said unto them, "Ye say that I am."

They said, "What need we any further witness? For we ourselves have heard of his own mouth."

When they had bound him, they led him away from Caiaphas unto the hall of judgment, to Pontius Pilate the | Matthew 27:2/ John 18:28-31 governor. It was early, and they themselves went not into the judgment hall lest they should be defiled, but that they might eat the passover.

Pilate then went out unto them and said, "What accusation bring ye against this man?"

They answered and said unto him, "If he were not a malefactor, we would not have delivered him up unto thee."

Pilate said unto them, "Then take ye him and judge him according to your law."

The Jews therefore said unto him, "It is not lawful for us to put any man to death." They began to accuse him, saying, "We found this fellow perverting the nation and forbidding to give tribute to Caesar, saying that he himself is Christ a King." The chief priests accused him of many things, but he answered nothing.   Luke 23:2

Mark 15:3

Then Pilate entered into the judgment hall again and called Jesus, and said unto him, "Hearest thou not how many things they witness against thee?" But Jesus yet answered nothing, insomuch that Pilate marvelled greatly.   Matthew 27:13/ John 18:33
Matthew 27:14/ Mark 15:5

Pilate asked him, "Art thou the King of the Jews?"   Mark 15:2

Jesus answered him, "Sayest thou this thing of thyself, or did others tell it thee of me?"   John 18:34-37

Pilate answered, "Am I a Jew? Thine own nation and the chief priests have delivered thee unto me. What hast thou done?"

Jesus answered, "My kingdom is not of this world. If my kingdom were of this world, then would my servants fight that I should not be delivered to the Jews. But now is my kingdom not from hence."

Pilate therefore said unto him, "Art thou a king then?"

Jesus answered, "Thou sayest that I am a king. To this end was I born and for this cause came I into the world, that I should bear witness unto the truth. Everyone that is of the truth heareth my voice."

Pilate said unto him, "What is truth?" And when he had said this, he went out again unto the chief priests and the Jews and said unto them, "I find no fault in this man at all."   Luke 23:4/ John 18:38

They were the more fierce, saying, "He stirreth up the people, teaching throughout all Jewry beginning from Galilee to this place."   Luke 23:5-12

When Pilate heard of Galilee, he asked whether the man were a Galilean. As soon as he knew that he belonged unto Herod's jurisdiction, he sent him to Herod,* who himself also was at Jerusalem at that time.

Herod Antipas

When Herod saw Jesus, he was exceeding glad, for he was desirous to see him of a long season because he had heard many things of him. He hoped to have seen some miracle done by him.

Then he questioned with him in many words, but he answered him nothing. The chief priests and scribes stood and vehemently accused him. Herod with his men of war set him at nought, mocked him, arrayed him in a gorgeous robe, and sent him again to Pilate.

The same day Pilate and Herod were made friends together, for before they were at enmity between themselves.

Now at that feast the governor was wont to release unto the people a prisoner, whomsoever they desired. They had then a notable prisoner called Barabbas, who for a certain sedition made in the city, and who had committed murder in the insurrection, was cast bound into prison with them that had made insurrection with him.

Matthew 27:15-16/
Mark 15:6-7
Luke 23:19

Pilate, when he had called together the chief priests and the rulers and the people, said unto them, "Ye have brought this man unto me as one that perverteth the people. Behold, having examined him before you, I have found no fault in this man touching those things whereof ye accuse him. No, nor yet Herod. For I sent you to him, and lo, nothing worthy of death is done unto him.

Luke 23:13-15

"But ye have a custom, that I should release unto you one prisoner at the passover. Whom will ye therefore that I release unto you? Barabbas, or Jesus which is called Christ?" For he knew that the chief priests had delivered him for envy.

Matthew 27:17/
Mark 15:6/
John 18:39
Mark 15:10

When he was set down on the judgment seat, his wife sent unto him, saying, "Have thou nothing to do with that just man, for I have suffered many things this day in a dream because of him."

Matthew 27:19

But the chief priests and elders persuaded the people that they should ask that he release Barabbas and destroy Jesus.

Matthew 27:20/
Mark 15:11

The governor answered and said unto them, "Whether of the twain will ye that I release unto you?"

Matthew 27:21/
Luke 23:18

They cried out all at once, saying, "Barabbas."

Pilate said unto them, "What shall I do then with Jesus which is called Christ, the King of the Jews?"

Matthew 27:22/
Mark 15:12

They all cried, saying, "Crucify him! Crucify him!" — Luke 23:21

The governor said, "Why? What evil hath he done?" — Matthew 27:23/

But they cried out the more, saying, "Crucify him!" — Mark 15:13/ Luke 23:22

He said unto them the third time, "I have found no cause of death in him. I will therefore chastise him and let him go."

They cried out the more exceedingly, "Crucify him." — Mark 15:14-15/

So Pilate, willing to content the people, released Barrabbas unto them. and took Jesus and scourged him. — John 19:1

The soldiers of the governor took Jesus into the common hall called Pretorium and gathered together the whole band of soldiers. They stripped him and clothed him with a purple robe. When they had platted a crown of thorns, they put it upon his head and a reed in his right hand. They bowed the knee before him and mocked him, saying, "Hail, King of the Jews!" They smote him with their hands, spit upon him, and took the reed and smote him on the head. — Matthew 27:27-28/ Mark 15:16-17

Matthew 27:29

Matthew 27:30/ John 19:3

Pilate therefore went forth again and said unto them, "Behold, I bring him forth to you, that ye may know that I find no fault in him." — John 19:4-15

Then came Jesus forth wearing the crown of thorns and the purple robe. Pilate said unto them, "Behold the man!"

When the chief priests therefore and officers saw him, they cried out, saying, "Crucify him! Crucify him!"

Pilate said unto them, "Take ye him and crucify him, for I find no fault in him."

The Jews answered him, "We have a law, and by our law he ought to die because he made himself the Son of God."

When Pilate therefore heard that saying, he was the more afraid, and went again into the judgment hall and said unto Jesus, "Whence art thou?"

But Jesus gave him no answer.

Then said Pilate unto him, "Speakest thou not unto me? Knowest thou not that I have power to crucify thee and have power to release thee?"

Jesus answered, "Thou couldest have no power at all against me, except it were given thee from above. Therefore he that delivered me unto thee hath the greater sin."

From thenceforth Pilate sought to release him. But the Jews cried out, saying, "If thou let this man go, thou art not Caesar's friend. Whosoever maketh himself a king speaketh against Caesar."

When Pilate therefore heard that saying, he brought Jesus forth and sat down in the judgment seat in a place that is called the Pavement, but in the Hebrew, *Gabbatha*. It was the preparation of the passover and about the sixth hour.

He said unto the Jews, "Behold your King!"

But they cried out, "Away with him! Away with him! Crucify him!"

Pilate said unto them, "Shall I crucify your King?"

The chief priest answered, "We have no king but Caesar." | Matthew 27:24-25

When Pilate saw that he could prevail nothing, but that rather a tumult was made, he took water and washed his hands before the multitude, saying, "I am innocent of the blood of this just person. See ye to it."

Then answered all the people and said, "His blood be on us and on our children."

Then delivered he him therefore unto them to be crucified. They took Jesus and, after they had mocked him, they took the robe off from him, and put his own clothes on him, and led him away to be crucified. | Matthew 27:31/ Mark 15:20/ John 19:16

Then Judas, which had betrayed him, when he saw that he was condemned, repented himself and brought again the thirty pieces of silver to the chief priests and elders, saying, "I have sinned in that I have betrayed the innocent blood." | Matthew 27:3-4

They said, "What is that to us? See thou to that."

He cast down the pieces of silver in the temple and departed, and went and hanged himself. Falling headlong, he burst asunder in the midst, and all his bowels gushed out. | Matthew 27:5 / Acts 1:18

The chief priests took the silver pieces and said, "It is not lawful for to put them into the treasury, because it is the price of blood." | Matthew 27:6-7

They took counsel and bought with them the potter's field to bury strangers in. It was known unto all the dwellers at Jerusalem, insomuch as that field is called in their proper tongue *Aceldama*, that is to say, "The field of blood," unto this day. | Matthew 27:8/ Acts 1:19

Then was fulfilled that which was spoken by Jeremiah the prophet, saying, "They took the thirty pieces of silver, the price of him that was valued, whom they of the children of Israel did value, and gave them for the potter's field, as the Lord appointed me."* | Matthew 27:9-10

Zechariah 11:13; No reference in Jeremiah

They took Jesus and led him away bearing his cross. | Luke 23:26,32/

There were also two other malefactors led with him to be put to death. As they came out, they laid hold upon a man of Cyrene, Simon by name, the father of Alexander and Rufus, who passed by coming out of the country. On him they laid the cross, compelled to bear it after Jesus.

    There followed him a great company of people, and of women which also bewailed and lamented him. But Jesus turning unto them said, "Daughters of Jerusalem, weep not for me, but weep for yourselves and for your children. For behold, the days are coming in the which they shall say, 'Blessed are the barren, and the wombs that never bare, and the paps which never gave suck.'

    "Then shall they begin to say to the mountains, 'Fall on us,' and to the hills, 'Cover us.' For if they do these things in a green tree, what shall be done in the dry?"

    When they were come unto a place called Calvary, which is called in the Hebrew *Golgotha*, which is, being interpreted, "The place of a skull," they gave him vinegar wine mingled with myrrh to drink. But when he had tasted thereof, he would not drink it.

    It was the third hour, and there they crucified him with the two thieves on either side and Jesus in the midst. The scripture was fulfilled which said, "And he was numbered with the transgressors."*

    Then said Jesus, "Father, forgive them, for they know not what they do."

    The soldiers took his garments and made four parts, to every soldier a part. Now the coat was without a seam, woven from the top throughout. They said therefore among themselves, "Let us not rend it, but cast lots for it, whose it shall be." These things the soldiers did that the scripture might be fulfilled which was spken by the prophet, "They parted my garments among them, and upon my vesture did they cast lots."*

    Sitting down, they watched him there.

    Pilate wrote a title in Greek, Latin, and Hebrew, and put it on the cross. The writing was, JESUS OF NAZARETH THE KING OF THE JEWS. This title then read many of the Jews, for the place where Jesus was crucified was nigh unto the city.

    Then said the chief priests of the Jews to Pilate, "Write not, 'The King of the Jews,' but that he said, 'I am King of the Jews.'"

John 19:16-17
Matthew 27:32/
Mark 15:21/
Luke 23:26

Luke 23:27-31

Matthew 27:33-34/
Mark 15:22-23/
Luke 23:33/
John 19:17

Mark 15:25,27-28/
Luke 23:33/
John 19:18
Isaiah 53:12

Luke 23:34

Matthew 27:35/
John 19:23-24

Psalm 22:18
Matthew 27:36
Luke 23:38/
John 19:19-20

John 19:21-22

Pilate answered, "What I have written, I have written."

The people stood beholding. They that passed by reviled him, wagging their heads and saying, "Thou that destroyest the temple and buildest it in three days, save thyself. If thou be the Son of God, come down from the cross." | Matthew 27:39-40/ Luke 23:35

Likewise also the chief priests, mocking him with the scribes and elders, said among themselves, "He saved others. Himself he cannot save. If he be Christ the King of Israel, the chosen of God, let him now come down from the cross, and we will believe him. He trusted in God. Let him deliver him now if he will have him, for he said, 'I am the Son of God.'" | Matthew 27:41-42/ Mark 15:31-32/ Luke 23:35

Matthew 27:43

The soldiers also mocked him, coming to him and offering him vinegar, and saying, "If thou be the king of the Jews, save thyself." | Luke 23:36-37

One of the thieves that were crucified with him reviled him, saying, "If thou be Christ, save thyself and us." | Matthew 27:44/ Mark 15:32/ Luke 23:39-43

But the other answering rebuked him, saying, "Dost not thou fear God, seeing thou art in the same condemnation? And we indeed justly, for we receive the due reward of our deeds. But this man hath done nothing amiss."

He said unto Jesus, "Lord, remember me when thou comest into thy kingdom."

Jesus said unto him, "Verily I say unto thee, today shalt thou be with me in paradise."

Now there stood by the cross of Jesus his mother and his mother's sister, Mary the wife of Cleophas, and Mary Magdalene. When Jesus therefore saw his mother and the disciple standing by whom he loved*, he said unto his mother, "Woman, behold thy son!" Then said he to the disciple, "Behold thy mother!" | John 19:25-27

John

From that hour that disciple took her unto his own home.

When the sixth hour was come, the sun was darkened, and there was darkness over all the earth until the ninth hour. | Mark 15:33/ Luke 23:44-45

About the ninth hour Jesus cried with a loud voice, saying, "Eloi, Eloi, lama sabachthani?" which is, being interpreted, "My God, my God, why hast thou forsaken me?" | Matthew 27:46/ Mark 15:34

Some of them that stood by, when they heard it, said, "This man calleth for Elijah." | Matthew 27:47/ Mark 15:35

After this, Jesus knowing that all things were now | John 19:28

accomplished, that the scripture might be fulfilled, said, "I thirst."* | *Psalm 69:21

There was set a vessel full of vinegar, and straightway one of them ran and filled a sponge full of vinegar, put it on a hyssop reed, and put it to his mouth to drink. The rest said, "Let alone! Let us see whether Elijah will come to save him." | Matthew 27:48-49/ Mark 15:36/ John 19:29

When Jesus therefore had received the vinegar, he said, "It is finished." When he had cried again with a loud voice, he said, "Father, into thy hands I commend my spirit." | Matthew 27:50/ Luke 23:46/ John 19:30

He bowed his head and gave up the ghost. Behold, the veil of the temple was rent in twain from the top to the bottom, and the earth did quake and the rocks rent. | Matthew 27:51

When the centurion which stood watching Jesus and they that were with him saw the earthquake and those things that were done, they feared greatly. He said, "Truly this man was the Son of God." | Matthew 27:54/ Mark 15:39

All the people that came together to that sight, beholding the things which were done, smote their breasts and returned. All his acquaintance and many women that came up with him from Galilee unto Jerusalem, who also, when he was in Galilee, followed him and ministered unto him, among whom was Mary Magdalene, Mary the mother of James and Joses, Salome, and the mother of Zebedee's children, stood afar off beholding these things. | Luke 23:48

Matthew 27:55-56/ Mark 15:40-41/ Luke 23:49

The Jews therefore, because it was the preparation—that is, the day before the sabbath—besought Pilate that their legs might be broken and that they might be taken away, that the bodies should not remain upon the cross on the sabbath day, for that sabbath day was a high day. | Mark 15:42/ John 19:31

Then came the soldiers and brake the legs of the first and of the other which was crucified with him. | John 19:32-37

But when they came to Jesus and saw that he was dead already, they brake not his legs. One of the soldiers with a spear pierced his side, and forthwith came there out blood and water. He that saw it bare record, and his record is true. He knoweth that he said true, that ye might believe.

For these things were done that the scripture should be fulfilled, "A bone of him shall not be broken."* | *Exodus 12:46; Numbers 9:12

Again another scripture said, "They shall look on him whom they pierced."§ | §Zechariah 12:10

When the even was come, there came a rich man named Joseph. He was of Arimathea, a city of the Jews, and he was a good and a just man, an honorable counsellor, who also himself was a disciple of Jesus, but secretly for fear of the Jews. He had not consented to the counsel and deed of them. This man went boldly unto Pilate and begged that he might take away the body of Jesus.	Matthew 27:57/ Mark 15:43/ Luke 23:50-52/ John 19:38
Pilate marvelled if he were already dead. Calling unto him the centurion, he asked him whether he had been any while dead.	Mark 15:44
When he knew it of the centurion, he commanded the body to be delivered to Joseph. He came therefore and took the body of Jesus.	Matthew 27:58/ Mark 15:45/ John 19:38
There came also Nicodemus, which at the first came to Jesus by night, and brought a mixture of myrrh and aloes, about a hundred pound weight.	John 19:39
He bought fine linen, took the body of Jesus down, and wrapped it in the linen clothes with the spices, as the manner of the Jews is to bury.	Mark 15:46/ John 19:40
Now in the place where he was crucified there was a garden, and in the garden a new sepulcher which Joseph had hewn in stone, wherein never man before was laid. There laid they Jesus therefore because of the Jews' preparation day. For the sepulcher was nigh at hand and the sabbath drew on.	Matthew 27:59-60/ Luke 23:53-54/ John 19:41-42
He rolled a great stone to the door of the sepulcher and departed.	
The women, also which came with him from Galilee, Mary Magdalene and Mary the mother of Joses, followed after and beheld the sepulcher and how his body was laid.	Mark 15:47/ Luke 23:55
They returned and prepared spices and ointments, and rested the sabbath day according to the commandment.	Luke 23:56

Saturday
The Sepulcher

The next day that followed the day of the preparation, the chief priests and Pharisees came together unto Pilate, saying, "Sir, we remember that that deceiver said while he was yet alive, 'After three days I will rise again.'	Matthew 27:62-66

"Command therefore that the sepulcher be made sure until the third day, lest his disciples come by night and steal him away and say unto the people, 'He is risen from the dead.' So the last error shall be worse than the first."

Pilate said unto them, "Ye have a watch. Go your way. Make it as sure as ye can."

So they went and made the sepulcher sure, sealing the stone and setting a watch.

THE RESURRECTION

1

Behold, there was a great earthquake. For the angel of the Lord descended from heaven, came and rolled back the stone from the door, and sat upon it. His countenance was like lightning, and his raiment white as snow. For fear of him the keepers did shake and became as dead men. — Matthew 28:2-4

The graves were opened, and many bodies of the saints which slept arose amd came out of the graves after his resurrection, and went into the holy city and appeared unto many. — Mathew 27:52-53

2

When the sabbath was past, Mary Magdalene, Mary the mother of James, Joanna, and Salome had bought sweet spices, that they might come and anoint him. — Mark 16:1/ Luke 24:10

Very early in the morning the first day of the week as it began to dawn, they came unto the sepulcher bringing the spices which they had prepared. They said among themselves, "Who shall roll us away the stone from the door of the sepulcher?" For it was very great. — Matthew 28:1/ Mark 16:2-3/ Luke 24:1

When they looked, they found the stone rolled away from the sepulcher. They entered in and found not the body of the Lord Jesus. — Mark 16:4/ Luke 24:2-3

It came to pass as they were much perplexed thereabout, behold, two men stood by them on the right side clothed in long shining garments. They were afraid and bowed down their faces to the earth. — Mark 16:5/ Luke 24:4-5

They said unto the women, "Fear not! Ye seek Jesus of Nazareth which was crucified. Why seek ye the living among the dead? — Matthew 28:5-6/ Mark 16:6/ Luke 24:5-8

"He is not here, for he is risen. Remember how he spake unto you when he was yet in Galilee, saying, 'The Son of man must be delivered into the hands of sinful men and be crucified, and the third day rise again.'"

They remembered his words.

"Come, see the place where the Lord lay. Go quickly and tell Peter and his disciples that he is risen from the dead. Behold, he goeth before you into Galilee. There shall ye see him, as he said unto you."

They trembled and were amazed, neither said they anything to any man, for they were afraid. They fled quickly from the sepulcher to bring his disciples word.

Mary Magdalene came to Simon Peter and the other disciple who Jesus loved,* and said unto them, "They have taken away the Lord out of the sepulcher, and we know not where they have laid him."

Then arose Peter and that other disciple, and both together ran to the sepulcher. The other disciple did outrun Peter and came first to the sepulcher. Stooping down and looking in, he saw the linen clothes lying, yet he went not in.

Then came Simon Peter, went into the sepulcher, and saw the linen clothes lie, and the napkin that was about his head not lying with the linen clothes, but wrapped together in a place by itself.

Then went in also that other disciple which came first to the sepulcher. He saw and believed, for as yet they knew not the scripture, that he must rise again from the dead.

Then the disciples went away again unto their own home, wondering at that which was come to pass.

Mary Magdalene stood without at the sepulcher weeping. As she wept, she stooped down and looked into the sepulcher.

"Woman, why weepest thou?"

Supposing him to be the gardener, she said, "Because they have taken away my Lord, and I know not where they have laid him."

"Whom seekest thou?"

She said unto him, "Sir, if thou have borne him hence, tell me where thou hast laid him, and I will take him away."

Jesus said unto her, "Mary."

She turned herself and said unto him, "Rabboni," which is to say, *Master.*

Jesus said unto her, "Touch me not, for I am not yet ascended to my Father. But go to my brethren and say

	Matthew 28:6-7/ Mark 16:7
	Matthew 28:8/ Mark 16:8/
	John 20:1-2 *John*
	Luke 24:12/ John 20:3-9
	Luke 24:12/ John 20:10
	Mark 16:9/ John 20:11
	John 20:15
	John 20:13
	John 20:15-17

unto them I ascend unto my Father and your Father, and to my God and your God."

She went and told the disciples, as they mourned and wept, that she had seen the Lord, and that he had spoken these things unto her. When they heard that he was alive and had been seen of her, they believed not. | Mark 16:10/ John 20:18 Mark 16:11

As the other women went, behold, Jesus met them, saying, "All hail." They came and held him by the feet and worshipped him. | Matthew 28:9-10/ Luke 24:10-11

Then said Jesus unto them, "Be not afraid. Go tell my brethren that they go into Galilee. There shall they see me."

They told all these things unto the disciples. Their words seemed to them as idle tales, and they believed them not.

3

Some of the watch came into the city and shewed unto the chief priests all the things that were done. When they were assembled with the elders and had taken counsel, they gave large money unto the soldiers, saying, "Say ye, 'His disciples came by night and stole him away while we slept.' If this come to the governor's ears, we will persuade him and secure you." | Matthew 28:11-15

They took the money and did as they were taught. This saying is commonly reported among the Jews until this day.

4

Two [disciples] went that same day to a village called Emmaus, which was from Jerusalem about threescore furlongs. They talked together of all these things which had happened. | Luke 24:13-32

It came to pass that, while they communed together and reasoned, Jesus himself drew near and went with them. But their eyes were holden that they should not know him.

He said unto them, "What manner of communications are these that ye have one to another as ye walk and are sad?"

One of them whose name was Cleopas, answering, said unto him, "Art thou only a stranger in Jerusalem and hast not known the things which are come to pass there in these days?"

He said unto them, "What things?"

They said unto him, "Concerning Jesus of Nazareth, which was a prophet mighty in deed and word before God and all the people. And how the chief priests and our rulers delivered him to be condemned to death, and have crucified him. But we trusted that it had been he which should have redeemed Israel. Beside all this, today is the third day since these things were done.

"Yea, and certain women also of our company which were early at the sepulcher made us astonished. When they found not his body, they came saying that they had also seen a vision of angels which said that he was alive. Certain of them which were with us went to the sepulcher and found it even so as the women had said. But him they saw not."

Then he said unto them, "O fools and slow of heart to believe all that the prophets have spoken, ought not Christ to have suffered these things and to enter into his glory?"

Beginning at Moses and all the prophets, he expounded unto them in all the scriptures the things concerning himself.

They drew nigh unto the village whither they went. He made as though he would have gone further, but they constrained him, saying, "Abide with us, for it is toward evening and the day is far spent."

He went in to tarry with them. It came to pass as he sat at meat with them, he took bread, blessed it, and brake, and gave to them. Their eyes were opened, and they knew him. He vanished out of their sight.

They said one to another, "Did not our heart burn within us while he talked with us by the way and while he opened to us the scriptures?"

They rose up the same hour and returned to Jerusalem. The same day at evening, being the first day of the week, found the disciples gathered together for fear of the Jews, and the doors were shut. They told what things were done in the way, and how he was known of them in breaking of bread, saying, "The Lord is risen indeed." | Luke 24:33/ John 20:19

Luke 24:35

Luke 24:34

As they thus spake, Jesus himself stood in the midst of them and said unto them, "Peace be unto you." | Luke 24:36-39

But they were terrified and affrighted, and supposed that they had seen a spirit. He said unto them, "Why are ye troubled? And why do thoughts arise in your hearts? Behold my hands and my feet, that it is I myself. Handle me and see, for a spirit hath not flesh and bones as ye see me have."

When he had thus spoken, he shewed them his hands and his feet and his side. While they yet believed not for joy and wondered, he said unto them, "Have ye here any meat?" | Luke 24:40-43/ John 20:20

They gave him a piece of a broiled fish and of a honeycomb. He took it and did eat before them. Then were the disciples glad when they saw the Lord.

He said unto them, "These are the words which I spake unto you while I was yet with you, that all things must be fulfilled which were written in the law of Moses, in the prophets, and in the psalms concerning me." | Luke 24:44-48

Then opened he their understanding, that they might understand the scriptures, and said unto them, "Thus it is written, and thus it behoved Christ to suffer and to rise from the dead the third day, that repentance and remission of sins should be preached in his name among all nations, beginning at Jerusalem. Ye are witnesses of these things."

Then said Jesus to them again, "Peace be unto you. As my Father hath sent me, even so send I you." | John 20:21-29

When he had said this, he breathed on them and said unto them, "Receive ye the Holy Ghost. Whose soever sins ye remit, they are remitted unto them, and whose soever sins ye retain, they are retained."

But Thomas called Didymus, one of the twelve, was not with them when Jesus came. The other disciples therefore said unto him, "We have seen the Lord."

But he said unto them, "Except I shall see in his hands the print of the nails, and put my finger into the print of the nails, and thrust my hand into his side, I will not believe."

After eight days again his disciples were within, and Thomas with them.

Then came Jesus, the doors being shut, and stood in the midst and said, "Peace be unto you."

Then said he to Thomas, "Reach hither thy finger and behold my hands. Reach hither thy hand and thrust it into my side. Be not faithless, but believing."

Thomas answered and said unto him, "My Lord and my God."

Jesus said unto him, "Thomas, because thou hast seen me, thou hast believed. Blessed are they that have not seen me and yet have believed."

5

The eleven disciples went away into Galilee. There were together Simon Peter, Thomas called Didymus, Nathanael of Cana in Galilee,* the sons of Zebedee§, and two other of his disciples. Matthew 28:16/
John 21:2
*Bartholomew
§James and John
John 21:3-23

Simon Peter said unto them, "I go a-fishing."

They said unto him, "We also go with thee."

They went forth and entered into a ship immediately. That night they caught nothing.

But when the morning was now come, Jesus stood on the shore, but the disciples knew not that it was Jesus.

Jesus said unto them, "Children, have ye any meat?"

They answered him, "No."

He said unto them, "Cast the net on the right side of the ship, and ye shall find."

They cast therefore, and now they were not able to draw it for the multitude of fishes. Therefore that disciple whom Jesus loved* saith unto Peter, "It is the Lord." *John

Now when Simon Peter heard that it was the Lord, he girt his fisher's coat unto him, for he was naked, and did cast himself into the sea. The other disciples came in a little ship, for they were not far from land, but as it were two hundred cubits, dragging the net with fishes.

As soon as they were come to land, they saw a fire of coals there, fish laid thereon, and bread. Jesus said unto them, "Bring of the fish which ye have now caught."

Simon Peter went up and drew the net to land full of great fishes, a hundred and fifty and three. For all there were so many, yet was not the net broken.

Jesus said unto them, "Come and dine."

None of the disciples durst ask him, "Who art thou?" knowing that it was the Lord. Jesus then came, took bread, and gave them, and fish likewise. This is now the third time that Jesus shewed himself to his disciples after that he was risen from the dead.

So when they had dined, Jesus saith to Simon Peter, "Simon, son of Jonah, lovest thou me more than these?"

He said unto him, "Yea, Lord. Thou knowest that I love thee."

He said unto him, "Feed my lambs."

He said again to him the second time, "Simon, son of Jonah, lovest thou me?"

He said unto him, "Yea, Lord. Thou knowest that I love thee."

He said unto him, "Feed my sheep."

He said unto him the third time, "Simon, son of Jonah, lovest thou me?"

Peter was grieved because he said unto him the third time, "Lovest thou me?" He said unto him, "Lord, thou knowest all things. Thou knowest that I love thee."

Jesus said unto him, "Feed my sheep.

"Verily, verily, I say unto thee, when thou wast young, thou girdedst thyself and walkedst wither thou wouldest. But when thou shalt be old, thou shalt stretch forth thy hands, and another shall gird thee and carry thee whither thou wouldest not."

This spake he, signifying by what death he should glorify God. When he had spoken this, he said unto him, "Follow me."

Then Peter, turning about, saw the disciple following whom Jesus loved* which also leaned on his breast at supper, and said, "Lord, which is he that betrayeth thee?"   *John*

Peter seeing him said to Jesus, "Lord, and what shall this man do?"

Jesus said unto him, "If I will that he tarry till I come, what is that to thee? Follow thou me."

Then went this saying abroad among the brethren, that that disciple should not die. Yet Jesus said not unto him, "He shall not die," but, "If I will that he tarry till I come, what is that to thee?"

6

Jesus came unto them into a mountain where Jesus had appointed them.   Matthew 28:16-18

When they saw him, they worshipped him, but some doubted.

He said unto them, "All power is given unto me in heaven and in earth. Go ye therefore into all the world and teach all nations. Preach the gospel to every creature, baptizing them in the name of the Father and of the Son and of the Holy Ghost, teaching them to observe all things whatsoever I have commanded you. He that believeth and is baptized shall be saved, but he that believeth not shall be damned. | Matthew 28:18-19/ Mark 16:15

Matthew 28:20 Mark 16:16-18

"These signs shall follow them that believe. In my name shall they cast out devils. They shall speak with new tongues. They shall take up serpents. If they drink any deadly thing, it shall not hurt them. They shall lay hands on the sick, and they shall recover.

"Lo, I am with you alway, even unto the end of the world. Amen." | Matthew 28:20

He led them out as far as to Bethany and assembled together with them [on] the mount called Olivet, which is from Jerusalem a sabbath day's journey. | Luke 24:50/ Acts 1:4,12

He lifted up his hands and blessed them. "Behold, I send the promise of my Father upon you. But tarry ye in the city of Jerusalem until ye be endued with power from on high. | Luke 25:49/ Acts 1:4

"But wait for the promise of the Father which ye have heard of me. For John truly baptized with water, but ye shall be baptized with the Holy Ghost not many days hence." | Acts 1:5-9/ Luke 24:51

They therefore asked of him, saying, "Lord, wilt thou at this time restore again the kingdom to Israel?"

He said unto them, "It is not for you to know the times or the seasons which the Father hath put in his own power. But ye shall receive power after that the Holy Ghost is come upon you. Ye shall be witnesses unto me both in Jerusalem, in all Judea, in Samaria, and unto the uttermost part of the earth.

When he had spoken these things, he blessed them. While they beheld, he was taken up, and a cloud received him out of their sight.

He was carried up into heaven and sat on the right hand of God. | Mark 16:19/ Luke 24:51

While they looked steadfastly toward heaven as he went up, behold, two men stood by them in white apparel | Acts 1:10-11 which also said, "Ye men of Galilee, why stand ye gazing up into heaven? This same Jesus, which is taken up from you into heaven, shall so come in like manner as ye have seen him go into heaven."

They worshipped him and returned to Jerusalem with great joy, and were continually in the temple, praising and blessing God. They went forth and preached everywhere, the Lord working with them and confirming the word with signs following.

Luke 24:52-53

Mark 16:20

EPILOG

These things understood not his disciples at the first. But when Jesus was glorified, then remembered they that these things were written of him, and that they had done these things unto him.

The people therefore that was with him when he called Lazarus out of his grave and raised him from the dead bare record. For this cause the people also met him, for that they had heard that he had done this miracle.

The Pharisees therefore said among themselves, "Perceive ye how ye prevail nothing? Behold, the world is gone after him."

There are also many other things which Jesus did in the presence of his disciples which are not written in this book. If they should be written every one, I suppose that even the world itself could not contain the books that should be written.

But these are written that ye might believe that Jesus is the Christ, the Son of God, and that believing ye might have life through his name.

Amen.

John 12:16-19

John 20:30/
John 21:25

BONUS NOVELETTE: THE APOSTLES

1

Peter, James, and John, Andrew, Philip, and Thomas, Bartholomew and Matthew, James the son of Alphaeus, Simon Zelotes, and Judas the brother of James abode in Jerusaleman. They went up into an upper room where these all continued with one accord in prayer and supplication with the women, Mary the mother of Jesus, and with his brethren.

In those days Peter stood up in the midst of the disciples, about a hundred and twenty, and said, "Men and brethren, this scripture must needs have been fulfilled, which the Holy Ghost by the mouth of David spake before concerning Judas, which was guide to them that took Jesus. For he was numbered with us, and had obtained part of this ministry.

"For it is written in the book of Psalms, 'Let his habitation be desolate, let no man dwell therein, and his bishopric let another take.'*

"Wherefore of these men which have companied with us all the time that the Lord Jesus went in and out among us, beginning from the baptism of John unto that same day that he was taken up from us, must one be ordained to be a witness with us of his resurrection.

They appointed two, Joseph called Barsabas who was surnamed Justus and Matthias. They prayed and said, "Thou, Lord, which knowest the hearts of all men, shew whether of these two thou hast chosen, that he may take part of this ministry and apostleship from which Judas by transgression fell, that he might go to his own place."

They gave forth their lots. The lot fell upon Matthias, and he was numbered with the eleven apostles.

Acts 1:12-17

Acts 1:20-26

Psalm 69:25, 109:8

2

When the day of Pentecost was fully come, they were all with one accord in one place.

Suddenly there came a sound from heaven as of a rushing mighty wind. It filled all the house where they were sitting. There appeared unto them cloven tongues like as of fire, and it sat upon each of them. They were all filled with the Holy Ghost and began to speak with other tongues, as the Spirit gave them utterance.

There were dwelling at Jerusalem Jews, devout men, out of every nation under heaven. Now when this was noised abroad, the multitude came together and were confounded, because that every man heard them speak in his own language.

They were all amazed and marveled, saying one to another, "Behold, are not all these which speak Galilaeans? How hear we every man in our own tongue, wherein we were born?

"Parthians, Medes, Elamites, the dwellers in Mesopotamia, and in Judaea and Cappadocia, in Pontus and Asia, Phrygia and Pamphylia, in Egypt and in the parts of Libya about Cyrene, and strangers of Rome, Jews and proselytes, Cretes and Arabians—we do hear them speak in our tongues the wonderful works of God."

They were all amazed and were in doubt, saying one to another, "What meaneth this?"

Others mocking said, "These men are full of new wine."

But Peter, standing up with the eleven, lifted up his voice and said unto them, "Ye men of Judea and all ye that dwell at Jerusalem, be this known unto you, and hearken to my words. For these are not drunken, as ye suppose, seeing it is but the third hour of the day.

"But this is that which was spoken by the prophet Joel, 'And it shall come to pass in the last days, saith God, I will pour out of my Spirit upon all flesh. Your sons and your daughters shall prophesy, your young men shall see visions, and your old men shall dream dreams. On my servants and on my handmaidens I will pour out in those days of my Spirit, and they shall prophesy. I will shew wonders in heaven above and signs in the earth beneath, blood, fire, and vapor of smoke. The sun shall be turned into darkness and the moon into blood before the great

Acts 2:1-47

and notable day of the Lord come. It shall come to pass that whosoever shall call on the name of the Lord shall be saved.'

"Ye men of Israel, hear these words. Jesus of Nazareth—a man approved of God among you by miracles and wonders and signs, which God did by him in the midst of you, as ye yourselves also know—him being delivered by the determinate counsel and foreknowledge of God, ye have taken and by wicked hands have crucified and slain whom God hath raised up, having loosed the pains of death, because it was not possible that he should be holden of it.

"For David speaketh concerning him, 'I foresaw the Lord always before my face, for he is on my right hand, that I should not be moved. Therefore did my heart rejoice, and my tongue was glad. Moreover also my flesh shall rest in hope because thou wilt not leave my soul in hell, neither wilt thou suffer thine Holy One to see corruption. Thou hast made known to me the ways of life. Thou shalt make me full of joy with thy countenance.'* *Psalm 16:8-11*

'Men and brethren, let me freely speak unto you of the patriarch David, that he is both dead and buried, and his sepulchre is with us unto this day. Therefore being a prophet, and knowing that God had sworn with an oath to him that of the fruit of his loins, according to the flesh, he would raise up Christ to sit on his throne, he seeing this before spake of the resurrection of Christ, that his soul was not left in hell, neither his flesh did see corruption.

"This Jesus hath God raised up, whereof we all are witnesses.

"Therefore, being by the right hand of God exalted and having received of the Father the promise of the Holy Ghost, he hath shed forth this which ye now see and hear.

"For David is not ascended into the heavens, but he saith himself, 'The Lord said unto my Lord, "Sit thou on my right hand until I make thy foes thy footstool."'

"Therefore let all the house of Israel know assuredly that God hath made the same Jesus, whom ye have crucified, both Lord and Christ."

Now when they heard this, they were pricked in their heart and said unto Peter and to the rest of the apostles, "Men and brethren, what shall we do?"

Then Peter said unto them, "Repent and be baptized every one of you in the name of Jesus Christ for the remission of sins, and ye shall receive the gift of the Holy Ghost. For the promise is unto you, and to your children, and to all that are afar off, even as many as the Lord our God shall call."

With many other words did he testify and exhort, saying, "Save yourselves from this untoward generation."

Then they that gladly received his word were baptized, and the same day there were added unto them about three thousand souls. They continued steadfastly in the apostles' doctrine and fellowship, and in breaking of bread and in prayers. Fear came upon every soul, and many wonders and signs were done by the apostles.

All that believed were together and had all things common, sold their possessions and goods and parted them to all men, as every man had need.

They, continuing daily with one accord in the temple, breaking bread from house to house, did eat their meat with gladness and singleness of heart, praising God, and having favor with all the people.

The Lord added to the church daily such as should be saved.

3

Peter and John went up together into the temple at the hour of prayer, being the ninth hour. A certain man, lame from his mother's womb, was carried, whom they laid daily at the gate of the temple which is called Beautiful, to ask alms of them that entered into the temple, who seeing Peter and John about to go into the temple asked an alms.

Peter, fastening his eyes upon him with John, said, "Look on us." He gave heed unto them, expecting to receive something of them.

Then Peter said, "Silver and gold have I none, but such as I have give I thee. In the name of Jesus Christ of Nazareth, rise up and walk"

He took him by the right hand and lifted him up. Immediately his feet and ankle bones received strength. He leaping up stood and walked and entered with them into

Acts 3:1-26

the temple, walking and leaping and praising God.

All the people saw him walking and praising God. They knew that it was he which sat for alms at the Beautiful gate of the temple, and they were filled with wonder and amazement at that which had happened unto him.

As the lame man which was healed held Peter and John, all the people ran together unto them in the porch that is called Solomon's, greatly wondering.

When Peter saw it, he answered unto the people, "Ye men of Israel, why marvel ye at this? Or why look ye so earnestly on us, as though by our own power or holiness we had made this man to walk? The God of Abraham and of Isaac and of Jacob, the God of our fathers, hath glorified his Son Jesus, whom ye delivered up and denied him in the presence of Pilate when he was determined to let him go.

"But ye denied the Holy One and the Just and desired a murderer to be granted unto you, and killed the Prince of life whom God hath raised from the dead, whereof we are witnesses. His name through faith hath made this man strong, whom ye see and know. Yea, the faith which is by him hath given him this perfect soundness in the presence of you all.

"Now, brethren, I wot that through ignorance ye did it, as did also your rulers. But those things which God before had shewed by the mouth of all his prophets, that Christ should suffer—he hath so fulfilled.

"Repent ye therefore and be converted, that your sins may be blotted out when the times of refreshing shall come from the presence of the Lord.

"He shall send Jesus Christ which before was preached unto you, whom the heaven must receive until the times of restitution of all things, which God hath spoken by the mouth of all his holy prophets since the world began.

"For Moses truly said unto the fathers, 'A prophet shall the Lord your God raise up unto you of your brethren, like unto me. Him shall ye hear in all things whatsoever he shall say unto you.'

"It shall come to pass that every soul which will not hear that prophet shall be destroyed from among the people. Yea, and all the prophets from Samuel and those that follow after, as many as have spoken, have likewise foretold of these days.

"Ye are the children of the prophets and of the covenant which God made with our fathers, saying unto Abraham, 'In thy seed shall all the kindreds of the earth be blessed.'

"Unto you first, God, having raised up his Son Jesus, sent him to bless you in turning away every one of you from his iniquities."

As they spake unto the people, the priests, the captain of the temple, and the Sadducees came upon them, being grieved that they taught the people and preached through Jesus the resurrection from the dead. They laid hands on them and put them in hold unto the next day, for it was now eventide. Acts 4:1-4

Howbeit many of them which heard the word believed, and the number of the men was about five thousand.

4

It came to pass on the morrow that their rulers, elders, scribes, and Annas the high priest, Caiaphas, John, and Alexander—as many as were of the kindred of the high priest—were gathered together at Jerusalem. Acts 4:5-32

When they had set them in the midst, they asked, "By what power or by what name have ye done this?"

Then Peter, filled with the Holy Ghost, said unto them, "Ye rulers of the people and elders of Israel, if we this day be examined of the good deed done to the impotent man, by what means he is made whole, be it known unto you all and to all the people of Israel that, by the name of Jesus Christ of Nazareth whom ye crucified, whom God raised from the dead, even by him doth this man stand here before you whole.

"This is the stone which was set at nought of you builders, which is become the head of the corner. Neither is there salvation in any other, for there is none other name under heaven given among men whereby we must be saved."

Now when they saw the boldness of Peter and John, and perceived that they were unlearned and ignorant men, they marveled. They took knowledge of them, that they had been with Jesus. And beholding the man which was healed standing with them, they could say nothing against it.

But when they had commanded them to go aside out of the council, they conferred among themselves, saying, "What shall we do to these men? For that indeed a notable miracle hath been done by them is manifest to all them that dwell in Jerusalem, and we cannot deny it.

"But that it spread no further among the people, let us straitly threaten them, that they speak henceforth to no man in this name."

They called them and commanded them not to speak at all nor teach in the name of Jesus.

"But Peter and John answered and said unto them, "Whether it be right in the sight of God to hearken unto you more than unto God, judge ye. For we cannot but speak the things which we have seen and heard."

So when they had further threatened them, they let them go, finding nothing how they might punish them because of the people, for all men glorified God for that which was done. For the man was above forty years old on whom this miracle of healing was shewed.

Being let go, they went to their own company and reported all that the chief priests and elders had said unto them. When they heard that, they lifted up their voice to God with one accord, and said, "Lord, thou art God which hast made heaven and earth and the sea and all that in them is. Who by the mouth of thy servant David hast said, 'Why did the heathen rage and the people imagine vain things? The kings of the earth stood up, and the rulers were gathered together against the Lord and against his Christ.'*

*Psalm 2:1-2

"For of a truth against thy holy child Jesus whom thou hast anointed, both Herod and Pontius Pilate, with the Gentiles and the people of Israel, were gathered together for to do whatsoever thy hand and thy counsel determined before to be done.

"And now, Lord, behold their threatenings, and grant unto thy servants, that with all boldness they may speak thy word by stretching forth thine hand to heal, that signs and wonders may be done by the name of thy holy child Jesus."

When they had prayed, the place was shaken where they were assembled together. They were all filled with the

Holy Ghost, and they spake the word of God with boldness. The multitude of them that believed were of one heart and of one soul. With great power gave the apostles witness of the resurrection of the Lord Jesus, and great grace was upon them all.

Acts 4:33

 Neither said any of them that ought of the things which he possessed was his own, but they had all things common. Neither was there any among them that lacked, for as many as were possessors of lands or houses sold them, brought the prices of the things that were sold, and laid them down at the apostles' feet. Distribution was made unto every man according as he had need.

Acts 4:32, 34-37

Joses, who by the apostles was surnamed Barnabas, which is being interpreted, *The son of consolation*, a Levite and of the country of Cyprus, having land, sold it, brought the money, and laid it at the apostles' feet.

But a certain man named Ananias, with Sapphira his wife also being privy to it, sold a possession, kept back part of the price, brought a certain part, and laid it at the apostles' feet.

Acts 5:1-11

But Peter said, "Ananias, why hath Satan filled thine heart to lie to the Holy Ghost and to keep back part of the price of the land? Whiles it remained, was it not thine own? And after it was sold, was it not in thine own power? Why hast thou conceived this thing in thine heart? Thou hast not lied unto men, but unto God."

Ananias, hearing these words, fell down and gave up the ghost.

Great fear came on all them that heard these things. The young men arose, wound him up, carried him out, and buried him.

It was about the space of three hours after, when his wife, not knowing what was done, came in. Peter answered unto her, "Tell me whether ye sold the land for so much?"

She said, "Yea, for so much."

Then Peter said unto her, "How is it that ye have agreed together to tempt the Spirit of the Lord? Behold, the feet of them which have buried thy husband are at the door and shall carry thee out."

Then fell she down straightway at his feet and yielded up the ghost The young men came in, found her dead, and carrying her forth, buried her by her husband.

Great fear came upon all the church, and upon as many as heard these things.

5

By the hands of the apostles were many signs and wonders wrought among the people. They were all with one accord in Solomon's porch. Of the rest durst no man join himself to them, but the people magnified them.

Believers were the more added to the Lord, multitudes both of men and women, insomuch that they brought forth the sick into the streets and laid them on beds and couches, that at the least the shadow of Peter passing by might overshadow some of them.

There came also a multitude out of the cities round about unto Jerusalem, bringing sick folks and them which were vexed with unclean spirits. They were healed every one.

Then the high priest rose up, and all they that were with him—which is the sect of the Sadducees—and were filled with indignation, laid their hands on the apostles, and put them in the common prison.

But the angel of the Lord by night opened the prison doors, brought them forth, and said, "Go, stand and speak in the temple to the people all the words of this life."

When they heard that, they entered into the temple early in the morning and taught.

But the high priest came, and they that were with him, and called the council together and all the senate of the children of Israel, and sent to the prison to have them brought.

But when the officers came and found them not in the prison, they returned and told, saying, "The prison truly found we shut with all safety and the keepers standing without before the doors. But when we had opened, we found no man within."

Now when the high priest and the captain of the temple and the chief priests heard these things, they doubted of them whereunto this would grow.

Then came one and told them, saying, "Behold, the men whom ye put in prison are standing in the temple and teaching the people."

Acts 5:12-42

Then went the captain with the officers and brought them without violence, for they feared the people lest they should have been stoned.

When they had brought them, they set them before the council. The high priest asked them, saying, "Did not we straitly command you that ye should not teach in this name? And behold, ye have filled Jerusalem with your doctrine, and intend to bring this man's blood upon us."

Then Peter and the other apostles answered and said, "We ought to obey God rather than men. The God of our fathers raised up Jesus, whom ye slew and hanged on a tree. Him hath God exalted with his right hand to be a Prince and a Savior, for to give repentance to Israel and forgiveness of sins.

"We are his witnesses of these things, and so is also the Holy Ghost, whom God hath given to them that obey him."

When they heard that, they were cut to the heart and took counsel to slay them.

Then stood there up one in the council, a Pharisee named Gamaliel, a doctor of the law had in reputation among all the people, and commanded to put the apostles forth a little space and said unto them, "Ye men of Israel, take heed to yourselves what ye intend to do as touching these men.

"For before these days rose up Theudas, boasting himself to be somebody, to whom a number of men, about four hundred, joined themselves who was slain, and all, as many as obeyed him, were scattered and brought to nought.

"After this man rose up Judas of Galilee in the days of the taxing, and drew away much people after him. He also perished, and all, even as many as obeyed him, were dispersed.

"I say unto you, refrain from these men and let them alone. For if this counsel or this work be of men, it will come to nought. But if it be of God, ye cannot overthrow it, lest haply ye be found even to fight against God."

To him they agreed. When they had called the apostles and beaten them, they commanded that they should not speak in the name of Jesus and let them go.

They departed from the presence of the council, rejoicing that they were counted worthy to suffer shame for his name.

Daily in the temple and in every house, they ceased not to teach and preach Jesus Christ.

6

In those days, when the number of the disciples was multiplied, there arose a murmuring of the Grecians against the Hebrews, because their widows were neglected in the daily ministration.

The twelve called the multitude of the disciples unto them and said, "It is not reason that we should leave the word of God and serve tables. Wherefore, brethren, look ye out among you seven men of honest report, full of the Holy Ghost and wisdom, whom we may appoint over this business. But we will give ourselves continually to prayer and to the ministry of the word."

The saying pleased the whole multitude. They chose Stephen, a man full of faith and of the Holy Ghost, and Philip, Prochorus, Nicanor, Timon, Parmenas, and Nicolas, a proselyte of Antioch, whom they set before the apostles. When they had prayed, they laid their hands on them.

The word of God increased, and the number of the disciples multiplied in Jerusalem greatly. A great company of the priests were obedient to the faith. And Stephen, full of faith and power, did great wonders and miracles among the people.

Then there arose certain of the synagogue which is called the synagogue of the Libertines, and Cyrenians, Alexandrians, and of them of Cilicia and of Asia, disputing with Stephen. They were not able to resist the wisdom and the spirit by which he spake.

Then they suborned men, which said, "We have heard him speak blasphemous words against Moses and against God."

They stirred up the people, the elders, and the scribes, and came upon him and caught him, and brought him to the council, and set up false witnesses which said, "This man ceaseth not to speak blasphemous words against this holy place and the law, for we have heard him say that this Jesus of Nazareth shall destroy this place and shall change the customs which Moses delivered us."

Acts 6:1-14

Then said the high priest, "Are these things so?" | Acts 7:1

All that sat in the council, looking steadfastly on him, saw his face as it had been the face of an angel. | Acts 6:15

He said, "Men, brethren, and fathers, hearken! The God of glory appeared unto our father Abraham when he was in Mesopotamia, before he dwelt in Charran, and said unto him, 'Get thee out of thy country and from thy kindred and come into the land which I shall shew thee.' | Acts 7:2-58

"Then came he out of the land of the Chaldeans and dwelt in Charran. From thence, when his father was dead, he removed him into this land wherein ye now dwell. And he gave him none inheritance in it—no, not so much as to set his foot on—yet he promised that he would give it to him for a possession and to his seed after him, when as yet he had no child.

"God spake on this wise, that his seed should sojourn in a strange land, that they should bring them into bondage, and entreat them evil four hundred years. 'The nation to whom they shall be in bondage will I judge,' said God, 'and after that shall they come forth and serve me in this place.'

"He gave him the covenant of circumcision. Abraham begat Isaac and circumcised him the eighth day. Isaac begat Jacob, and Jacob begat the twelve patriarchs. And the patriarchs, moved with envy, sold Joseph into Egypt.

"But God was with him and delivered him out of all his afflictions, and gave him favor and wisdom in the sight of Pharaoh king of Egypt. He made him governor over Egypt and all his house.

"Now there came a dearth over all the land of Egypt and Canaan, and great affliction. Our fathers found no sustenance.

"But when Jacob heard that there was corn in Egypt, he sent out our fathers first. At the second time, Joseph was made known to his brethren, and Joseph's kindred was made known unto Pharaoh. Then sent Joseph and called his father Jacob to him, and all his kindred, threescore and fifteen souls.

"So Jacob went down into Egypt and died, he and our fathers, and were carried over into Sychem and laid in the sepulchre that Abraham bought for a sum of money of the sons of Emmor the father of Sychem.

"But when the time of the promise drew nigh which

God had sworn to Abraham, the people grew and multiplied in Egypt till another king arose, which knew not Joseph. The same dealt subtlely with our kindred. Evil entreated our fathers, so that they cast out their young children to the end they might not live.

"In which time Moses was born, was exceeding fair, and nourished up in his father's house three months. When he was cast out, Pharaoh's daughter took him up and nourished him for her own son.

"Moses was learned in all the wisdom of the Egyptians and was mighty in words and in deeds. When he was full forty years old, it came into his heart to visit his brethren the children of Israel.

"Seeing one of them suffer wrong, he defended him and avenged him that was oppressed, and smote the Egyptian, for he supposed his brethren would have understood how that God by his hand would deliver them. But they understood not.

"The next day he shewed himself unto them as they strove, and would have set them at one again, saying, 'Sirs, ye are brethren. Why do ye wrong one to another?'

"But he that did his neighbour wrong thrust him away, saying, 'Who made thee a ruler and a judge over us? Wilt thou kill me, as thou diddest the Egyptian yesterday?'

"Then fled Moses at this saying, and was a stranger in the land of Madian where he begat two sons. When forty years were expired, there appeared to him in the wilderness of mount Sinai an angel of the Lord in a flame of fire in a bush.

"When Moses saw it, he wondered at the sight. As he drew near to behold it, the voice of the Lord came unto him, saying, 'I am the God of thy fathers, the God of Abraham, the God of Isaac, and the God of Jacob.'

"Then Moses trembled and durst not behold. Then said the Lord to him, 'Put off thy shoes from thy feet, for the place where thou standest is holy ground. I have seen, I have seen the affliction of my people which is in Egypt. I have heard their groaning and am come down to deliver them. Now come, I will send thee into Egypt.'

"This Moses whom they refused, saying, 'Who made thee a ruler and a judge?'—the same did God send to be a ruler and a deliverer by the hand of the angel which appeared to him in the bush. He brought them out after that he had shewed wonders and signs in the land of Egypt, in the Red Sea, and in the wilderness forty years. This is that Moses which said unto the children of Israel, 'A prophet shall the Lord your God raise up unto you of your brethren, like unto me. Him shall ye hear.'

"This is he that was in the church in the wilderness with the angel which spake to him in the Mount Sinai, and with our fathers who received the lively oracles to give unto us, to whom our fathers would not obey, but thrust him from them, and in their hearts turned back again into Egypt, saying unto Aaron, 'Make us gods to go before us. As for this Moses which brought us out of the land of Egypt, we wot not what is become of him.'

"They made a calf in those days, offered sacrifice unto the idol, and rejoiced in the works of their own hands. Then God turned and gave them up to worship the host of heaven. As it is written in the book of the prophets, 'O ye house of Israel, have ye offered to me slain beasts and sacrifices by the space of forty years in the wilderness? Yea, ye took up the tabernacle of Moloch and the star of your god Remphan, figures which ye made to worship them, and I will carry you away beyond Babylon.'* *Amos 5:25-27

"Our fathers had the tabernacle of witness in the wilderness as he had appointed, speaking unto Moses, that he should make it according to the fashion that he had seen. Which also our fathers that came after brought in with Jesus into the possession of the Gentiles, whom God drave out before the face of our fathers unto the days of David, who found favor before God, and desired to find a tabernacle for the God of Jacob.

"But Solomon built him an house.

"Howbeit the most High dwelleth not in temples made with hands. As said the prophet, 'Heaven is my throne, and earth is my footstool, saith the Lord. What house will ye build me? Or what is the place of my rest? Hath not my hand made all these things?'* *Isaiah 66:1-2

"Ye stiffnecked and uncircumcised in heart and ears, ye do always resist the Holy Ghost. As your fathers did, so do ye. Which of the prophets have not your fathers persecuted? They have slain them which shewed before of the coming of the Just One, of whom ye have been now the betrayers and murderers, who have received the law by the disposition of angels and have not kept it."

When they heard these things, they were cut to the heart, and they gnashed on him with their teeth.

But he, being full of the Holy Ghost, looked up steadfastly into heaven and saw the glory of God, and Jesus standing on the right hand of God, and said, "Behold, I see the heavens opened and the Son of man standing on the right hand of God."

Then they cried out with a loud voice, stopped their ears, ran upon him with one accord, and cast him out of the city. The witnesses laid down their clothes at a young man's feet whose name was Saul.

They stoned Stephen. He kneeled down and cried with a loud voice, "Lord Jesus, receive my spirit. Lay not this sin to their charge." | Acts 7:59-60

When he had said this, he fell asleep. Devout men carried Stephen to his burial and made great lamentation over him. | Acts 8:2

And Saul was consenting unto his death. | Acts 8:1

7

At that time there was a great persecution against the church which was at Jerusalem. They were all scattered abroad throughout the regions of Judaea and Samaria, except the apostles. Therefore they that were scattered abroad went everywhere preaching the word. | Acts 8:1

| Acts 8:4-40

Then Philip went down to the city of Samaria and preached Christ unto them. The people with one accord gave heed unto those things which Philip spake, hearing and seeing the miracles which he did. For unclean spirits, crying with loud voice, came out of many that were possessed with them, and many taken with palsies and that were lame were healed. There was great joy in that city.

But there was a certain man called Simon, which beforetime in the same city used sorcery and bewitched the people of Samaria, giving out that himself was some great one to whom they all gave heed from the least to the greatest, saying, "This man is the great power of God."

To him they had regard because that of long time he had bewitched them with sorceries.

But when they believed Philip preaching the things concerning the kingdom of God and the name of Jesus

Christ, they were baptized, both men and women.

Then Simon himself believed also. When he was baptized, he continued with Philip and wondered, beholding the miracles and signs which were done.

Now when the apostles which were at Jerusalem heard that Samaria had received the word of God, they sent unto them Peter and John who, when they were come down, prayed for them that they might receive the Holy Ghost. For as yet he was fallen upon none of them. Only they were baptized in the name of the Lord Jesus.

Then laid they their hands on them, and they received the Holy Ghost.

When Simon saw that through laying on of the apostles' hands the Holy Ghost was given, he offered them money, saying, "Give me also this power, that on whomsoever I lay hands, he may receive the Holy Ghost."

But Peter said unto him, "Thy money perish with thee, because thou hast thought that the gift of God may be purchased with money. Thou hast neither part nor lot in this matter, for thy heart is not right in the sight of God. Repent therefore of this thy wickedness, and pray God if perhaps the thought of thine heart may be forgiven thee. For I perceive that thou art in the gall of bitterness, and in the bond of iniquity."

Then answered Simon and said, "Pray ye to the Lord for me that none of these things which ye have spoken come upon me."

They, when they had testified and preached the word of the Lord, returned to Jerusalem and preached the gospel in many villages of the Samaritans.

The angel of the Lord spake unto Philip, saying, "Arise and go toward the south unto the way that goeth down from Jerusalem unto Gaza, which is desert." He arose and went.

Behold, a man of Ethiopia—a eunuch of great authority under Candace, Queen of the Ethiopians, who had the charge of all her treasure and had come to Jerusalem for to worship—was returning, and sitting in his chariot read Isaiah the prophet.

Then the Spirit said unto Philip, "Go near and join thyself to this chariot."

Philip ran thither to him and heard him read the prophet Isaiah, and said, "Understandest thou what thou readest?"

He said, "How can I, except some man should guide me?" He desired Philip that he would come up and sit with him.

The place of the scripture which he read was this, "He was led as a sheep to the slaughter, and like a lamb dumb before his shearer, so opened he not his mouth. In his humiliation his judgment was taken away, and who shall declare his generation? For his life is taken from the earth."* *Isaiah 53:7-8*

The eunuch answered Philip and said, "I pray thee, of whom speaketh the prophet this? Of himself, or of some other man?"

Then Philip opened his mouth and began at the same scripture, and preached unto him Jesus.

As they went on their way, they came unto a certain water. The eunuch said, "See, here is water. What doth hinder me to be baptized?"

Philip said, "If thou believest with all thine heart, thou mayest."

He answered and said, "I believe that Jesus Christ is the Son of God."

He commanded the chariot to stand still. They went down into the water, both Philip and the eunuch, and he baptized him.

When they were come up out of the water, the Spirit of the Lord caught away Philip, that the eunuch saw him no more. He went on his way rejoicing.

But Philip was found at Azotus. Passing through, he preached in all the cities till he came to Caesarea.

As for Saul, he made havoc of the church, entering into every house and, haling men and women, committed them to prison. Acts 8:3

Saul, yet breathing out threatenings and slaughter against the disciples of the Lord, went unto the high priest and desired of him letters to Damascus to the synagogues, that if he found any of this way, whether they were men or women, he might bring them bound unto Jerusalem. Acts 9:1-23

As he journeyed, he came near Damascus. Suddenly there shined round about him a light from heaven. He fell to the earth and heard a voice saying unto him, "Saul, Saul, why persecutest thou me?"

He said, "Who art thou, Lord?"

The Lord said, "I am Jesus whom thou persecutest. It is hard for thee to kick against the pricks."

He trembling and astonished said, "Lord, what wilt thou have me to do?"

The Lord said unto him, "Arise and go into the city, and it shall be told thee what thou must do."

The men which journeyed with him stood speechless, hearing a voice, but seeing no man.

Saul arose from the earth. When his eyes were opened, he saw no man, but they led him by the hand and brought him into Damascus.

He was three days without sight, and neither did eat nor drink.

There was a certain disciple at Damascus named Ananias. To him said the Lord in a vision, "Ananias."

He said, "Behold, I am here, Lord."

The Lord said unto him, "Arise and go into the street which is called Straight, and enquire in the house of Judas for one called Saul of Tarsus. For behold, he prayeth and hath seen in a vision a man named Ananias coming in and putting his hand on him, that he might receive his sight."

Then Ananias answered, "Lord, I have heard by many of this man, how much evil he hath done to thy saints at Jerusalem. And here he hath authority from the chief priests to bind all that call on thy name."

But the Lord said unto him, "Go thy way, for he is a chosen vessel unto me to bear my name before the Gentiles and kings and the children of Israel. For I will shew him how great things he must suffer for my name's sake."

Ananias went his way and entered into the house, and putting his hands on him said, "Brother Saul, the Lord, even Jesus that appeared unto thee in the way as thou camest, hath sent me, that thou mightest receive thy sight and be filled with the Holy Ghost."

Immediately there fell from his eyes as it had been scales, and he received sight forthwith, and arose and was baptized.

When he had received meat, he was strengthened. Then was Saul certain days with the disciples which were at Damascus.

Straightway he preached Christ in the synagogues, that he is the Son of God.

But all that heard him were amazed and said, "Is not this he that destroyed them which called on this name in Jerusalem, and came hither for that intent, that he might bring them bound unto the chief priests?"

But Saul increased the more in strength and confounded the Jews which dwelt at Damascus, proving that this is very Christ.

After that many days were fulfilled, the Jews took counsel to kill him. They watched the gates day and night to kill him. | Acts 9:24

But their laying await was known of Saul. Then the disciples took him by night and let him down by the wall in a basket. | Acts 9:25-31

When Saul was come to Jerusalem, he assayed to join himself to the disciples. But they were all afraid of him and believed not that he was a disciple. But Barnabas took him and brought him to the apostles, and declared unto them how he had seen the Lord in the way, that he had spoken to him, and how he had preached boldly at Damascus in the name of Jesus.

He was with them coming in and going out at Jerusalem. He spake boldly in the name of the Lord Jesus and disputed against the Grecians.

But they went about to slay him. Which when the brethren knew, they brought him down to Caesarea and sent him forth to Tarsus.

Then had the churches rest throughout all Judaea and Galilee and Samaria, and were edified, and walking in the fear of the Lord and in the comfort of the Holy Ghost, were multiplied.

8

It came to pass as Peter passed throughout all quarters, he came down also to the saints which dwelt at Lydda. There he found a certain man named Aeneas, which had kept his bed eight years and was sick of the palsy. | Acts 9:32-43

Peter said unto him, "Aeneas, Jesus Christ maketh thee whole. Arise and make thy bed."

He arose immediately. All that dwelt at Lydda and Saron saw him and turned to the Lord.

Now there was at Joppa a certain disciple named Tabitha, which by interpretation is called Dorcas. This woman was full of good works and alms deeds which she did.

It came to pass in those days that she was sick and died, whom when they had washed, they laid her in an upper chamber.

Forasmuch as Lydda was nigh to Joppa, and the disciples had heard that Peter was there, they sent unto him two men, desiring him that he would not delay to come to them.

Then Peter arose and went with them. When he was come, they brought him into the upper chamber, and all the widows stood by him weeping, and shewing the coats and garments which Dorcas made while she was with them.

But Peter put them all forth, kneeled down and prayed, and turning him to the body said, "Tabitha, arise."

She opened her eyes. When she saw Peter, she sat up. He gave her his hand and lifted her up, and when he had called the saints and widows, presented her alive.

It was known throughout all Joppa, and many believed in the Lord.

It came to pass that he tarried many days in Joppa with one Simon, a tanner.

There was a certain man in Caesarea called Cornelius, a centurion of the band called the Italian band, a devout man and one that feared God with all his house, which gave much alms to the people, and prayed to God always.

Acts 10:1-48

He saw in a vision evidently about the ninth hour of the day an angel of God coming in to him and saying unto him, "Cornelius."

When he looked on him, he was afraid and said, "What is it, Lord?"

He said unto him, "Thy prayers and thine alms are come up for a memorial before God. Now send men to Joppa and call for one Simon whose surname is Peter. He lodgeth with one Simon a tanner, whose house is by the seaside. He shall tell thee what thou oughtest to do."

"When the angel which spake unto Cornelius was departed, he called two of his household servants and a devout soldier of them that waited on him continually. When he had declared all these things unto them, he sent them to Joppa.

On the morrow as they went on their journey and drew nigh unto the city, "Peter went up upon the housetop to pray about the sixth hour. He became very hungry and would have eaten, but while they made ready, he fell into a trance and saw heaven opened and a certain vessel descending upon him, as it had been a great sheet knit at the four corners and let down to the earth, wherein were all manner of four-footed beasts of the earth, wild beasts, creeping things, and fowls of the air.

There came a voice to him, "Rise, Peter. Kill and eat."

But Peter said, "Not so, Lord. For I have never eaten any thing that is common or unclean."

The voice spake unto him again the second time, "What God hath cleansed, that call not thou common."

This was done thrice, and the vessel was received up again into heaven.

Now while Peter doubted in himself what this vision which he had seen should mean, behold, the men which were sent from Cornelius had made enquiry for Simon's house and stood before the gate, and called and asked whether Simon, which was surnamed Peter, were lodged there.

While Peter thought on the vision, the Spirit said unto him, "Behold, three men seek thee. Arise therefore and get thee down and go with them, doubting nothing, for I have sent them."

Then Peter went down to the men which were sent unto him from Cornelius and said, "Behold, I am he whom ye seek. What is the cause wherefore ye are come?"

They said, "Cornelius the centurion, a just man, one that feareth God, and of good report among all the nation of the Jews, was warned from God by a holy angel to send for thee into his house and to hear words of thee."

Then called he them in and lodged them. On the morrow Peter went away with them, and certain brethren from Joppa accompanied him. The morrow after they entered into Caesarea.

Cornelius waited for them. He had called together his kinsmen and near friends. As Peter was coming in, Cornelius met him, fell down at his feet, and worshipped him.

But Peter took him up, saying, "Stand up. I myself also am a man." As he talked with him, he went in and found many that were come together.

He said unto them, "Ye know how that it is an unlawful thing for a man that is a Jew to keep company or come unto one of another nation. But God hath shewed me that I should not call any man common or unclean. Therefore came I unto you without gainsaying, as soon as I was sent for. I ask therefore for what intent ye have sent for me?"

Cornelius said, "Four days ago I was fasting until this hour. At the ninth hour I prayed in my house, and behold, a man stood before me in bright clothing and said, 'Cornelius, thy prayer is heard, and thine alms are had in remembrance in the sight of God. Send therefore to Joppa and call hither Simon, whose surname is Peter. He is lodged in the house of one Simon, a tanner by the sea side, who when he cometh shall speak unto thee.'

"Immediately therefore I sent to thee, and thou hast well done that thou art come. Now therefore are we all here present before God to hear all things that are commanded thee of God."

Then Peter opened his mouth and said, "Of a truth I perceive that God is no respecter of persons, but in every nation, he that feareth him and worketh righteousness is accepted with him.

"The word which God sent unto the children of Israel, preaching peace by Jesus Christ—he is Lord of all—that word I say ye know, which was published throughout all Judaea and began from Galilee after the baptism which John preached, how God anointed Jesus of Nazareth with the Holy Ghost and with power, who went about doing good and healing all that were oppressed of the devil, for God was with him.

"We are witnesses of all things which he did both in the land of the Jews and in Jerusalem whom they slew and hanged on a tree—him God raised up the third day and shewed him openly. Not to all the people, but unto witnesses chosen before God, even to us, who did eat and drink with him after he rose from the dead.

"He commanded us to preach unto the people and to testify that it is he which was ordained of God to be the Judge of quick and dead. To him give all the prophets witness, that through his name whosoever believeth in him shall receive remission of sins."

While Peter yet spake these words, the Holy Ghost fell on all them which heard the word. They of the circumcision which believed were astonished, as many as came with Peter, because that on the Gentiles also was poured out the gift of the Holy Ghost. For they heard them speak with tongues and magnify God.

Then answered Peter, "Can any man forbid water, that these should not be baptized, which have received the Holy Ghost as well as we?"

He commanded them to be baptized in the name of the Lord. Then prayed they him to tarry certain days.

The apostles and brethren that were in Judea heard that the Gentiles had also received the word of God. When Peter was come up to Jerusalem, they that were of the circumcision contended with him, saying, "Thou wentest in to men uncircumcised and didst eat with them."

Acts 11:1-18

But Peter rehearsed the matter from the beginning and expounded it by order unto them, saying, "I was in the city of Joppa praying, and in a trance I saw a vision. A certain vessel descend, as it had been a great sheet let down from heaven by four corners. It came even to me, upon the which when I had fastened mine eyes, I considered and saw four-footed beasts of the earth, wild beasts, creeping things, and fowls of the air.

"I heard a voice saying unto me, 'Arise, Peter. Slay and eat.'

"But I said, 'Not so, Lord. For nothing common or unclean hath at any time entered into my mouth.'

"But the voice answered me again from heaven, 'What God hath cleansed, that call not thou common.'

"This was done three times, and all were drawn up again into heaven.

"And, behold, immediately there were three men already come unto the house where I was, sent from Caesarea unto me. The Spirit bade me go with them, nothing doubting. Moreover these six brethren accompanied me, and we entered into the man's house.

"He shewed us how he had seen an angel in his house, which stood and said unto him, 'Send men to Joppa and call for Simon, whose surname is Peter, who shall tell thee words whereby thou and all thy house shall be saved.'

"As I began to speak, the Holy Ghost fell on them as on us at the beginning. Then remembered I the word of the Lord, how that he said, 'John indeed baptized with water, but ye shall be baptized with the Holy Ghost.' Forasmuch then as God gave them the like gift as he did unto us who believed on the Lord Jesus Christ, what was I, that I could withstand God?"

When they heard these things, they held their peace and glorified God, saying, "Then hath God also to the Gentiles granted repentance unto life."

9

Now they which were scattered abroad upon the persecution that arose about Stephen travelled as far as Phenice, Cyprus, and Antioch, preaching the word to none but unto the Jews only. Some of them were men of Cyprus and Cyrene, which when they were come to Antioch, spake unto the Grecians, preaching the Lord Jesus. The hand of the Lord was with them. A great number believed and turned unto the Lord.

Then tidings of these things came unto the ears of the church which was in Jerusalem. They sent forth Barnabas, that he should go as far as Antioch, who when he came and had seen the grace of God, was glad and exhorted them all that with purpose of heart they would cleave unto the Lord. For he was a good man, full of the Holy Ghost and of faith, and much people was added unto the Lord.

Then departed Barnabas to Tarsus, for to seek Saul. When he had found him, he brought him unto Antioch. It came to pass that a whole year they assembled themselves with the church and taught much people.

The disciples were called Christians first in Antioch.

In these days came prophets from Jerusalem unto Antioch. There stood up one of them named Agabus and signified by the Spirit that there should be great dearth throughout all the world, which came to pass in the days of Claudius Caesar.

Then the disciples, every man according to his ability, determined to send relief unto the brethren which dwelt in Judea, which also they did, and sent it to the elders by the hands of Barnabas and Saul.

Acts 11:19-30

10

About that time Herod the king stretched forth his hands to vex certain of the church. Then were the days of unleavened bread.	Acts 12:1,3
He killed James the brother of John with the sword. Because he saw it pleased the Jews, he proceeded further to take Peter also.	Acts 12:2-3
When he had apprehended him, he put him in prison and delivered him to four quaternions of soldiers to keep him, intending after Easter to bring him forth to the people.	Acts 12:4-23

Peter therefore was kept in prison. But prayer was made without ceasing of the church unto God for him.

When Herod would have brought him forth, the same night Peter was sleeping between two soldiers, bound with two chains, and the keepers before the door kept the prison.

Behold, the angel of the Lord came upon him, and a light shined in the prison. He smote Peter on the side and raised him up, saying, "Arise up quickly."

His chains fell off from his hands.

The angel said unto him, "Gird thyself and bind on thy sandals."

And so he did.

He said unto him, "Cast thy garment about thee, and follow me."

He went out and followed him, and wist not that it was true which was done by the angel, but thought he saw a vision.

When they were past the first and the second ward, they came unto the iron gate that leadeth unto the city, which opened to them of his own accord. They went out and passed on through one street.

Forthwith the angel departed from him.

When Peter was come to himself, he said, "Now I know of a surety that the Lord hath sent his angel and hath delivered me out of the hand of Herod, and from all the expectation of the people of the Jews."

When he had considered the thing, he came to the house of Mary the mother of John, whose surname was Mark, where many were gathered together praying.

As Peter knocked at the door of the gate, a damsel

came to hearken named Rhoda. When she knew Peter's voice, she opened not the gate for gladness, but ran in and told how Peter stood before the gate.

They said unto her, "Thou art mad!"

But she constantly affirmed that it was even so. Then said they, "It is his angel."

But Peter continued knocking.

When they had opened the door and saw him, they were astonished. But he, beckoning unto them with the hand to hold their peace, declared unto them how the Lord had brought him out of the prison.

He said, "Go shew these things unto James and to the brethren." He departed and went into another place.

As soon as it was day, there was no small stir among the soldiers what was become of Peter. When Herod had sought for him and found him not, he examined the keepers and commanded that they should be put to death.

He went down from Judea to Caesarea and there abode. Herod was highly displeased with them of Tyre and Sidon, but they came with one accord to him and, having made Blastus the king's chamberlain their friend, desired peace because their country was nourished by the king's country.

Upon a set day Herod, arrayed in royal apparel, sat upon his throne and made an oration unto them. The people gave a shout, saying, "It is the voice of a god, and not of a man."

Immediately the angel of the Lord smote him because he gave not God the glory. He was eaten of worms and gave up the ghost.

11

The word of God grew and multiplied. Barnabas and Saul returned from Jerusalem when they had fulfilled their ministry and took with them John, whose surname was Mark. | Acts 12:24-25

Now there were in the church that was at Antioch certain prophets and teachers—Barnabas, Simeon that was called Niger, Lucius of Cyrene, Manaen which had been brought up with Herod the tetrarch, and Saul who also is called Paul. | Acts 13:1,9

As they ministered to the Lord and fasted, the Holy Ghost said, "Separate me Barnabas and Saul for the work whereunto I have called them."

When they had fasted and prayed and laid their hands on them, they sent them away. So they, being sent forth by the Holy Ghost, departed unto Seleucia, and from thence they sailed to Cyprus.

When they were at Salamis, they preached the word of God in the synagogues of the Jews, and they had also John to their minister. When they had gone through the isle unto Paphos, they found a certain sorcerer—a false prophet, a Jew—whose name was Bar-Jesus, which was with the deputy of the country, Sergius Paulus—a prudent man—who called for Barnabas and Saul and desired to hear the word of God.

Elymas the sorcerer—for so is his name by interpretation—withstood them, seeking to turn away the deputy from the faith.

Then Saul, filled with the Holy Ghost, set his eyes on him and said, "O full of all subtlety and all mischief, thou child of the devil, thou enemy of all righteousness, wilt thou not cease to pervert the right ways of the Lord? And now, behold, the hand of the Lord is upon thee, and thou shalt be blind, not seeing the sun for a season."

Immediately there fell on him a mist and a darkness. He went about seeking some to lead him by the hand. Then the deputy, when he saw what was done, believed, being astonished at the doctrine of the Lord.

Now when Paul and his company loosed from Paphos, they came to Perga in Pamphylia. John, departing from them, returned to Jerusalem.

But when they departed from Perga, they came to Antioch in Pisidia, went into the synagogue on the sabbath day, and sat down.

After the reading of the law and the prophets the rulers of the synagogue sent unto them, saying, "Ye men and brethren, if ye have any word of exhortation for the people, say on."

Then Paul stood up and, beckoning with his hand, said, "Men of Israel and ye that fear God, give audience. The God of this people of Israel chose our fathers and exalted the people when they dwelt as strangers in the land of Egypt, and with a high arm brought he them out of it.

Acts 13:2-9

Acts 13:9-52

And about the time of forty years suffered he their manners in the wilderness.

"When he had destroyed seven nations in the land of Canaan, he divided their land to them by lot. After that he gave unto them judges about the space of four hundred and fifty years, until Samuel the prophet.

"Afterward they desired a king. God gave unto them Saul the son of Cis, a man of the tribe of Benjamin, by the space of forty years. When he had removed him, he raised up unto them David to be their king, to whom also he gave their testimony and said, 'I have found David the son of Jesse, a man after mine own heart which shall fulfill all my will.'

"Of this man's seed hath God according to his promise raised unto Israel a Savior, Jesus, when John had first preached before his coming the baptism of repentance to all the people of Israel.

"As John fulfilled his course, he said, 'Whom think ye that I am? I am not he. But behold, there cometh one after me whose shoes of his feet I am not worthy to loose.'

"Men and brethren, children of the stock of Abraham, and whosoever among you feareth God, to you is the word of this salvation sent. For they that dwell at Jerusalem and their rulers, because they knew him not nor yet the voices of the prophets which are read every sabbath day, they have fulfilled them in condemning him. Though they found no cause of death in him, yet desired they Pilate that he should be slain.

"When they had fulfilled all that was written of him, they took him down from the tree and laid him in a sepulcher.

"But God raised him from the dead. He was seen many days of them which came up with him from Galilee to Jerusalem, who are his witnesses unto the people.

"We declare unto you glad tidings, how that the promise which was made unto the fathers, God hath fulfilled the same unto us their children, in that he hath raised up Jesus again. As it is also written in the second psalm, 'Thou art my Son. This day have I begotten thee.'* **Psalm 2:7*

"As concerning that he raised him up from the dead, now no more to return to corruption, he said on this wise, 'I will give you the sure mercies of David.'§ *§Isaiah 55:3*

"Wherefore he said also in another psalm, 'Thou shalt not suffer thine Holy One to see corruption.'*

*Psalm 16:10

"For David, after he had served his own generation by the will of God, fell on sleep and was laid unto his fathers, and saw corruption. But he whom God raised again, saw no corruption.

"Be it known unto you therefore, men and brethren, that through this man is preached unto you the forgiveness of sins, By him all that believe are justified from all things, from which ye could not be justified by the law of Moses.

"Beware therefore, lest that come upon you which is spoken of in the prophets, 'Behold, ye despisers, and wonder and perish. For I work a work in your days, a work which ye shall in no wise believe, though a man declare it unto you.'"*

*Habakkuk 1:5

When the Jews were gone out of the synagogue, the Gentiles besought that these words might be preached to them the next sabbath. Now when the congregation was broken up, many of the Jews and religious proselytes followed Paul and Barnabas, who speaking to them, persuaded them to continue in the grace of God.

The next sabbath day came almost the whole city together to hear the word of God. But when the Jews saw the multitudes, they were filled with envy and spake against those things which were spoken by Paul, contradicting and blaspheming.

Then Paul and Barnabas waxed bold and said, "It was necessary that the word of God should first have been spoken to you. But seeing ye put it from you and judge yourselves unworthy of everlasting life, lo, we turn to the Gentiles. For so hath the Lord commanded us, saying, 'I have set thee to be a light of the Gentiles, that thou shouldest be for salvation unto the ends of the earth.'"*

*Isaiah 49:6

When the Gentiles heard this, they were glad and glorified the word of the Lord, and as many as were ordained to eternal life believed.

The word of the Lord was published throughout all the region. But the Jews stirred up the devout and honorable women and the chief men of the city, and raised persecution against Paul and Barnabas, and expelled them out of their coasts.

But they shook off the dust of their feet against them and came unto Iconium. And the disciples were filled with joy and with the Holy Ghost.

It came to pass in Iconium, that they went both together into the synagogue of the Jews and so spake, that a great multitude both of the Jews and also of the Greeks believed. But the unbelieving Jews stirred up the Gentiles, and made their minds evil affected against the brethren.

Acts 14:1-28

Long time therefore abode they speaking boldly in the Lord, which gave testimony unto the word of his grace and granted signs and wonders to be done by their hands. But the multitude of the city was divided. Part held with the Jews, and part with the apostles.

When there was an assault made, both of the Gentiles and also of the Jews with their rulers, to use them despitefully and to stone them, they were ware of it and fled unto Lystra and Derbe, cities of Lycaonia, and unto the region that lieth round about, and there they preached the gospel.

There sat a certain man at Lystra, impotent in his feet, being a cripple from his mother's womb, who never had walked. The same heard Paul speak, who steadfastly beholding him and perceiving that he had faith to be healed, said with a loud voice, "Stand upright on thy feet."

He leaped and walked. When the people saw what Paul had done, they lifted up their voices, saying in the speech of Lycaonia, "The gods are come down to us in the likeness of men." They called Barnabas Jupiter, and Paul Mercury, because he was the chief speaker.

Then the priest of Jupiter, which was before their city, brought oxen and garlands unto the gates and would have done sacrifice with the people. Which when the apostles Barnabas and Paul heard of, they rent their clothes and ran in among the people, crying out and saying, "Sirs, why do ye these things? We also are men of like passions with you, and preach unto you that ye should turn from these vanities unto the living God which made heaven, earth, and the sea, and all things that are therein, who in times past suffered all nations to walk in their own ways.

"Nevertheless he left not himself without witness in that he did good, and gave us rain from heaven and fruitful seasons, filling our hearts with food and gladness."

With these sayings scarce restrained they the people, that they had not done sacrifice unto them.

There came thither certain Jews from Antioch and Iconium, who persuaded the people, and having stoned Paul, drew him out of the city, supposing he had been dead. Howbeit as the disciples stood round about him, he rose up and came into the city. The next day he departed with Barnabas to Derbe.

When they had preached the gospel to that city and had taught many, they returned again to Lystra, Iconium, and Antioch, confirming the souls of the disciples and exhorting them to continue in the faith, and that we must through much tribulation enter into the kingdom of God.

When they had ordained them elders in every church and had prayed with fasting, they commended them to the Lord on whom they believed.

After they had passed throughout Pisidia, they came to Pamphylia. When they had preached the word in Perga, they went down into Attalia and thence sailed to Antioch, from whence they had been recommended to the grace of God for the work which they fulfilled.

When they were come and had gathered the church together, they rehearsed all that God had done with them, and how he had opened the door of faith unto the Gentiles.

There they abode long time with the disciples.

12

Certain men which came down from Judea taught the brethren and said, "Except ye be circumcised after the manner of Moses, ye cannot be saved."

When therefore Paul and Barnabas had no small dissension and disputation with them, they determined that Paul and Barnabas and certain other of them, should go up to Jerusalem unto the apostles and elders about this question.

Being brought on their way by the church, they passed through Phoenicia and Samaria declaring the conversion of the Gentiles, and they caused great joy unto all the brethren.

When they were come to Jerusalem, they were received of the church and of the apostles and elders, and

Acts 15:1-41

they declared all things that God had done with them, but there rose up certain of the sect of the Pharisees which believed, saying that it was needful to circumcise them and to command them to keep the law of Moses.

The apostles and elders came together for to consider of this matter. When there had been much disputing, Peter rose up and said unto them, "Men and brethren, ye know how that a good while ago God made choice among us, that the Gentiles by my mouth should hear the word of the gospel and believe. God, which knoweth the hearts, bare them witness, giving them the Holy Ghost, even as he did unto us and put no difference between us and them, purifying their hearts by faith.

"Now therefore why tempt ye God to put a yoke upon the neck of the disciples, which neither our fathers nor we were able to bear? But we believe that through the grace of the Lord Jesus Christ we shall be saved, even as they."

Then all the multitude kept silence and gave audience to Barnabas and Paul, declaring what miracles and wonders God had wrought among the Gentiles by them.

After they had held their peace, James answered, saying, "Men and brethren, hearken unto me. Simeon hath declared how God at the first did visit the Gentiles, to take out of them a people for his name. To this agree the words of the prophets, as it is written, 'After this I will return and will build again the tabernacle of David, which is fallen down. I will build again the ruins thereof, and I will set it up that the residue of men might seek after the Lord, and all the Gentiles upon whom my name is called, saith the Lord, who doeth all these things.'*

*Amos 9:11-12

"Known unto God are all his works from the beginning of the world. Wherefore my sentence is that we trouble not them which from among the Gentiles are turned to God, but that we write unto them that they abstain from pollutions of idols, from fornication, from things strangled, and from blood. For Moses of old time hath in every city them that preach him, being read in the synagogues every sabbath day."

Then pleased it the apostles and elders with the whole church to send chosen men of their own company to Antioch with Paul and Barnabas, namely Judas surnamed Barsabas and Silas, chief men among the brethren. They wrote letters by them after this manner:

"The apostles and elders and brethren send greeting unto the brethren which are of the Gentiles in Antioch and Syria and Cilicia. Forasmuch as we have heard that certain which went out from us have troubled you with words, subverting your souls, saying, 'Ye must be circumcised and keep the law,' to whom we gave no such commandment, it seemed good unto us, being assembled with one accord, to send chosen men unto you with our beloved Barnabas and Paul, men that have hazarded their lives for the name of our Lord Jesus Christ.

"We have sent therefore Judas and Silas, who shall also tell you the same things by mouth. For it seemed good to the Holy Ghost and to us to lay upon you no greater burden than these necessary things, that ye abstain from meats offered to idols, and from blood, and from things strangled, and from fornication, from which if ye keep yourselves, ye shall do well.

"Fare ye well."

So when they were dismissed, they came to Antioch. When they had gathered the multitude together, they delivered the epistle, which when they had read, they rejoiced for the consolation. Judas and Silas, being prophets also themselves, exhorted the brethren with many words and confirmed them.

After they had tarried there a space, they were let go in peace from the brethren unto the apostles. Notwithstanding it pleased Silas to abide there still.

Paul also and Barnabas continued in Antioch, teaching and preaching the word of the Lord with many others also.

Some days after, Paul said unto Barnabas, "Let us go again and visit our brethren in every city where we have preached the word of the Lord and see how they do."

Barnabas determined to take with them John, whose surname was Mark. But Paul thought not good to take him with them, who departed from them from Pamphylia, and went not with them to the work. The contention was so sharp between them, that they departed asunder one from the other.

So Barnabas took Mark and sailed unto Cyprus.

Paul chose Silas and departed, being recommended by the brethren unto the grace of God. He went through Syria and Cilicia, confirming the churches. Then came he to Derbe and Lystra.

Acts 16:1-31

Behold, a certain disciple was there named Timothy, the son of a certain woman which was a Jewess and believed—but his father was a Greek—which was well reported of by the brethren that were at Lystra and Iconium. Him would Paul have to go forth with him, and took and circumcised him because of the Jews which were in those quarters, for they knew all that his father was a Greek.

As they went through the cities, they delivered them the decrees for to keep, that were ordained of the apostles and elders which were at Jerusalem. So were the churches established in the faith and increased in number daily.

Now when they had gone throughout Phrygia and the region of Galatia, and were forbidden of the Holy Ghost to preach the word in Asia, after they were come to Mysia they assayed to go into Bithynia, but the Spirit suffered them not. They passing by Mysia came down to Troas.

A vision appeared to Paul in the night. There stood a man of Macedonia and prayed him, saying, "Come over into Macedonia and help us."

After he had seen the vision, immediately we* endeavored to go into Macedonia, assuredly gathering that the Lord had called us for to preach the gospel unto them.

Therefore loosing from Troas, we came with a straight course to Samothracia, and the next day to Neapolis, and from thence to Philippi, which is the chief city of that part of Macedonia and a colony.

We were in that city abiding certain days. On the sabbath we went out of the city by a river side where prayer was wont to be made. We sat down and spake unto the women which resorted thither.

A certain woman named Lydia, a seller of purple of the city of Thyatira which worshipped God, heard us, whose heart the Lord opened that she attended unto the things which were spoken of Paul. When she was baptized and her household, she besought us, saying, "If ye have judged me to be faithful to the Lord, come into my house and abide there." And she constrained us.

It came to pass, as we went to prayer, a certain damsel possessed with a spirit of divination met us which brought her masters much gain by soothsaying. The same followed Paul and us and cried, saying, "These men are the servants

---

*Since Acts is reputably written by Luke, the sudden appearance of "we" is considered to indicate that Luke joined the others in their travels.

of the most high God, which shew unto us the way of salvation."

This did she many days. But Paul, being grieved, turned and said to the spirit, "I command thee in the name of Jesus Christ to come out of her."

He came out the same hour. When her masters saw that the hope of their gains was gone, they caught Paul and Silas, drew them into the marketplace unto the rulers, and brought them to the magistrates, saying, "These men, being Jews, do exceedingly trouble our city and teach customs which are not lawful for us to receive, neither to observe, being Romans."

The multitude rose up together against them, and the magistrates rent off their clothes and commanded to beat them.

When they had laid many stripes upon them, they cast them into prison, charging the jailor to keep them safely, who having received such a charge, thrust them into the inner prison and made their feet fast in the stocks.

At midnight Paul and Silas prayed and sang praises unto God, and the prisoners heard them.

Suddenly there was a great earthquake, so that the foundations of the prison were shaken. Immediately all the doors were opened, and every one's bands were loosed.

The keeper of the prison, awaking out of his sleep and seeing the prison doors open, he drew out his sword and would have killed himself, supposing that the prisoners had been fled.

But Paul cried with a loud voice, saying, "Do thyself no harm, for we are all here."

Then he called for a light, sprang in and came trembling, and fell down before Paul and Silas, and brought them out and said, "Sirs, what must I do to be saved?"

They said, "Believe on the Lord Jesus Christ, and thou shalt be saved, and thy house."

He took them the same hour of the night and washed their stripes. When he had brought them into his house, he set meat before them. They spake unto him the word of the Lord, and to all that were in his house. He was baptized and all his straightway and rejoiced, believing in God with all his house. *Acts 16:32-34*

When it was day, the magistrates sent the sergeants, saying, "Let those men go." *Acts 16:35-40*

The keeper of the prison told this saying to Paul, "The magistrates have sent to let you go. Now therefore depart and go in peace."

But Paul said unto them, "They have beaten us openly uncondemned, being Romans, and have cast us into prison, and now do they thrust us out privily? Nay verily, but let them come themselves and fetch us out."

The sergeants told these words unto the magistrates, and they feared when they heard that they were Romans. They came and besought them and brought them out, and desired them to depart out of the city.

They went out of the prison and entered into the house of Lydia. When they had seen the brethren, they comforted them and departed.

13

Now when they had passed through Amphipolis and Apollonia, they came to Thessalonica where was a synagogue of the Jews. Paul as his manner was went in unto them and three sabbath days reasoned with them out of the scriptures, opening and alleging that Christ must needs have suffered and risen again from the dead, and that "this Jesus, whom I preach unto you, is Christ."

Some of them believed and consorted with Paul and Silas, and of the devout Greeks a great multitude, and of the chief women not a few.

But the Jews which believed not, moved with envy, took unto them certain lewd fellows of the baser sort and gathered a company, and set all the city on an uproar, assaulted the house of Jason, and sought to bring them out to the people. When they found them not, they drew Jason and certain brethren unto the rulers of the city, crying, "These that have turned the world upside down are come hither also, whom Jason hath received. These all do contrary to the decrees of Caesar, saying that there is another king, one Jesus."

They troubled the people and the rulers of the city when they heard these things. When they had taken security of Jason and of the other, they let them go.

The brethren immediately sent away Paul and Silas by night unto Berea, who coming thither went into the

Acts 17:1-34

synagogue of the Jews. These were more noble than those in Thessalonica, in that they received the word with all readiness of mind and searched the scriptures daily, whether those things were so.

Therefore many of them believed, also of honorable women which were Greeks, and of men not a few.

But when the Jews of Thessalonica had knowledge that the word of God was preached of Paul at Berea, they came thither also, and stirred up the people. Then immediately the brethren sent away Paul to go as it were to the sea, but Silas and Timothy abode there still.

They that conducted Paul brought him unto Athens and, receiving a commandment unto Silas and Timothy for to come to him with all speed, they departed.

Now while Paul waited for them at Athens, his spirit was stirred in him when he saw the city wholly given to idolatry. Therefore disputed he in the synagogue with the Jews, with the devout persons, and in the market daily with them that met with him.

Then certain philosophers of the Epicureans and of the Stoics encountered him. Some said, "What will this babbler say?"

Other some, "He seemeth to be a setter forth of strange gods," because he preached unto them Jesus and the resurrection.

They took him and brought him unto Areopagus, saying, "May we know what this new doctrine whereof thou speakest is? For thou bringest certain strange things to our ears. We would know therefore what these things mean."

For all the Athenians and strangers which were there spent their time in nothing else, but either to tell or to hear some new thing.

Then Paul stood in the midst of Mars' hill and said, "Ye men of Athens, I perceive that in all things ye are too superstitious. For as I passed by and beheld your devotions, I found an altar with this inscription, *To the Unknown God*. Whom therefore ye ignorantly worship, him declare I unto you.

"God that made the world and all things therein, seeing that he is Lord of heaven and earth, dwelleth not in temples made with hands, neither is worshipped with men's hands—as though he needed anything, seeing he giveth to all life and breath and all things, and hath made of one blood all nations of men for to dwell on all the face of the earth, and hath determined the times before appointed and the bounds of their habitation, that they should seek the Lord, if haply they might feel after him and find him, though he be not far from every one of us.

"For in him we live and move and have our being, as certain also of your own poets have said, 'For we are also his offspring.' Forasmuch then as we are the offspring of God, we ought not to think that the Godhead is like unto gold or silver or stone, graven by art and man's device.

"The times of this ignorance God winked at, but now commandeth all men every where to repent, because he hath appointed a day in the which he will judge the world in righteousness by that man whom he hath ordained, whereof he hath given assurance unto all men in that he hath raised him from the dead."

When they heard of the resurrection of the dead, some mocked. Others said, "We will hear thee again of this matter." So Paul departed from among them.

Howbeit certain men clave unto him and believed, among the which was Dionysius the Areopagite, and a woman named Damaris, and others with them.

After these things Paul departed from Athens and came to Corinth, and found a certain Jew named Aquila, born in Pontus, lately come from Italy with his wife Priscilla—because that Claudius had commanded all Jews to depart from Rome—and came unto them. *Acts 18:1-28*

Because he was of the same craft, he abode with them and wrought, for by their occupation they were tentmakers. He reasoned in the synagogue every sabbath and persuaded the Jews and the Greeks.

When Silas and Timotheus were come from Macedonia, Paul was pressed in the spirit and testified to the Jews that Jesus was Christ. When they opposed themselves and blasphemed, he shook his raiment and said unto them, "Your blood be upon your own heads. I am clean. From henceforth I will go unto the Gentiles."

He departed thence and entered into a certain man's house named Justus, one that worshipped God, whose house joined hard to the synagogue. Crispus, the chief ruler of the synagogue, believed on the Lord with all his house. Many of the Corinthians hearing believed and were baptized.

Then spake the Lord to Paul in the night by a vision. "Be not afraid, but speak and hold not thy peace. For I am with thee, and no man shall set on thee to hurt thee, for I have much people in this city."

He continued there a year and six months, teaching the word of God among them.

When Gallio was the deputy of Achaia, the Jews made insurrection with one accord against Paul and brought him to the judgment seat, saying, This fellow persuadeth men to worship God contrary to the law."

When Paul was now about to open his mouth, Gallio said unto the Jews, "If it were a matter of wrong or wicked lewdness, O ye Jews, reason would that I should bear with you. But if it be a question of words and names and of your law, look ye to it, for I will be no judge of such matters." He drave them from the judgment seat.

Then all the Greeks took Sosthenes, the chief ruler of the synagogue, and beat him before the judgment seat. And Gallio cared for none of those things.

Paul after this tarried there yet a good while, then took his leave of the brethren and sailed thence into Syria, and with him Priscilla and Aquila, having shorn his head in Cenchrea, for he had a vow. He came to Ephesus and left them there, but he himself entered into the synagogue and reasoned with the Jews.

When they desired him to tarry longer time with them, he consented not, but bade them farewell, saying, "I must by all means keep this feast that cometh in Jerusalem. But I will return again unto you, if God will."

He sailed from Ephesus. When he had landed at Caesarea, and gone up and saluted the church, he went down to Antioch. After he had spent some time there, he departed and went over all the country of Galatia and Phrygia in order, strengthening all the disciples.

A certain Jew named Apollos, born at Alexandria, an eloquent man and mighty in the scriptures, came to Ephesus. This man was instructed in the way of the Lord. Being fervent in the spirit, he spake and taught diligently the things of the Lord, knowing only the baptism of John.

He began to speak boldly in the synagogue, whom when Aquila and Priscilla had heard, they took him unto them and expounded unto him the way of God more perfectly.

When he was disposed to pass into Achaia, the brethren wrote, exhorting the disciples to receive him, who when he was come, helped them much which had believed through grace. For he mightily convinced the Jews, and that publicly, shewing by the scriptures that Jesus was Christ.

14

It came to pass that while Apollos was at Corinth, Paul having passed through the upper coasts came to Ephesus. Finding certain disciples, he said unto them, "Have ye received the Holy Ghost since ye believed?"

They said unto him, "We have not so much as heard whether there be any Holy Ghost."

He said unto them, "Unto what then were ye baptized?"

They said, "Unto John's baptism."

Then said Paul, "John verily baptized with the baptism of repentance, saying unto the people that they should believe on him which should come after him, that is, on Christ Jesus."

When they heard this, they were baptized in the name of the Lord Jesus. When Paul had laid his hands upon them, the Holy Ghost came on them, and they spake with tongues and prophesied. All the men were about twelve.

He went into the synagogue and spake boldly for the space of three months, disputing and persuading the things concerning the kingdom of God. But when divers were hardened and believed not, but spake evil of that way before the multitude, he departed from them and separated the disciples, disputing daily in the school of one Tyrannus.

This continued by the space of two years, so that all they which dwelt in Asia heard the word of the Lord Jesus, both Jews and Greeks.

God wrought special miracles by the hands of Paul, so that from his body were brought unto the sick handkerchiefs or aprons, and the diseases departed from them, and the evil spirits went out of them.

Then certain of the vagabond Jews, exorcists, took upon them to call over them which had evil spirits the

Acts 19:1-41

name of the Lord Jesus, saying, "We adjure you by Jesus whom Paul preacheth." There were seven sons of one Sceva, a Jew, and chief of the priests which did so.

The evil spirit answered and said, "Jesus I know, and Paul I know. But who are ye?"

The man in whom the evil spirit was leaped on them, overcame them, and prevailed against them, so that they fled out of that house naked and wounded.

This was known to all the Jews and Greeks also dwelling at Ephesus, and fear fell on them all. The name of the Lord Jesus was magnified. Many that believed came, confessed, and shewed their deeds.

Many of them also which used curious arts brought their books together and burned them before all men. They counted the price of them, and found it fifty thousand pieces of silver.

So mightily grew the word of God and prevailed.

After these things were ended, Paul purposed in the spirit, when he had passed through Macedonia and Achaia, to go to Jerusalem, saying, "After I have been there, I must also see Rome."

So he sent into Macedonia two of them that ministered unto him, Timothy and Erastus. But he himself stayed in Asia for a season.

The same time there arose no small stir about that way. For a certain man named Demetrius, a silversmith which made silver shrines for Diana, brought no small gain unto the craftsmen, whom he called together with the workmen of like occupation and said, "Sirs, ye know that by this craft we have our wealth. Moreover ye see and hear that not alone at Ephesus, but almost throughout all Asia, this Paul hath persuaded and turned away much people, saying that they be no gods which are made with hands. So that not only this our craft is in danger to be set at nought, but also that the temple of the great goddess Diana should be despised, and her magnificence should be destroyed, whom all Asia and the world worshippeth."

When they heard these sayings, they were full of wrath and cried out, saying, "Great is Diana of the Ephesians!"

The whole city was filled with confusion. Having caught Gaius and Aristarchus, men of Macedonia, Paul's companions in travel, they rushed with one accord into the theater.

When Paul would have entered in unto the people, the disciples suffered him not. Certain of the chief of Asia which were his friends sent unto him, desiring him that he would not adventure himself into the theater.

Some therefore cried one thing, and some another, for the assembly was confused, and the more part knew not wherefore they were come together.

They drew Alexander out of the multitude, the Jews putting him forward. Alexander beckoned with the hand and would have made his defence unto the people. But when they knew that he was a Jew, all with one voice about the space of two hours cried out, "Great is Diana of the Ephesians!"

When the town clerk had appeased the people, he said, "Ye men of Ephesus, what man is there that knoweth not how that the city of the Ephesians is a worshipper of the great goddess Diana, and of the image which fell down from Jupiter? Seeing then that these things cannot be spoken against, ye ought to be quiet, and to do nothing rashly.

"For ye have brought hither these men, which are neither robbers of churches nor yet blasphemers of your goddess. Wherefore if Demetrius and the craftsmen which are with him have a matter against any man, the law is open, and there are deputies. Let them implead one another.

"But if ye inquire anything concerning other matters, it shall be determined in a lawful assembly. For we are in danger to be called in question for this day's uproar, there being no cause whereby we may give an account of this concourse."

When he had thus spoken, he dismissed the assembly.

Acts 20:1-38

After the uproar was ceased, Paul called unto him the disciples, embraced them, and departed for to go into Macedonia. When he had gone over those parts and had given them much exhortation, he came into Greece, and there abode three months.

When the Jews laid wait for him, as he was about to sail into Syria, he purposed to return through Macedonia.

There accompanied him into Asia Sopater of Berea, and of the Thessalonians, <u>Aristarchus</u> and Secundus, and Gaius of Derbe, and Timothy, and of Asia, Tychicus and Trophimus. These going before tarried for us at Troas.

We sailed away from Philippi after the days of unleavened bread and came unto them to Troas in five days, where we abode seven days.

Upon the first day of the week, when the disciples came together to break bread, Paul preached unto them, ready to depart on the morrow, and continued his speech until midnight. There were many lights in the upper chamber where they were gathered together.

There sat in a window a certain young man named Eutychus, being fallen into a deep sleep. As Paul was long preaching, he sunk down with sleep, fell down from the third loft, and was taken up dead.

Paul went down and fell on him, and embracing him said, "Trouble not yourselves, for his life is in him."

When he therefore was come up again and had broken bread and eaten, and talked a long while, even till break of day, so he departed. They brought the young man alive, and were not a little comforted.

We went before to ship and sailed unto Assos, there intending to take in Paul. For so had he appointed, minding himself to go afoot. When he met with us at Assos, we took him in and came to Mitylene.

We sailed thence and came the next day over against Chios. The next day we arrived at Samos and tarried at Trogyllium. The next day we came to Miletus.

For Paul had determined to sail by Ephesus, because he would not spend the time in Asia. For he hasted, if it were possible, for him to be at Jerusalem the day of Pentecost.

From Miletus he sent to Ephesus and called the elders of the church. When they were come to him, he said unto them, "Ye know, from the first day that I came into Asia, after what manner I have been with you at all seasons. Serving the Lord with all humility of mind, with many tears, and temptations which befell me by the lying in wait of the Jews.

"How I kept back nothing that was profitable unto you, but have shewed you and have taught you publicly, and from house to house, testifying both to the Jews and also to the Greeks repentance toward God and faith toward our Lord Jesus Christ.

"Now behold, I go bound in the spirit unto Jerusalem,

not knowing the things that shall befall me there, save that the Holy Ghost witnesseth in every city, saying that bonds and afflictions abide me.

"But none of these things move me, neither count I my life dear unto myself, so that I might finish my course with joy, and the ministry which I have received of the Lord Jesus to testify the gospel of the grace of God.

"Now behold, I know that ye all, among whom I have gone preaching the kingdom of God, shall see my face no more. Wherefore I take you to record this day, that I am pure from the blood of all men. For I have not shunned to declare unto you all the counsel of God.

"Take heed therefore unto yourselves, and to all the flock over the which the Holy Ghost hath made you overseers to feed the church of God, which he hath purchased with his own blood.

"For I know this, that after my departing shall grievous wolves enter in among you, not sparing the flock. Also of your own selves shall men arise, speaking perverse things to draw away disciples after them. Therefore watch and remember, that by the space of three years I ceased not to warn everyone night and day with tears.

"Now brethren, I commend you to God and to the word of his grace, which is able to build you up and to give you an inheritance among all them which are sanctified. I have coveted no man's silver or gold or apparel.

"Yea, ye yourselves know that these hands have ministered unto my necessities, and to them that were with me. I have shewed you all things, how that so laboring ye ought to support the weak and to remember the words of the Lord Jesus, how he said, 'It is more blessed to give than to receive.'"

When he had thus spoken, he kneeled down and prayed with them all. They all wept sore and fell on Paul's neck and kissed him, sorrowing most of all for the words which he spake, that they should see his face no more.

They accompanied him unto the ship.

15

It came to pass that, after we were gotten from them and had launched, we came with a straight course unto

Acts 21:1-40

Coos, and the day following unto Rhodes, and from thence unto Patara. Finding a ship sailing over unto Phoenicia, we went aboard and set forth.

Now when we had discovered Cyprus, we left it on the left hand, sailed into Syria, and landed at Tyre, for there the ship was to unlade her burden.

Finding disciples, we tarried there seven days, who said to Paul through the Spirit that he should not go up to Jerusalem.

When we had accomplished those days, we departed and went our way. They all brought us on our way, with wives and children, till we were out of the city. We kneeled down on the shore and prayed. When we had taken our leave one of another, we took ship, and they returned home again.

When we had finished our course from Tyre, we came to Ptolemais and saluted the brethren, and abode with them one day. The next day we that were of Paul's company departed and came unto Caesarea. We entered into the house of Philip the evangelist, which was one of the seven, and abode with him. The same man had four daughters, virgins which did prophesy.

As we tarried there many days, there came down from Judea a certain prophet named Agabus. When he was come unto us, he took Paul's girdle, bound his own hands and feet, and said, "Thus saith the Holy Ghost, 'So shall the Jews at Jerusalem bind the man that owneth this girdle, and shall deliver him into the hands of the Gentiles.'"

When we heard these things, both we and they of that place besought him not to go up to Jerusalem.

Then Paul answered, "What mean ye to weep and to break mine heart? For I am ready not to be bound only, but also to die at Jerusalem for the name of the Lord Jesus."

When he would not be persuaded, we ceased, saying, "The will of the Lord be done."

After those days we took up our carriages and went up to Jerusalem. There went with us also certain of the disciples of Caesarea and brought with them one Mnason of Cyprus, an old disciple with whom we should lodge. When we were come to Jerusalem, the brethren received us gladly.

The day following Paul went in with us unto James. All the elders were present. When he had saluted them, he declared particularly what things God had wrought among the Gentiles by his ministry.

When they heard it, they glorified the Lord and said unto him, "Thou seest, brother, how many thousands of Jews there are which believe. And they are all zealous of the law. They are informed of thee, that thou teachest all the Jews which are among the Gentiles to forsake Moses, saying that they ought not to circumcise their children, neither to walk after the customs.

"What is it therefore? The multitude must needs come together, for they will hear that thou art come. Do therefore this that we say to thee.

"We have four men which have a vow on them. Them take, and purify thyself with them. Be at charges with them, that they may shave their heads, and all may know that those things whereof they were informed concerning thee are nothing, but that thou thyself also walkest orderly and keepest the law.

"As touching the Gentiles which believe, we have written and concluded that they observe no such thing, save only that they keep themselves from things offered to idols, and from blood, and from strangled, and from fornication."

Then Paul took the men and, the next day purifying himself with them, entered into the temple to signify the accomplishment of the days of purification, until that an offering should be offered for every one of them.

When the seven days were almost ended, the Jews which were of Asia, when they saw him in the temple, stirred up all the people and laid hands on him, crying out, "Men of Israel, help! This is the man that teacheth all men everywhere against the people and the law and this place, and further brought Greeks also into the temple, and hath polluted this holy place."

For they had seen before with him in the city Trophimus an Ephesian, whom they supposed that Paul had brought into the temple.

All the city was moved. The people ran together, and they took Paul and drew him out of the temple. Forthwith the doors were shut.

As they went about to kill him, tidings came unto the

chief captain of the band that all Jerusalem was in an uproar, who immediately took soldiers and centurions and ran down unto them. When they saw the chief captain and the soldiers, they left beating of Paul.

The chief captain came near, took him, and commanded him to be bound with two chains, and demanded who he was and what he had done. Some cried one thing, some another among the multitude. When he could not know the certainty for the tumult, he commanded him to be carried into the castle.

When he came upon the stairs, so it was that he was borne of the soldiers for the violence of the people. For the multitude of the people followed after, crying, "Away with him."

As Paul was to be led into the castle, he said unto the chief captain, "May I speak unto thee?"

Who said, "Canst thou speak Greek? Art not thou that Egyptian, which before these days madest an uproar and leddest out into the wilderness four thousand men that were murderers?"

But Paul said, "I am a man which am a Jew of Tarsus, a city in Cilicia, a citizen of no mean city. I beseech thee, suffer me to speak unto the people.

When he had given him license, Paul stood on the stairs and beckoned with the hand unto the people. When there was made a great silence, he spake unto them in the Hebrew tongue, saying, "Men, brethren, and fathers, hear ye my defense which I make now unto you."

When they heard that he spake in the Hebrew tongue to them, they kept the more silence.

He said, "I am verily a man which am a Jew, born in Tarsus, a city in Cilicia, yet brought up in this city at the feet of Gamaliel, and taught according to the perfect manner of the law of the fathers, and was zealous toward God, as ye all are this day.

"I persecuted this way unto the death, binding and delivering into prisons both men and women. As also the high priest doth bear me witness, and all the estate of the elders, from whom also I received letters unto the brethren and went to Damascus to bring them which were there bound unto Jerusalem, for to be punished.

"It came to pass that, as I made my journey and was come nigh unto Damascus about noon, suddenly there

Acts 22:1-29

shone from heaven a great light round about me. I fell unto the ground and heard a voice saying unto me, 'Saul, Saul, why persecutest thou me?'

"I answered, 'Who art thou, Lord?'

"He said unto me, 'I am Jesus of Nazareth, whom thou persecutest.'

"They that were with me saw indeed the light and were afraid, but they heard not the voice of him that spake to me.

"I said, 'What shall I do, Lord?'

"The Lord said unto me, 'Arise and go into Damascus. There it shall be told thee of all things which are appointed for thee to do.

"When I could not see for the glory of that light, being led by the hand of them that were with me, I came into Damascus. One Ananias, a devout man according to the law, having a good report of all the Jews which dwelt there, came unto me, stood and said unto me, 'Brother Saul, receive thy sight.'

"The same hour I looked up upon him.

"He said, 'The God of our fathers hath chosen thee, that thou shouldest know his will and see that Just One, and shouldest hear the voice of his mouth. For thou shalt be his witness unto all men of what thou hast seen and heard. Now why tarriest thou? Arise and be baptized, and wash away thy sins, calling on the name of the Lord.'

"It came to pass that, when I was come again to Jerusalem, even while I prayed in the temple, I was in a trance and saw him saying unto me, 'Make haste and get thee quickly out of Jerusalem, for they will not receive thy testimony concerning me.'

"I said, 'Lord, they know that I imprisoned and beat in every synagogue them that believed on thee, and when the blood of thy martyr Stephen was shed, I also was standing by and consenting unto his death, and kept the raiment of them that slew him.'

"He said unto me, 'Depart! For I will send thee far hence unto the Gentiles.'"

They gave him audience unto this word, then lifted up their voices and said, "Away with such a fellow from the earth, for it is not fit that he should live."

As they cried out, cast off their clothes, and threw dust into the air, the chief captain commanded him to be brought into the castle and bade that he should be examined by scourging, that he might know wherefore they cried so against him.

As they bound him with thongs, Paul said unto the centurion that stood by, "Is it lawful for you to scourge a man that is a Roman and uncondemned?"

When the centurion heard that, he went and told the chief captain, saying, "Take heed what thou doest, for this man is a Roman."

Then the chief captain came and said unto him, "Tell me, art thou a Roman?"

He said, "Yea."

The chief captain answered, "With a great sum obtained I this freedom."

Paul said, "But I was free born."

Then straightway they departed from him which should have examined him. The chief captain also was afraid after he knew that he was a Roman and because he had bound him.

16

On the morrow, because he would have known the certainty wherefore he was accused of the Jews, he loosed him from his bands and commanded the chief priests and all their council to appear, and brought Paul down and set him before them. | Acts 22:30

Paul, earnestly beholding the council, said, "Men and brethren, I have lived in all good conscience before God until this day." | Acts 23:1-35

The high priest Ananias commanded them that stood by him to smite him on the mouth.

Then said Paul unto him, "God shall smite thee, thou whited wall. For sittest thou to judge me after the law, and commandest me to be smitten contrary to the law?"

They that stood by said, "Revilest thou God's high priest?"

Then said Paul, "I wist not, brethren, that he was the high priest. For it is written, 'Thou shalt not speak evil of the ruler of thy people.'"* | *Exodus 22:28*

But when Paul perceived that the one part were Sadducees and the other Pharisees, he cried out in the council, "Men and brethren, I am a Pharisee, the son of a Pharisee. Of the hope and resurrection of the dead I am called in question."

When he had so said, there arose a dissension between the Pharisees and the Sadducees, and the multitude was divided. For the Sadducees say that there is no resurrection, neither angel nor spirit. But the Pharisees confess both.

There arose a great cry. The scribes that were of the Pharisees' part arose and strove, saying, "We find no evil in this man, but if a spirit or an angel hath spoken to him, let us not fight against God."

When there arose a great dissension, the chief captain, fearing lest Paul should have been pulled in pieces of them, commanded the soldiers to go down and to take him by force from among them, and to bring him into the castle.

The night following, the Lord stood by him and said, "Be of good cheer, Paul. For as thou hast testified of me in Jerusalem, so must thou bear witness also at Rome."

When it was day, certain of the Jews banded together and bound themselves under a curse, saying that they would neither eat nor drink till they had killed Paul. They were more than forty which had made this conspiracy.

They came to the chief priests and elders and said, "We have bound ourselves under a great curse, that we will eat nothing until we have slain Paul.

"Now therefore ye with the council signify to the chief captain that he bring him down unto you tomorrow, as though ye would inquire something more perfectly concerning him. And we, or ever he come near, are ready to kill him."

When Paul's sister's son heard of their lying in wait, he went and entered into the castle and told Paul. Then Paul called one of the centurions unto him and said, "Bring this young man unto the chief captain, for he hath a certain thing to tell him."

So he took him and brought him to the chief captain, and said, "Paul the prisoner called me unto him and prayed me to bring this young man unto thee, who hath something to say unto thee."

Then the chief captain took him by the hand, went with him aside privately, and asked him, "What is that thou hast to tell me?"

He said, "The Jews have agreed to desire thee that thou wouldest bring down Paul tomorrow into the council, as though they would inquire somewhat of him more perfectly. But do not thou yield unto them, for there lie in wait for him of them more than forty men, which have bound themselves with an oath that they will neither eat nor drink till they have killed him, and now are they ready, looking for a promise from thee."

So the chief captain then let the young man depart and charged him, "See thou tell no man that thou hast shewed these things to me."

He called unto him two centurions, saying, "Make ready two hundred soldiers to go to Caesarea, and horsemen threescore and ten, and spearmen two hundred, at the third hour of the night. Provide them beasts that they may set Paul on and bring him safe unto Felix the governor."

He wrote a letter after this manner:

"Claudius Lysias unto the most excellent governor Felix sendeth greeting.

"This man was taken of the Jews and should have been killed of them. Then came I with an army and rescued him, having understood that he was a Roman.

"when I would have known the cause wherefore they accused him, I brought him forth into their council, whom I perceived to be accused of questions of their law, but to have nothing laid to his charge worthy of death or of bonds.

"When it was told me how that the Jews laid wait for the man, I sent straightway to thee, and gave commandment to his accusers also to say before thee what they had against him.

"Farewell."

Then the soldiers, as it was commanded them, took Paul and brought him by night to Antipatris. On the morrow they left the horsemen to go with him and returned to the castle, who, when they came to Caesarea and delivered the epistle to the governor, presented Paul also before him.

When the governor had read the letter, he asked of what province he was. When he understood that he was of Cilicia, "I will hear thee," said he, "when thine accusers are also come."

He commanded him to be kept in Herod's judgment hall.

After five days, Ananias the high priest descended with the elders and with a certain orator named Tertullus, who informed the governor against Paul. When he was called forth, Tertullus began to accuse him, saying, "Seeing that by thee we enjoy great quietness, and that very worthy deeds are done unto this nation by thy providence, we accept it always and in all places, most noble Felix, with all thankfulness.

"Notwithstanding, that I be not further tedious unto thee, I pray thee that thou wouldest hear us of thy clemency a few words. For we have found this man a pestilent fellow, a mover of sedition among all the Jews throughout the world, and a ringleader of the sect of the Nazarenes who also hath gone about to profane the temple, whom we took and would have judged according to our law.

"But the chief captain Lysias came upon us, and with great violence took him away out of our hands, commanding his accusers to come unto thee, by examining of whom thyself mayest take knowledge of all these things, whereof we accuse him.

"And the Jews also assented, saying that these things were so."

Then Paul, after that the governor had beckoned unto him to speak, answered, "Forasmuch as I know that thou hast been of many years a judge unto this nation, I do the more cheerfully answer for myself, because that thou mayest understand that there are yet but twelve days since I went up to Jerusalem for to worship.

They neither found me in the temple disputing with any man, neither raising up the people, neither in the synagogues, nor in the city. Neither can they prove the things whereof they now accuse me.

"But this I confess unto thee, that after the way which they call heresy, so worship I the God of my fathers, believing all things which are written in the law and in the prophets, and have hope toward God which they themselves also allow, that there shall be a resurrection of the dead, both of the just and unjust.

"Herein do I exercise myself to have always a conscience void of offense toward God and toward men.

"Now after many years I came to bring alms to my

Acts 24:1-27

nation, and offerings. Whereupon certain Jews from Asia found me purified in the temple, neither with multitude, nor with tumult. Who ought to have been here before thee and object, if they had ought against me.

"Or else let these same here say if they have found any evil doing in me, while I stood before the council. Except it be for this one voice, that I cried standing among them touching the resurrection of the dead I am called in question by you this day."

When Felix heard these things, having more perfect knowledge of that way, he deferred them and said, "When Lysias the chief captain shall come down, I will know the uttermost of your matter."

He commanded a centurion to keep Paul, and to let him have liberty, and that he should forbid none of his acquaintance to minister or come unto him.

After certain days when Felix came with his wife Drusilla, which was a Jewess, he sent for Paul and heard him concerning the faith in Christ.

As he reasoned of righteousness, temperance, and judgment to come, Felix trembled and answered, "Go thy way for this time. When I have a convenient season, I will call for thee."

He hoped also that money should have been given him of Paul, that he might loose him, wherefore he sent for him the oftener and communed with him.

But after two years Porcius Festus came into Felix' room, and Felix, willing to shew the Jews a pleasure, left Paul bound.

Now when Festus was come into the province, after three days he ascended from Caesarea to Jerusalem. Then the high priest and the chief of the Jews informed him against Paul, besought him and desired favor against him, that he would send for him to Jerusalem, laying wait in the way to kill him.

But Festus answered that Paul should be kept at Cæsarea, and that he himself would depart shortly thither. "Let them therefore," said he, "which among you are able, go down with me and accuse this man, if there be any wickedness in him."

When he had tarried among them more than ten days, he went down unto Caesarea, and the next day sitting on the judgment seat commanded Paul to be brought.

Acts 25:1-12

When he was come, the Jews which came down from Jerusalem stood round about and laid many grievous complaints against Paul, which they could not prove. While he answered for himself, "Neither against the law of the Jews, neither against the temple, nor yet against Cæsar, have I offended anything at all."

But Festus, willing to do the Jews a pleasure, answered Paul and said, "Wilt thou go up to Jerusalem and there be judged of these things before me?"

Then said Paul, "I stand at Caesar's judgment seat, where I ought to be judged. To the Jews have I done no wrong, as thou very well knowest. For if I be an offender or have committed anything worthy of death, I refuse not to die. But if there be none of these things whereof these accuse me, no man may deliver me unto them. I appeal unto Caesar!"

Then Festus, when he had conferred with the council, answered, "Hast thou appealed unto Caesar? Unto Cæsar shalt thou go."

17

After certain days, king Agrippa and Bernice came unto Caesarea to salute Festus. When they had been there many days, Festus declared Paul's cause unto the king, saying, "There is a certain man left in bonds by Felix, about whom, when I was at Jerusalem, the chief priests and the elders of the Jews informed me, desiring to have judgment against him. To whom I answered, 'It is not the manner of the Romans to deliver any man to die, before that he which is accused have the accusers face to face and have licence to answer for himself concerning the crime laid against him.'

"Therefore when they were come hither without any delay on the morrow, I sat on the judgment seat and commanded the man to be brought forth. Against whom when the accusers stood up, they brought none accusation of such things as I supposed, but had certain questions against him of their own superstition and of one Jesus which was dead, whom Paul affirmed to be alive.

"Because I doubted of such manner of questions, I asked him whether he would go to Jerusalem and there be

Acts 25:13-27

judged of these matters. But when Paul had appealed to be reserved unto the hearing of Augustus, I commanded him to be kept till I might send him to Caesar."

Then Agrippa said unto Festus, "I would also hear the man myself."

"Tomorrow," said he, "thou shalt hear him."

On the morrow, when Agrippa was come, and Bernice with great pomp, and was entered into the place of hearing with the chief captains and principal men of the city, at Festus' commandment Paul was brought forth.

Festus said, "King Agrippa and all men which are here present with us, ye see this man about whom all the multitude of the Jews have dealt with me, both at Jerusalem and also here, crying that he ought not to live any longer. But when I found that he had committed nothing worthy of death, and that he himself hath appealed to Augustus, I have determined to send him, of whom I have no certain thing to write unto my lord.

"Wherefore I have brought him forth before you, and specially before thee, O king Agrippa, that after examination had, I might have somewhat to write. For it seemeth to me unreasonable to send a prisoner and not withal to signify the crimes laid against him."

Then Agrippa said unto Paul, "Thou art permitted to speak for thyself."

Acts 26:1-32

Then Paul stretched forth the hand and answered for himself. "I think myself happy, king Agrippa, because I shall answer for myself this day before thee touching all the things whereof I am accused of the Jews. Especially because I know thee to be expert in all customs and questions which are among the Jews, wherefore I beseech thee to hear me patiently.

"My manner of life from my youth, which was at the first among mine own nation at Jerusalem, know all the Jews which knew me from the beginning if they would testify, that after the most straitest sect of our religion I lived a Pharisee.

"Now I stand and am judged for the hope of the promise made of God unto our fathers, unto which promise our twelve tribes, instantly serving God day and night, hope to come. For which hope's sake, king Agrippa, I am accused of the Jews. Why should it be thought a thing incredible with you, that God should raise the dead?

"I verily thought with myself that I ought to do many things contrary to the name of Jesus of Nazareth, which thing I also did in Jerusalem. Many of the saints did I shut up in prison, having received authority from the chief priests, and when they were put to death, I gave my voice against them.

"I punished them oft in every synagogue and compelled them to blaspheme. Being exceedingly mad against them, I persecuted them even unto strange cities.

"Whereupon as I went to Damascus with authority and commission from the chief priests, at midday, O king, I saw in the way a light from heaven above the brightness of the sun, shining round about me and them which journeyed with me. When we were all fallen to the earth, I heard a voice speaking unto me and saying in the Hebrew tongue, 'Saul, Saul, why persecutest thou me? It is hard for thee to kick against the pricks.'

"I said, 'Who art thou, Lord?'

"He said, 'I am Jesus whom thou persecutest. But rise and stand upon thy feet, for I have appeared unto thee for this purpose, to make thee a minister and a witness, both of these things which thou hast seen and of those things in the which I will appear unto thee delivering thee from the people and from the Gentiles, unto whom now I send thee to open their eyes and to turn them from darkness to light and from the power of Satan unto God, that they may receive forgiveness of sins and inheritance among them which are sanctified by faith that is in me.'

"Whereupon, O king Agrippa, I was not disobedient unto the heavenly vision, but shewed first unto them of Damascus, and at Jerusalem, and throughout all the coasts of Judea, then to the Gentiles, that they should repent and turn to God and do works meet for repentance.

"For these causes the Jews caught me in the temple and went about to kill me.

"Having therefore obtained help of God, I continue unto this day, witnessing both to small and great, saying none other things than those which the prophets and Moses did say should come—that Christ should suffer, that he should be the first that should rise from the dead, and should shew light unto the people and to the Gentiles."

As he thus spake for himself, Festus said with a loud

voice, "Paul, thou art beside thyself! Much learning doth make thee mad."

But he said, "I am not mad, most noble Festus, but speak forth the words of truth and soberness. For the king knoweth of these things before whom also I speak freely. For I am persuaded that none of these things are hidden from him, for this thing was not done in a corner.

"King Agrippa, believest thou the prophets? I know that thou believest."

Agrippa said unto Paul, "Almost thou persuadest me to be a Christian."

Paul said, "I would to God that, not only thou, but also all that hear me this day were both almost and altogether such as I am—except these bonds."

When he had thus spoken, the king rose up, and the governor and Bernice and they that sat with them. When they were gone aside, they talked between themselves, saying, "This man doeth nothing worthy of death or of bonds."

Then said Agrippa unto Festus, "This man might have been set at liberty if he had not appealed unto Caesar."

18

When it was determined that we should sail into Italy, they delivered Paul and certain other prisoners unto one named Julius, a centurion of Augustus' band. Entering into a ship of Adramyttium, we launched, meaning to sail by the coasts of Asia, one Aristarchus, a Macedonian of Thessalonica, being with us.

The next day we touched at Sidon. Julius courteously entreated Paul and gave him liberty to go unto his friends to refresh himself.

When we had launched from thence, we sailed under Cyprus because the winds were contrary. When we had sailed over the sea of Cilicia and Pamphylia, we came to Myra, a city of Lycia. There the centurion found a ship of Alexandria sailing into Italy, and he put us therein.

When we had sailed slowly many days and scarce were come over against Cnidus, the wind not suffering us, we sailed under Crete over against Salmone and, hardly

Acts 27:1-44

passing it, came unto a place which is called The Fair Havens, nigh whereunto was the city of Lasea.

Now when much time was spent, and when sailing was now dangerous, because the fast was now already past, Paul admonished them and said unto them, "Sirs, I perceive that this voyage will be with hurt and much damage, not only of the lading and ship, but also of our lives."

Nevertheless the centurion believed the master and the owner of the ship more than those things which were spoken by Paul. And because the haven was not commodious to winter in, the more part advised to depart thence also, if by any means they might attain to Phoenicia and there to winter, which is a haven of Crete and lieth toward the southwest and northwest.

When the south wind blew softly—supposing that they had obtained their purpose—loosing thence, they sailed close by Crete. But not long after, there arose against it a tempestuous wind called Euroclydon. When the ship was caught and could not bear up into the wind, we let her drive.

Running under a certain island which is called Clauda, we had much work to come by the boat which, when they had taken up, they used helps undergirding the ship, and fearing lest they should fall into the quicksands, strake sail and so were driven.

We being exceedingly tossed with a tempest, the next day they lightened the ship. The third day we cast out with our own hands the tackling of the ship.

When neither sun nor stars in many days appeared and no small tempest lay on us, all hope that we should be saved was then taken away.

But after long abstinence Paul stood forth in the midst of them and said, "Sirs, ye should have hearkened unto me and not have loosed from Crete, to have gained this harm and loss.

"Now I exhort you to be of good cheer, for there shall be no loss of any man's life among you, but of the ship. For there stood by me this night the angel of God, whose I am and whom I serve, saying, 'Fear not, Paul. Thou must be brought before Caesar, and lo, God hath given thee all them that sail with thee.'

"Wherefore, sirs, be of good cheer, for I believe God,

that it shall be even as it was told me. Howbeit we must be cast upon a certain island."

When the fourteenth night was come, as we were driven up and down in Adria, about midnight the shipmen deemed that they drew near to some country, sounded and found it twenty fathoms. When they had gone a little further, they sounded again and found it fifteen fathoms.

Fearing lest we should have fallen upon rocks, they cast four anchors out of the stern and wished for the day.

As the shipmen were about to flee out of the ship, when they had let down the boat into the sea under color as though they would have cast anchors out of the foreship, Paul said to the centurion and to the soldiers, "Except these abide in the ship, ye cannot be saved."

The soldiers cut off the ropes of the boat and let her fall off.

While the day was coming on, Paul besought them all to take meat, saying, "This day is the fourteenth day that ye have tarried and continued fasting, having taken nothing. Wherefore I pray you to take some meat, for this is for your health. For there shall not a hair fall from the head of any of you."

When he had thus spoken, he took bread and gave thanks to God in presence of them all. When he had broken it, he began to eat. Then were they all of good cheer, and they also took some meat. We were, in all, in the ship two hundred threescore and sixteen souls.

When they had eaten enough, they lightened the ship and cast out the wheat into the sea. And when it was day, they knew not the land. But they discovered a certain creek with a shore, into the which they were minded, if it were possible, to thrust in the ship.

When they had taken up the anchors, they committed themselves unto the sea and loosed the rudder bands, hoised up the mainsail to the wind, and made toward shore.

Falling into a place where two seas met, they ran the ship aground. The forepart stuck fast and remained unmovable, but the hinder part was broken with the violence of the waves.

The soldiers' counsel was to kill the prisoners, lest any of them should swim out and escape. But the centurion, willing to save Paul, kept them from their purpose and commanded that they which could swim should cast themselves first into the sea and get to land, and the rest, some on boards and some on broken pieces of the ship. So it came to pass that they escaped all safe to land.

19

When they were escaped, then they knew that the island was called Melita. The barbarous people shewed us no little kindness, for they kindled a fire and received us every one because of the present rain and because of the cold.

When Paul had gathered a bundle of sticks and laid them on the fire, there came a viper out of the heat and fastened on his hand. When the barbarians saw the venomous beast hang on his hand, they said among themselves, "No doubt this man is a murderer whom, though he hath escaped the sea, yet vengeance suffereth not to live."

He shook off the beast into the fire, and felt no harm. Howbeit they looked when he should have swollen, or fallen down dead suddenly. But after they had looked a great while and saw no harm come to him, they changed their minds and said that he was a god.

In the same quarters were possessions of the chief man of the island whose name was Publius. who received us and lodged us three days courteosly. It came to pass that the father of Publius lay sick of a fever and of a bloody flux, to whom Paul entered in, prayed, laid his hands on him, and healed him.

So when this was done, others also which had diseases in the island came and were healed, who also honored us with many honors. When we departed, they laded us with such things as were necessary.

After three months we departed in a ship of Alexandria which had wintered in the isle, whose sign was Castor and Pollux. Landing at Syracuse, we tarried there three days.

From thence we fetched a compass and came to Rhegium. After one day the south wind blew, and we came the next day to Puteoli where we found brethren, and were desired to tarry with them seven days.

So we went toward Rome. From thence, when the

Acts 28:1-31

brethren heard of us, they came to meet us as far as Appii Forum and The Three Taverns, whom when Paul saw, he thanked God and took courge.

When we came to Rome, the centurion delivered the prisoners to the captain of the guard, but Paul was suffered to dwell by himself with a soldier that kept him.

It came to pass that after three days, Paul called the chief of the Jews together. When they were come together, he said unto them, "Men and brethren, though I have committed nothing against the people or customs of our fathers, yet was I delivered prisoner from Jerusalem into the hands of the Romans. Who when they had examined me would have let me go, because there was no cause of death in me.

"But when the Jews spake against it, I was constrained to appeal unto Caesar—not that I had ought to accuse my nation of.

"For this cause therefore have I called for you, to see you and to speak with you, because that for the hope of Israel I am bound with this chain."

They said unto him, "We neither received letters out of Judea concerning thee, neither any of the brethren that came shewed or spake any harm of thee. But we desire to hear of thee what thou thinkest, for as concerning this sect, we know that everywhere it is spoken against."

When they had appointed him a day, there came many to him into his lodging, to whom he expounded and testified the kingdom of God, persuading them concerning Jesus, both out of the law of Moses and out of the prophets, from morning till evening. Some believed the things which were spoken, and some believed not.

When they agreed not among themselves, they departed, after that Paul had spoken one word, "Well spake the Holy Ghost by Isaiah the prophet unto our fathers, saying, 'Go unto this people and say, "Hearing ye shall hear and shall not understand, and seeing ye shall see and not perceive. For the heart of this people is waxed gross, and their ears are dull of hearing, and their eyes have they closed, lest they should see with their eyes and hear with their ears and understand with their heart and should be converted, and I should heal them.'"*

*Isaiah 6:9-10

"Be it known therefore unto you that the salvation of God is sent unto the Gentiles, and that they will hear it."

When he had said these words, the Jews departed and had great reasoning among themselves.

Paul dwelt two whole years in his own hired house and received all that came in unto him, preaching the kingdom of God and teaching those things which concern the Lord Jesus Christ with all confidence, no man forbidding him.

20

He which testifieth these things saith, "Surely I come quickly." Even so. Come, Lord Jesus. | Revelation 22:20-21

The grace of our Lord Jesus Christ be with you all. Amen.

ABOUT THE EDITOR

D. Michael Martindale is a storyteller. It doesn't matter which medium the story is told in—whether it be film or television or books or music—what's important is telling stories that people enjoy.

He was born in Minnesota and has been telling stories since before he could write. He started out by drawing comic strips and having his mother fill in the dialog balloons for him. He developed a taste for science fiction and fantasy, and although he's written screenplays in all sorts of genres, he continues to gravitate back to speculative fiction in his written work.

Martindale earned an Associate Degree in Film Production at Salt Lake Community College and a Bachelor Degree in Screenwriting and Cinematography at Utah Valley University.

For a period of time, he focused on telling stories about his religious community, Mormons. He considered the quality of Mormon literature subpar and preachy and wanted to tell stories about his people that he'd want to read, quality stories that were honest and edgy and not the least bit preachy. He's glad to see that the quality of Mormon art has been improving over the years.

He served three years on the board of the Association for Mormon Letters, a nonprofit organization that promotes Mormon literature and other arts, and acted as their Writers Conference chairperson for four years. He wrote a number of articles and book and film reviews for their literary journal *Irreantum*.

He worked for a time as a staff writer for *The Sugar Beet*, an Internet publication of Mormon satire patterned after the infamous website *The Onion*. Many of these online articles of alleged Mormon "news" were eventually collected into the popular book *The Mormon Tabernacle Enquirer*.

The editor of *The Mormon Tabernacle Enquirer* decided to start his own publishing company, Zarahemla Books, and chose as its flagship publication Martindale's second novel *Brother Brigham*, which he categorizes as "Mormon speculative fiction." *Brother Brigham* went on to receive substantial critical acclaim and was even used as reading material in a college comparative religion class one semester. He also had a science fiction short story "Bokev Momen" published in the anthology *Monsters and Mormons*, which has been included in Worldsmith Stories' *Twisted Minds* anthology.

Inspired by *Jesus Christ Superstar*, he composed the musical *General Prophet Joseph Smith*, based on the events leading up to the assassination of the Mormon prophet Joseph Smith. He produced a concept album recording of it on CDs, and is currently developing a film adaptation of it. He calls it "Les Mis for Mormons."

Martindale has written two other novels. His first, *The Power of the Seeker*, is the beginning installment of a science fiction series called *The Reincarnate*. It remains unpublished, as he describes it as "crap." He may rewrite it someday. Maybe.

His third novel is a fantasy called *Celeste & the White Dragon* which has been published by Woroldsmith Stories. It's the first volume of a fantasy series.

For nine years Martindale focused on screenwriting and film making as a director and editor. Film is his favorite medium in which to tell stories. He wrote, produced, directed, and edited eight short films and a feature-length fantasy film called *Geeks and Goblins, Elves and Elliot*. He has multiple other screenplays ready to be developed into feature-length films, including an adaptation of his short story "Solar Butterfly" that also appears in *Twisted Minds*. Additionally, he's been on the development team for three television/web series.

He resides in Salt Lake City, Utah, and is the father of three grown children and the grandfather of two of the most adorable granddaughters in the world. Do not debate him on this.

Brother Brigham
by D. Michael Martindale

Like many young boys, C.H. Young grew up with an imaginary friend. In his case, it was his ancestor Brigham Young—or rather, "Brother Brigham" as C.H. knew him. During his formative years, Brother Brigham filled the boy's head with grand expectations of an important mission in life.

Now grown up with a wife and two young sons, C.H. has sacrificed his dreams to earn a living for his family. Brother Brigham is just a distant memory—until one day he returns in a most unexpected way. As Brother Brigham's appearances and instructions grow increasingly bold, C.H. struggles to hold together his faith, his marriage, and his sanity.

brotherbrigham.worldsmithstories.com

Twisted Mind:
6 Science Fiction Stories
by D. Michael Martindale

From the twisted mind of D. Michael come six science fiction stories that disrupt the status quo of our world in the spirit of *The Twilight Zone* and *Black Mirror*. Whether the new world that arises is better or worse is a question each individual will have to decide for themselves.

A Growth in the Backyard
Eternal Rectangle
Solar Butterfly
Bokev Momen
Mary Mother of Nanites
Eyes of the Beholder
Bonus story: **Time Forks**

twistedstories.worldsmithstories.com

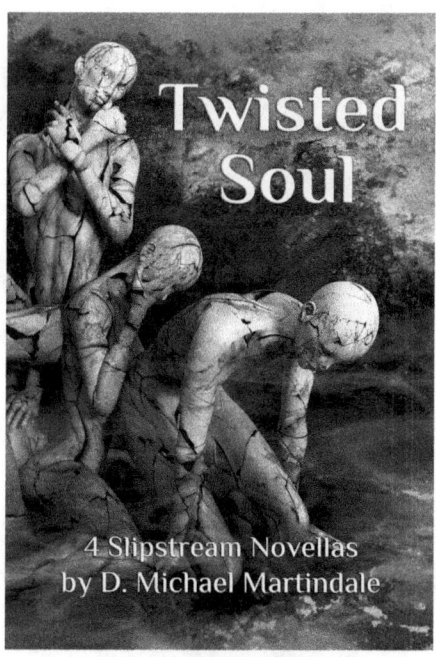

Twisted Soul:
4 Slipstream Novellas
by D. Michael Martindale

From the twisted soul of D. Michael come four slipstream novellas that explore the twists and turns of human spirituality and psychic powers. The hidden worlds they reveal may inspire or disturb, but the souls that experience them will never be the same again.

Alexandra
   A strange young girl enters young Noah's life. He tries to find out her secret and is sucked into the horror that is her life.
The First Mormons in the Moon
   Mormon prophet Brigham Young travels to the moon to convert the moon people which Joseph Smith claimed live there.
A Face in the Window
   Engaged couple Amy and Tyler face a life threatening nemesis that can't be stopped by any means.
Godblind
   Blinders is Godblind—unable to hear the Gods speak in his head. His community fears him because of this, but why?
Bonus novelette: **The Dreamcatcher**

twistedstories.worldsmithstories.com

Celeste & the White Dragon
by D. Michael Martindale

Queen Tamara, thrown into a dungeon by the rogue sorceress Gwendolyn, is about to give birth. There's something about her baby that makes Gwendolyn want to possess it, and when Tamara delivers, Gwendolyn will kill her and take the baby.

But Tamara's chambermaid Zenia will not let that happen. At great risk to her life, she rescues Tamara and helps her flee out of the kingdom of Gallea. But in the midst of Fenweald Forest, Tamara dies while giving birth to the baby, and Zenia discovers the terrible secret that makes Gwendolyn want to possess it. She puts her life in peril seeking a way to hide the infant.

A great search for the child begins, with kings and sorceresses and wizards and accursed monsters and village witches all struggling to find and possess the young princess, whom Zenia names Celeste. The fate of three continents depends on who succeeds.

celeste.worldsmithstories.com

www.ingramcontent.com/pod-product-compliance
Lightning Source LLC
LaVergne TN
LVHW051826080426
835512LV00018B/2745